Praise ...

TREJO

"[A] story with compassion and unsparing candor . . . It's all enough to make you believe in the possibility of a Hollywood ending."

—*The New York Times Book Review*

"An often eye-popping personal narrative that belongs among the great California memoirs."

—*Los Angeles Times*

"Quintessential Hollywood bad guy Trejo delivers a powerful and expertly crafted memoir that is tougher, more frightening, and more memorable than any of his films . . . This page-turner will thrill the legend's huge fan base."

—*Publishers Weekly*

"A raw and deeply engrossing salvation story."

—*Kirkus Reviews*

"*Trejo* proves an engaging read from the jump-off. Danny Trejo and Donal Logue have compiled a redemption story that is unparalleled . . . An autobiography with a depth of soul."

—*San Francisco Book Review*

"The perspective and clarity captured in the words of his story will hit home with many."

—*Nerds & Beyond*

"From ex-con to icon. Danny's incredible life story shows that even though we may fall down at some point in our lives, it's what we do when we stand back up that really counts."

—Robert Rodriguez, creator of *Spy Kids*,
Desperado, and *Machete*

"Trejo's tale as told by Logue is an inspirational study in the definition of character. Danny's journey of recovery and self-discovery is like a road map for those of us who are still struggling to figure ourselves out."

—Kevin Smith, filmmaker,
podcaster, and author

"*Trejo* is a celebration of a life fully lived. With brutal honesty, Trejo shows us that we can turn our lives around, rewrite our most difficult moments into proud accomplishments, and transform our deepest pain into our greatest joy."

—Reyna Grande, author of National Book Critics
Circle finalist *The Distance Between Us*

"Brimming with heart and generosity, wicked humor, and hard-won wisdom, *Trejo* reaches across generations, cultures, and borders to leave readers with a righteous, inspirational high."

—Francisco Cantú, *New York Times* bestselling
author of *The Line Becomes a River*

"Danny Trejo is an American treasure. I've been a fan of his since I was nine years old. He's had one of the most legendary runs in Hollywood history, in my opinion. If you're a fan like I am, this is definitely the book for you."

—Pete Davidson, actor, producer, and
cast member of *Saturday Night Live*

"Danny Trejo's unflinching, exquisitely written memoir, *Trejo*, unpacks his extraordinary journey from the hole at Folsom Prison and the notorious B Section at San Quentin to the dizzy heights of leading roles in Hollywood movies. Trejo tells his story with grace, humor, humility, as well as a terrifying immediacy during the more violent portions of his troubled early years."

—Adrian McKinty, *New York Times*
bestselling author of *The Chain*

"*Trejo* is a story of survival, of power, of transformation, and ultimately, of love. Hollywood couldn't have written a script this dramatic—this is the real-life rebirth of a man who wrote his own story in life and now finally shares it with us."

—Eric Garcetti, mayor of Los Angeles

"This is more, much more, than a celebrity memoir. It's a gutsy, wrenching, inspiring account of personal redemption and one man's discovery of a higher purpose, written as though Trejo's life depended on it. And once you read his story, you'll know that it does."

—Walter Kirn, *New York Times* bestselling author of
*Blood Will Out: The True Story of a Murder,
a Mystery, and a Masquerade*

"I was incredibly fortunate to shoot *Blood In, Blood Out* inside San Quentin, the Big House. We had three hundred active inmates working every day as extras next to the eleven actors I'd cast for the main roles. Danny Trejo was a graduate of 'Q,' so in addition to playing Geronimo in the film, he served as my unofficial prison advisor—he knew the territory intimately. We shot in cell block C, on tier 5, in the actual cell where Danny had spent two years of his life. It wasn't just that Trejo was the real deal—he turned out to be a terrific actor."

—Taylor Hackford, director and
producer of *Blood In, Blood Out*

TREJO

*My Life of Crime,
Redemption, and Hollywood*

DANNY TREJO

with DONAL LOGUE

ATRIA PAPERBACK
New York London Toronto Sydney New Delhi

ATRIA
PAPERBACK

An Imprint of Simon & Schuster, Inc.
1230 Avenue of the Americas
New York, NY 10020

Copyright © 2021 by Danny Trejo

All rights reserved, including the right to reproduce this book or portions thereof in any form whatsoever. For information, address Atria Books Subsidiary Rights Department, 1230 Avenue of the Americas, New York, NY 10020.

First Atria Paperback edition April 2022

ATRIA PAPERBACK and colophon are trademarks of Simon & Schuster, Inc.

For information about special discounts for bulk purchases, please contact Simon & Schuster Special Sales at 1-866-506-1949 or business@simonandschuster.com.

The Simon & Schuster Speakers Bureau can bring authors to your live event. For more information or to book an event, contact the Simon & Schuster Speakers Bureau at 1-866-248-3049 or visit our website at www.simonspeakers.com.

Interior design by Jill Putorti

Manufactured in the United States of America

5 7 9 10 8 6

Library of Congress Cataloging-in-Publication Data

Names: Trejo, Danny, 1944– author. | Logue, Donal, 1966– author.
Title: Trejo : my life of crime, redemption, and Hollywood / Danny Trejo with Donal Logue.
Description: First Atria Books hardcover edition. | New York : Atria Books, 2021.
Identifiers: LCCN 2020058142 (print) | LCCN 2020058143 (ebook) |
ISBN 9781982150822 (hardcover) | ISBN 9781982150846 (ebook)
Subjects: LCSH: Trejo, Danny, 1944– | Actors—United States—Biography. | Hispanic American actors—Biography. | Ex-convicts—United States—Biography. | Drug addicts—United States—Biography.
Classification: LCC PN2287.T736 A3 2021 (print) | LCC PN2287.T736 (ebook) |
DDC 791.4302/8092 [B]—dc23
LC record available at https://lccn.loc.gov/2020058142
LC ebook record available at https://lccn.loc.gov/2020058143

ISBN 978-1-9821-5082-2
ISBN 978-1-9821-5083-9 (pbk)
ISBN 978-1-9821-5084-6 (ebook)

For Maeve, Danielle, Gilbert, Danny Boy, Theo, and Sam.
Family is everything.

To all the incarcerated men and women throughout the world, know that through God all things are possible. You can not only make it out of your current circumstances, but you can know a freedom and happiness you never thought possible. You can't even dream the kind of life you can have. I love you and I'm praying for you every day.

CONTENTS

CONTENTS

Part Three
INMATE #1   127

Part Four
FROM A SON   211

TREJO

PROLOGUE

1949

Mary Carmen ran in our room yelling. She said, "I found a mudda cat!" Her sisters Coke; Coke's twin, Toni; Salita; and I followed her to the alley. These were my cousins. We shared a room at my grandmother's house, and we never rolled anywhere without each other.

I've always been in a gang of some sort, even if it was five- and six-year-old girls.

Lying next to a trash can in high grass was a dead cat with big tits. Mary Carmen was right. She was a mother cat.

A group of men stood outside a factory, smoking.

One of them said, "Get away from that thing. Can't you see a dog got to it?"

Salita said, "We have to save her babies. Where are her babies?"

We searched through the grass and up the alley for kittens but couldn't find any.

Coke had the idea to bury the cat and give her a proper funeral. We had to hurry because the evening was spreading out against the sky. We got a stick, pushed the cat onto a piece of plywood, and carried her to my grandmother's backyard.

The ground was harder than I thought. After a few minutes of digging I wanted to quit.

"It's probably deep enough."

1

We slid the cat off the board and covered her with dirt. Just then, my dad burst out the back door.

"What the hell's going on? If you kids don't get in this house, I'm going to smack some asses."

"A mudda cat died," said Mary Carmen, but my dad had already disappeared back into the house. Blackie, our dog, slipped through the screen door and started pawing at the grave.

"No, Blackie, no!" I said.

We tied Blackie up to keep the mother cat safe. Salita made the sign of the cross and we started to pray.

Later that night my uncle Art came running into the house, his shirt torn and bloody. He said he'd gotten jumped in a bar off San Fernando Road. Without missing a beat, he and the rest of my uncles grabbed sticks and bats and ran out the door.

About an hour later the men of the family swaggered back into the house, bragging about how many people they'd fucked up. My grandma grabbed us kids and made us kneel with her in the corner of the living room to say the rosary. I watched out of the corner of my eye while our abuelito stomped around, pumping his fist, yelling about how macho we Trejos were. My uncles were laughing, passing beers, doing play-by-plays of what had gone down. My grandmother made us pray louder.

Looking at my cousins and me, kneeling in prayer for the second time that day, you'd never guess that every one of us would go to jail or prison. But we did. No matter how close to God my grandmother wanted us to be, we were already on a path. We were Trejos. If my family had a legacy, that was it.

And you'd never guess that the baddest of the bad—me—would make it out of the prison system and instead of dying in the street as a stone-cold junkie and killer, I'd end up being shot, stabbed, decapitated, blown up, hanged, flattened by an elevator, and disintegrated into a pool table until my eyeballs rolled into the pockets in a career that made me the most-killed actor in Hollywood history; that I'd meet presidents and have murals of my face painted on walls in different continents; that companies would want me as their spokesman because I was not only loved but trusted; and that I'd have an official day named after me in Los Angeles. Because the Danny Trejo who I was before I got clean and became a drug counselor, or before the world got to know me through my acting career, was no one anyone would want to paint or honor. Because back then, I was the Mexican you didn't want to fuck with.

Part One

ESCAPE

Chapter 1

SOLEDAD

1968

I felt like shit. I was high on heroin, pruno, reds, and whiskey.

I was three years into a ten-year stretch, which for a Mexican was more likely to be a twenty-year stretch, a life stretch, a death stretch.

I always figured I'd die in prison.

It was Cinco de Mayo 1968, in Soledad State Prison. To Mexicans, real Mexicans, Corazón Mexicans, Cinco de Mayo doesn't mean the Mexican day of independence (it's not); it doesn't signify the day the Mexicans defeated the French at Puebla; it doesn't even mean the fifth of May. Cinco de Mayo means "Get bail money ready."

I was already inside, so no need for bail.

Mexicans had been planning a *un chingón volar* for weeks. Since I was running the gym next to the loading docks, I got my hands on all the contraband coming in: cigarettes, speed, heroin, even women's underwear and makeup (if that was your thing). As long as you could pay for it, I could get it.

I ran the heroin bag, so I was well stocked. I also had hundreds of pills I collected from inmates who saved their meds and used them to pay gambling debts, traded them for contraband, or needed protection. I had a few pints of whiskey, two ounces of weed, and the batches of pruno we'd been making for weeks. A connect in the kitchen got us the raisins, oranges, sugar, and yeast to mix it with. We'd pour it into garbage bags, twist them tight, wrap them in T-shirts, and stash them in the heating vents. When it was ready, we'd strain it through tube socks.

We started early the day before and went all night. That next morning, I was settling in when the Captain's voice came over the loudspeaker. He announced we were having an outside activity that day: a local junior college baseball team would be playing a team of inmates in an exhibition game.

Bringing a group of civilians into a California prison on Cinco de Mayo is the stupidest fucking thing on earth you could do; over half the prison was already wasted. Plus, whenever there's an outside activity it means extra guards, extra security, extra guns, extra everything.

After the announcement about the Cinco de Mayo ball game, we were ordered out of our cells. On the Yard, I held my face to the sun for a minute to let it touch me, but when I closed my eyes, I felt queasy. The pruno wasn't sitting right. I took a spot on the bleachers along the third base line with Ray Pacheco and Henry Quijada, two old crime partners from my juvie days. Ray was incredibly strong, a hell of an athlete. We knew each other from when we played football in the street when we were thirteen, before Ray joined the White Fence gang. Henry was a tall, thin kid from Azusa. They were both housed in Ranier, another section within the prison.

We settled in to watch the game between the junior college and a team of inmates. I took in the fact there was no fence—only ten feet of air separated us from the junior college kids. We watched the teams warm up. A big, Mickey Mantle–looking white kid was playing third base. I remember thinking that he'd be a highly prized punk inside.

He was chomping on a big wad of gum.

Ray turned to me and said, "Man, I wish I had some *chicle.*"

Gum was special. We couldn't get gum in prison. We certainly couldn't get the sugary kind the college kid was chomping on.

Ray turned into a child. "I want gum."

Ray'd come to Soledad from Atascadero, a full lockdown mental facility. Ray had brutally murdered his ex-girlfriend and her new boyfriend. He didn't just murder them—the court found there were "special circumstances." I don't remember the particulars, but they were bad—the-kind-you-read-about-in-the-newspaper bad, the-recoil-in-shock kind of bad. To old-school Mexicans like Ray, there was no such thing as an ex-girlfriend— once you were his, you were his forever. The crime was so vicious, the court figured no one in their right mind could have done it, so he was found "guilty but insane." In exchange for years of electroshock therapy and medical experiments, Ray got a reduced sentence of seven years.

The treatments only made him worse.

Back in Central, sometimes I'd sneak behind Ray and make *zzzzhhhhhh* sounds like he was being electrocuted to fuck with him. Normally he didn't mind, but when I did it to him that morning, it was clear he wasn't in the mood for fucking around.

The game started. I was exhausted. I felt like shit from the wine, weed, pills, and whiskey. The sun, which for a few seconds was comforting, felt like a magnifying glass aimed at my forehead. Everyone in my area was drunk, high, uncomfortable. I could feel something simmering. I recognized it; it was the desire for violence. Aggression and fear among the inmates released pheromones. Once they're out, they're out, and the air at that moment was full of them.

In the second inning, Ray yelled at the third baseman, "*¡Dame chicle, pinchi güero!*"

The kid pretended not to hear. He just pounded his fist into his mitt and kept chomping away. *Chomp. Chomp. Chomp.* He was like a cow chewing cud.

"You heard me, bitch! Throw me some gum!"

The kid didn't turn. He just stared forward, pounding his fist into his mitt and chomping his gum. Out of the corner of his mouth, he said, "We're not supposed to talk to you guys."

"What?"

"We were told not to talk to the inmates."

Chomp. Chomp.

With every chomp, Ray got crazier. A switch flipped behind his eyes. He was like a great white shark with its eyes rolled back. He was grinding his teeth and clenching his jaw like he was fighting demons. He was back chewing leather strips with hundreds of volts of electricity blasting through him, back in a straitjacket he'd worn for four months.

Ray was gone.

"Fuck you, bitch. We ain't good enough to talk to?"

"We were told not to interact with you."

I knew it was useless, but I tried to calm Ray. I told him every kind of bullshit I could think of.

"Don't fuck with that kid, holmes, he knows karate," I said. And: "They got a special sniper guarding that dude."

I should have known better. Telling a loaded killer they can't fuck with someone is a direct invitation to fuck with them.

The third baseman was scared shitless. Every inning, he drifted farther from third base and closer to second. It got to the point where the third baseman, the shortstop, and the second baseman were standing next to each other in the middle of the infield. None of them wanted to be there. They wanted to be with their girlfriends, driving their trucks, drinking beer, listening to country music on some canal bank, anywhere other than playing baseball with a bunch of thieves and killers in a prison. Whatever worst-case scenario they might have been briefed about concerning visiting a high-security prison was going down in real time—especially for the third baseman, who was getting shit from a stone-cold killer no more than twenty feet away.

I had to piss. I was afraid to leave Ray, but I was going to piss my pants. I told Ray to come with me, but he said no, he wanted to stay with Henry. I jammed to the bathroom, doing the weird hop-skip thing you do when you have to piss but can't fully run. Standing at the urinal, I cussed myself for how much I had to pee. It felt like I had a gallon in my bladder. I was nauseous. The crowd outside sounded eerie. The air had changed. Things were electric.

I was hurrying back to the field when I saw Ray fly out of the stands and punch the third baseman in the face. At that moment, everything exploded. The only thing I can compare it to is when the baboons went crazy on Damien in the safari adventure park in *The Omen*, or when every dog in a dog park gets in a fight. In an instant a thousand animals were fighting for their lives.

I'd been locked up, in and out but mostly in, since 1956. In those twelve years, I put to use everything I learned from my uncle Gilbert about being incarcerated. The first time I got taken to Eastlake Juvenile Hall, I remember saying to myself, *What did Gilbert teach me?*

To stick with the Mexicans, first off. Secondly, find three or four specific homies who'd always have my back. Gilbert told me I'd develop instincts I never knew I had. I'd learn to master how to go to sleep in a chaotic tier full of people screaming and running around and learn to spring awake in an instant if someone stopped even for a moment in front of my cell. He taught me if someone was looking at me for just a second too long I'd have to respond with "What the fuck do you want?" Only six years older, Gilbert was my mentor. He ran every joint he'd been in. He taught me how to deal, steal, intimidate, how to spot weakness, when it was best to terrify, and when it was right to comfort. He taught me never to bully people weaker than me, but if I had to fight, the goal was to win.

The first time I got hauled off to a police station, I was ten. By twelve, I was a regular at juvenile hall. My parents sent me to live with relatives in Texas for a while to avoid getting locked up after I kicked some kid's ass for squirting ink on me in art class. But at that point I was incorrigible. My stay in Texas didn't last long. Even though my aunt Margaret and my uncle Rudy Cantú's place was deep in the sticks, miles outside of San Antonio, I still found my way to the hopping night scene in La Colonia. My aunt and uncle, who were proper, religious people, realized they couldn't control me, so they sent me back to Los Angeles.

I wasn't scared of being busted, I wasn't scared of being locked up, and when a kid loses fear of consequences, that's when society has lost them. Halfway through tenth grade, I was sent to North Hollywood High School, my fifth school in a year. I'd been kicked out of four others for fighting. I had caused excitement in the last three because, as the only Mexican, I was a novelty. Not only was I Latino, I wore yellow-and-white Sir Guy shirts with matching vests and pleated khakis. If I wore Levi's, they were ironed with Folsom cuffs. I was sharp, I was clean. I stood out. At North Hollywood, Barbara D., a beautiful Italian girl who was the homecoming queen, loved me. I loved her back. One day, she saw me sitting on a bench in the quad and looked alarmed.

"You can't sit there, Danny, that's the Caballeros' bench." I thought, *What the fuck? They got a bench? For that matter, who the fuck are the Caballeros, and why would they call themselves a Spanish name?*

A big, goofy white dude and a smaller guy walked up. The big guy got puffy. He said, "Are you going to get off the Caballeros' bench, or am I going to have to take you off?"

If he'd just said, "That's the Caballeros' bench," I might have gotten up and left. But because he challenged me, I stood on the bench and kicked him in the throat.

"Take me off this bench now, bitch."

The guy started choking. Then the little one said the magic words: "Just wait till after school, beaner."

Big mistake. The trigger wasn't *beaner.* It was the "wait till after school" part. Normal high schoolers are worried about getting in trouble, real trouble. I didn't have that problem. I was the kind of Mexican who couldn't wait until after school. The whole day, my rage kept growing. The final bell couldn't come fast enough. I positioned myself outside the school gates. The throat-kick guy and five of his Caballero friends showed up with the whole school behind them, ready for the show. This was good. I was ready to introduce them to a level of violence that wasn't even on their radar.

It was like a scene of out the movie *Grease,* except they were stuck in PG mode, and I was rated X. As soon as the leader opened his mouth, I grabbed him by his neck and took a chunk out of his face with my teeth. People gasped. I saw two girls cover their faces. No one in North Hollywood High School was ready for me. That Caballero certainly wasn't.

While the guy flailed around, screaming, I jammed to Leonard's Burger Shop across the street, jumped the counter, grabbed a cleaver, and ran back out on the street. I was going to take out the whole school if I had to. Leonard came running out of the restaurant with a cleaver of his own and took up a spot beside me. I faced off against a ring of what seemed like every kid at North Hollywood High. No one dared take a step toward me. That's the power of crazy, that's the power of being willing to go to a place unimaginable to your foes. But that kind of power comes with a cost—by exercising it, you reveal to the world the only place you belong is a state penitentiary.

I took what Gilbert taught me to heart. I didn't fight to gain respect. I fought to win. I took a sick pleasure in it. I respected people who showed me respect, but if they didn't, I wanted whoever fucked with me to wake up years in the future, when they were old and walking with a cane, to look at their faces in the mirror, see the deep, ugly scars, and remember the huge mistake they made one afternoon long ago when they messed with Danny Trejo.

When a riot goes down, everybody knows what to do: survive and go after your enemies. Mexicans jumped Blacks; whites stood back-to-back, squaring off, trying to fight a path back to their own; Blacks were swinging on whites and Mexicans. Aryans, Blacks, Mexicans, all executing hit orders that had been in the pipeline for months. I was dropping motherfuckers. I'd throw a left, *bam.* A right, *bam.* A left, right, left, right. I had no fear. There was no time for that. If fear ever creeped in, I turned it to rage immediately. It was adrenaline-fueled. If a child's trapped under a car and his mother's stuck in fear, the kid's screwed; if she turns it to rage, she lifts that car.

I had car-lifting strength. Mack Truck–lifting strength.

In my periphery, I saw sissies running for safety at the edge of the Yard. I don't mean *sissy* as a derogatory term, because it isn't in the pen. We shared time with everyone and everyone had value. The homosexuals pooled money, kept their books stacked, paid for protection, looked after the homosexual guys coming in, and had all the intel. Taking care of gay inmates meant a hundred eyes had your back. Baseball players swung bats to keep inmates from killing them. Dudes threw trash cans, rocks, whatever they could grab. I remember having a rock or a chunk of concrete, but it's a blur.

The noise was inhuman.

I was back-to-back with Ray, slugging it out with anyone who rolled up, when I saw Captain Rogers, one of the head bulls, pointing at us. He was signaling the gun tower to shoot. Ray and I took off, swerving in different directions. Like a couple of rodeo clowns, we ended up running into each other, knocking each other down.

Flat on the ground, facedown, we laced our fingers behind the backs of our heads. Ray turned into a little kid again. He was terrified.

"Danny, don't let them hurt me."

Captain Rogers ran up and said, "Trejo, did you get him?" I guessed he was asking if I took Ray out to stop him from running. I didn't know how to answer, so I said, "Yeah."

The guards pulled us to our feet and hauled us off.

Out of the over one thousand prisoners involved in the riot that day, they singled out only Henry, Ray, and me. It was alleged that I threw the rock that hit a guard named Lieutenant Gibbons in the head. Everyone saw Ray assault a free person. Henry was charged with kicking Coach Stalmeyer in the testicles and causing them to rupture. All capital crimes.

We were looking at the death penalty.

What can change in an instant? *Todo.*

It wasn't totally a surprise. Whether it was juvie, camp, Tracy, YTS, Wayside, Chino, Vacaville, San Quentin, Folsom, anywhere I'd been locked up, I never expected I'd get out alive. I knew I'd be in prison until I was dead. I just didn't know when, how, or where.

I guessed it was there. Soledad.

Most teachers I had said, "He has real potential." Or more precisely, they'd say, "He has enormous potential if he would just *change*." Even parole officers said I had incredible potential.

In the hole, I thought, *What the fuck is potential?*

Just when I had things going right in Soledad, everything changed. I was going to die and it was going to be the gas chamber. That it was in the hands of the state was something I couldn't wrap my mind around. I knew I was a fighter and could go out fighting, but when they walked me to my death, how would I act?

Would I be brave?

Henry yelled from down the hall, "They're going to top us, Danny! They're going to kill us good!"

There's a movie from the 1930s called *Angels with Dirty Faces*. James Cagney plays Rocky, a straight-up gangster who gets involved in a shoot-out with the police. When he's surrounded, he yells, "Come and get me, coppers!"

After he's arrested, his crew in the neighborhood says, "He's going to spit in those coppers' eyes!"

But when Rocky's sentenced to death, he cries like a bitch. On the way to the electric chair he weeps and begs for mercy. The next day, his gang reads in the newspaper that he died a yellow-bellied coward.

The message to me was clear: *Don't be a bitch when you die.*

Just a year later, George Jackson would write about the O Wing in Soledad: "The strongest hold out for no more than a couple of weeks . . . When a white con leaves here, he's ruined for life. No black leaves Max Row walking." But O Wing wasn't even the max, not close, certainly not in terms of punishment and degradation. X Wing was, and X Wing was where Henry, Ray, and I were. O Wing, comparatively, was a cakewalk, and we dreamed of going there someday. I sat on the naked iron bed. I was sick, detoxing off pills and alcohol. I was freezing. On the wall across from me, someone had written *Fuck God* in shit.

I said, "God, if You're there, me, Henry, and Ray will be alright. If You're not, we're fucked."

Chapter 2

NINETY DAYS OF FREEDOM

1965

Soledad was, for me, the current link in a chain of lockups. I had ended up there only ninety days after I got out of Youth Training School, a prison in Chino that was unofficially known as "Gladiator School." There are prep schools in America that prepare students for the best colleges, and that's what YTS was for kids like me: it prepared us to fill the pens in California.

I was twenty-one years old when I was released from YTS in 1965. They gave me a bus ticket home and some cash. At a liquor store next to the Greyhound bus terminal in Ontario, California, I bought two bottles of Ripple.

Before the internet, Greyhound bus stations were the dark web of their day—they were where hustlers and hookers and runaways, pimps with cool street names, soldiers on leave, and prisoners fresh from the pen all mixed together in a place you could pay a dime to watch TV for a fifteen-minute chunk. Until I was in my thirties, I didn't even know proper wine came with a cork. Ripple wine was made without grapes and came with a screw top. I took those two short dogs on the Greyhound with me and crouched down in my seat to drink them as fast as I could. A sign above me read: "Drinking alcohol on this bus is a violation of the civil code—punishable by a fine, imprisonment, or both." I laughed and cracked open the other bottle.

When we pulled into downtown LA, I stepped off the bus and I heard a whistle. A sketchy-looking Mexican asked me, "*¿Qué quieres?*"

I said, "What do you got?"

"It's good."

Every dealer says what they've got is good. A dealer never says, "It's actually shit cut with lactose."

"Do you have an outfit?"

He nodded, and we went down an alley and shot up.

Bam. When it hit me, the boogeyman was gone. The boogeyman was that feeling of regret about the past and fear about the future. Like a lot of addicts, I was full of myself while at the same time exploding with self-hatred. I'd feel remorse, then fear, then anger in that order and sometimes I'd move through the first two in less than a second. My anger turned outward, to blame. I would blame outside people, places, and things for the fucked-up state I found myself in, never once taking a hard look at myself and taking responsibility for the situation I was in. All of these conflicting feelings would overwhelm me and that's where heroin stepped in. Heroin was my escape hatch. It had been ever since I first used it, at twelve, to avoid the anger in my house.

My state jacket transformed into a cashmere coat—I was floating off the ground. That was a Friday, and I made it home five days later with a black eye. My mother said, "What happened, *mijo*?" I had no idea. I took off again, and a couple of weeks later ended up at the house of an old partner of mine from the neighborhood, Frank Russo. As kids, Frank and I had been in a gang we called the Ulans. We prided ourselves on having all been kicked out of other gangs for being too wild. Then we'd been at YTS together a couple of rounds earlier.

At YTS, Frank had attended meetings for a twelve-step group to help with his drinking problem. He knew I was a drunk and an addict. To be honest, I knew it, too; I just didn't care. Frank suggested I join him at the meetings, but he did it in a way he knew would get my interest.

"They have broads there, Danny." For a teenager who'd been cooped up in YTS for a while, that was intriguing.

"Really?"

"Yeah, outsiders come to the meetings."

I went straight into my counselor's office and wrote down that I had a problem with drugs and alcohol and wanted to attend meetings. That move would turn out to be a blessing and a curse, but at first all I saw was the curse. First of all, it was now on my jacket that I had a problem with drugs (the specific wording was something like "Inmate expresses he has acute alcohol and narcotics issues requiring counseling"), and your jacket stays with you for your entire journey through the prison system and with parole officers on the outside. I didn't know it at the time, but just because I wanted to see women, I opened myself to years of extra testing and forced meeting attendance. Second, I went to that first meeting and while there were indeed two women there, they were two one-hundred-year-old women. I could've kicked Frank's ass.

I'd stayed on the wide and not-so-straight path, but Frank had stayed clean and sober since those first meetings in YTS. Now he looked at me and shook his head.

"Jesus, Danny, you look like shit. What have you been doing?"

"Mostly alcohol."

"Man, let's get you cleaned up and go to a meeting. Oh shit," he said.

"What?"

"You're still wearing your state-issued brogans. Anyone who's done time is gonna know just where you came from."

I'd been in touch with Frank before I got released. He said he'd have everything ready for me when I got back to the Valley. In the old days that usually meant a crash pad, a broad, a gun, and a car, but Frank was all about recovery now. What he meant in 1965 was that he'd have a directory of twelve-step meetings and a *Big Book*. Part of me was jealous of how Frank could be so committed to sobriety. I knew twelve-step programs worked; I knew they worked for OGs like Jhonnie Harris; I just didn't want to work them. But I knew if I started using again, I'd go back to prison. More immediately, hitting meetings was a condition of my parole.

"You have to give me a ride home so I can change."

I changed into the prison-issued khakis they gave me when I got out—they were all I had. Frank and I went to a meeting, and afterward I checked into some Fed-contracted halfway house my parole officer had assigned me. He knew I had beef with my parents and thought it was better for me to live under supervision. It was a condition of my parole. The place wasn't too bad. We had roommates and a ten o'clock curfew on the weekends, which was fine. I was used to restrictions, and besides, compared to prison, curfew was nothing.

Frank had studied auto body repair at YTS and taken his skills to a guy we all used to work for in our teens, Frank Carlisi. Carlisi was a constant in all our lives. A bit of a gangster who had a huge heart for other gangsters, Carlisi hired us when we got out of jail or prison without any questions asked. We were lucky to have Carlisi. Most places won't look at you if you have a record. POs are always hassling ex-cons about getting jobs, but it's tough when no one will hire you.

Carlisi had expanded his wrecking yard to include a shop where Frank Russo could do auto bodywork. I worked with Frank at Carlisi's and promised him and Carlisi I'd get my shit together. Frank and I would sand cars, Bondo them up, and paint them, and at night we'd go to meetings.

Now that I was out and going to meetings, I asked Frank what I should do about Laura, the wife who had divorced me while I was in prison.

The last time I'd gotten out of prison, in '62, I went to Frank's house to see him and meet the girlfriend he had written me about when I was in the joint. But what really got my attention was his girlfriend's younger sister. Laura was wearing a short skirt. Her hair was long and red. She was tall, slender, and breathtakingly gorgeous. She sat on the other side of the living room and kept staring at me. I'd catch her eye, and she'd look away and smile. It was absolutely love at first sight for me. For both of us. I said, "Come on over here."

She got up and crossed the room. She was like a vision. I said, "Sit on my lap." She was only eighteen. So was I, but I'd already been through so much that I felt old. Laura liked that. Laura liked rebels, bad guys, tough guys, ex-cons. Being attracted to bad guys is one thing. Living with one is a completely different story.

Laura and I got serious real fast. Her parents hated Mexicans and convicts and they certainly hated the fact their youngest daughter was dating someone who was both, so they kicked her out of the house. She had nowhere to go, so we decided to get married. We had the wedding in the backyard of my parents' house. A lot of people came, and it was a nice affair. There was plenty of beer, tacos, and tamales. She looked beautiful. She was the kind of woman who would walk away and my friends, aunts, cousins, and uncles would all give me this look like, "How'd you score that, *ese*?"

I was sitting on top of the world. I had this beautiful wife and good job. I was working for the famous developer Saul Pick, building the first concrete geodesic roof in the world for the Cinerama Dome. I was making big cash working concrete and big cash selling bennies to all the workers. Since the heat was on us to work around the clock to get the roof built, I dealt bennies (amphetamines) to help people to stay up, then reds (Seconal, barbiturates) for them to crash out.

But just a few months into our marriage, Laura came home from her job answering phones at some electrical company and found broads on the couch and drugs all over the apartment. She had that look on her face, that look of deep hurt. I'd seen it before, and I'd see it again. There it was, and then the trembling lip that someone gets right before they cry. I didn't care. I honestly didn't, because, to me, women's feelings didn't rate. It's a terrible thing to say and it's embarrassing to admit, but that's the truth about how I felt at the time.

The bad-boy appeal diminishes when the person is actually bad. It's all very sexy and mysterious until you have to deal with the reality. Laura left in tears and went to her sister and Frank's place for the night. Frank was my best friend, but he knew if I was using, the tears weren't going to stop. It would go downhill from there.

The women Laura caught on my couch were Rita and Donna, a couple of wild girls from the Valley who were down for anything. Laura wasn't as gangster as I think she might have thought she was when we first met. Rita and Donna were.

I left my marriage to Laura for prison the night I told Rita to drive me over to my cousin Ponchee's house. Ponchee was my cousin by marriage. He was married to my cousin Mary Carmen (who we'd nicknamed "Muddacat" ever since that day in the alley), and I had them selling weed for me. I'd delivered them two kilos, and they were supposed to have a big payday waiting. Rita stayed out in the street, and I went up on the porch. As soon as I knocked, the door swung open. It was Officer Mullins, a North Hollywood narcotics officer I'd crossed paths with before.

I jumped over the railing and ran around the side of the house, where a big cop grabbed me and stuck a pistol under my chin.

"Move, Trejo, and I'll blow your fucking brains out!"

"Fuck you." I was fronting like I wasn't scared, but my legs were jelly. I knew the game was up.

The cop pulled me up on the porch, and I saw Rita burning off down the block. Inside the house, Officer Mullins was standing by the door; another cop was standing next to Ponchee; and Mary's five kids were sitting on the floor crying. There was a pile of weed on the coffee table and bundles of cash.

Ponchee said, *"Les dije que es mío, no digas nada. Les dije que es mío."* He was saying he'd told them it was his and I shouldn't say anything.

Mullins nodded toward the kids on the floor. "What you going to do here, Trejo?"

"Fuck you," I said. "It's mine. It's all mine."

Ponchee said, *"¡No, es mío!"*

"Fuck them, Ponchee," I said. "I'll get probation."

All the cops laughed because they knew that was bullshit. I had already violated probation. I was looking at way more than six months. I was looking at years. I was smiling and bobbing my head like it was all no big deal, but my soul was crushed.

I was cuffed and led outside. "That was the right thing you did back there, Danny," Officer Mullins said. "The right thing." I think Mullins was relieved he didn't have to process everyone, especially the children. We both knew if Ponchee and Mary Carmen were arrested, the kids would be placed in homes or juvenile hall.

I was booked at the North Hollywood Police Department before being taken to County. I was with some other dudes in a holding cell, a couple of drunks they'd pulled off the streets. Things were pretty sleepy when we heard this loud screech and a car crashed into the back door of the police station. The door came right off the hinges. It was Rita and Donna. Those gangsters tried to break me out. They had no idea I was locked up in a cell and had no way of getting to the door.

Like I said, a couple of gangsters.

Some cops went outside in the alley and saw the driver had taken off. The car was stolen and there was no way to trace it. They laughed at the absurdity of it.

"Friends of yours, Trejo?"

It was all pretty funny, but that arrest was why I was sent to YTS. Not surprisingly, while I was there, Laura served me with divorce papers. I used them to keep score when I played dominoes. It was an act of bullshit bravado. I didn't want to be one of those suckers with an old lady on the outside. I didn't want to wait for letters and cards that might or might not come. I didn't want to feel that hurt.

Now that I'd served that three-year sentence and was out and going to meetings, I asked Frank to ask his girlfriend if I should make amends to Laura. Frank said, "The best amends you can make that poor girl, Danny, is to stay as far away from her as possible." So that's what I did.

This time I did alright for twenty-nine days. I remember it being twenty-nine because I was a day away from a thirty-day chip. A few weeks into going to meetings with Frank, I felt better. I wanted to be better. Being sober wasn't just something I was doing to please my PO; I desperately wanted to stay the fuck out of jail. I knew if I got fucked up, I'd be back doing crime. But knowing what the stakes are doesn't mean you'll do the right thing. And bad decisions were brewing inside me. When Frank took me to a Friday-night meeting in Burbank, I was in a foul mood.

This old guy started to speak. "I drank alcohol for fifty years . . ." Already, he'd lost me. I was twenty-one years old. I was an armed robber, a bad motherfucker. If this guy drank for fifty years, I still had decades to go. He went on about how he started with beer, and moved to harder liquor, bourbon and whiskey, and ended up in his sixties drinking wine in an alley.

Fuck this, I thought, *I started drinking wine in an alley.*

He said, "If you want what we have . . ." He talked about having a car, a boat, a house, and a cabin in Mammoth. I was really confused. What the hell did a woolly mammoth have to do with anything? I looked at his old lady, literally an old lady of about seventy-five, and I sure as fuck didn't want any of that.

The next guy shared. He started with, "I drank for sixty years . . ."

That was enough for me. I said to Frank, "Listen, I might have a problem with alcohol, but if these guys are alcoholics, I'm definitely not a fucking alcoholic. I'm a dope fiend." This is a classic dope fiend argument. We think heroin is our only problem, but give us a few beers and the heroin we promised we'd never touch again suddenly seems like a good idea.

Frank said, "Danny, be careful, it sounds like you might be setting yourself up for 'experimental' drinking."

I took what he said as a suggestion that I experiment with some drinking. So I split.

I went by a bowling alley that was near my halfway house, hoping there might be some broads there. I was twenty-one; I'd been locked up for almost three years and was looking for anything. I waited around for about half an hour, but there wasn't anybody in there except middle-aged motherfuckers with their spouses.

I went out front to a taco stand to get myself something to eat, and I saw it—the Retreat bar. I hadn't been to a bar in years. I went in and sat. The bartender asked if I wanted something to drink. I asked for a Coke. I remember the thick, old-school Coca-Cola glass it was served in. It was frosty cold. The bartender smiled. He knew me. At that point, every Mexican in the Valley knew me. When you're a high school kid who gets kicked out of school for tearing off a kid's face with your teeth, then later maims a sailor with a broken beer bottle, you get a reputation.

I was working on my second Coke when an older lady came in the bar. She must have been in her sixties. She wandered to the pool table looking lost. She couldn't even figure out that you had to put a quarter in the table to start a game.

"You need help?"

"Would you mind?"

I'd busted out of the meeting after listening to the old dudes, but now it didn't matter if she was sixty. When you're a *vato* and a lady shows up around a pool table, all of a sudden you become Willie Mosconi or Minnesota Fats. Then I asked the fucked-up, slippery-slope question: "Can I get you a drink?"

"I'll take a beer, thank you."

I whistled. "Hey, bartender, get the lady a beer." He nodded and then said, "Danny, would you like a . . ." and he made a swirly move with his finger that I immediately knew was sign language for soda pop. I was enraged. Here I was, a bad motherfucker, an armed robber, a *maimer*, and this asshole was making a swirly finger like I was a little kid.

"Get me a beer, too."

I don't remember the pool game. Turns out, when you're an addict, there's no such thing as experimental drinking. For someone like me, one is too many and a thousand is never enough.

The next thing I knew, the bartender announced last call.

I looked up at the clock. It was a quarter to two in the morning. I was supposed to be back at the halfway house by ten. *Fuck*, I thought, *this is definitely a parole violation.*

The broad was gone. I went up to the bartender and ordered a couple of shots and a six-pack of beer to go. He looked at me like I was a wild animal. Because I was.

I walked down the street. A '59 Impala, white and red with a B&M Hydramatic transmission, burned a *U* in front of me and crashed into the curb. The driver yelled my name. "Trejo! Trejo!" I stumbled over to the passenger side and saw that it was a dude named Dennis I knew from around the Valley. Dennis had only been a youngster when I'd gone away; he was still only about eighteen now. He was a skinny, pretty, blond white boy who looked like he could be in the Beach Boys, but right now he was in a panic.

"The cops are after me. I just spilled a jar of reds."

A jar holds a thousand Seconals. I hopped in the car and immediately grabbed a fistful of reds and started stuffing them in my mouth. Dennis did the same. He asked me for a beer and we washed the reds down with Budweiser.

"Dennis, I don't see no cops."

"They're after me, I know it."

We took off. That was a Saturday morning around two thirty. I woke up when Dennis's car crashed into a tree in North Hollywood Park at dawn on Sunday. I'd lost a whole day. The experimental drinking phase had officially failed.

Dennis was freaking out. "Grab the guns, grab the guns!" I saw two revolvers in the back seat and reached for them. "Not those," said Dennis. "The guns in the trunk!" I grabbed his keys and went around the back of the car. No one was up yet except for the birds, chirping away. It was a beautiful morning, and I felt dark as a devil. Opening the trunk, I saw two sawed-off shotguns, a machine gun, and a hand grenade.

I thought, *This is definitely a violation.* We scooped up the guns and whatever was left in the jar of reds and headed down Magnolia. We were looking for Richard Berry's house. Richard was the big heroin dealer in the Valley at that time. Dennis suggested we trade the guns for heroin.

Richard gave us enough to keep us high for a few days with some left over to sell. We grabbed a motel room, stashed the drugs and the guns we hadn't traded, and went back to the park. To my astonishment, the car was still there, smashed up against the tree. Dennis turned it over and stuck it in reverse. The good news was it was still running. The bad news was it was still running. We had wheels to continue our spree. We went to the motel, got the guns, and started an epic forty-five-day run of dealing, stealing, and drugging.

A lot went down in a month and a half—we crashed at cheap, eight-dollar-a-night joints like The Pink and The Rose. We weren't alone. I knew all the broads working the streets and a lot of them stayed with us for drugs and sex. There were scared faces, wasted faces, empty faces. Dennis and I robbed a Big Boy restaurant, a White Front (which was the Best Buy of the day), and other stores; we ripped off dealers, we burned people on drug deals and told them where we were staying, daring them to come find us. I pulled three robberies using the grenade that Dennis had in his trunk. I got the idea from something I'd heard at a meeting in YTS. A guy confessed that he used to go into banks and pull the pin on a grenade he stole from his brother who was in the Army. I said that sounded like a good idea to Jhonnie Harris. Jhonnie was a sober ex-con who'd done serious stretches at Quentin. He came to meetings in the joint to try and help out younger people. Jhonnie's only response to the grenade scheme was to say, "Danny, the only thing that's going to beat you to San Quentin are the lights on the bus." I thought he meant it as a compliment.

Dennis kept saying, "I can't believe I'm with Trejo!" like I was his idol. He stood up in a motel room full of broads, grabbed a gun, and said, "We'll hold court in the streets! They'll have to kill us!" It was embarrassing. Dennis was never meant to be a robber. He became one with me. I felt like I was living in that cartoon *Chester and Spike*, where the little dog (Chester) cruises around with a big dog (Spike) and bothers him, kisses his ass, and gets smacked around. Dennis was Chester, a yapping shit talker. Our journey only had two possible outcomes—jail or death. When I was fucked up, I'd tell Dennis what would happen to him in the joint in the most graphic terms. I terrified him. Dennis had never been to prison.

"But not if we're in there together, right, Danny?"

This is where I was most evil.

"The guy who pretends to be your best friend is the one that gets you first." And that's how I set myself up for what happened next.

Part of me didn't give a shit if we held court in the street and died in a hail of gunfire. I hated myself. I was on a train heading off a cliff with no idea how to get off. I hated my life. I would never have killed myself intentionally, but if I shot too much dope or got shot in the street by the cops, I wouldn't have cared. I was going to ride out this run until it found its natural end.

That didn't take long.

One day, Dennis came back to the motel and told me he'd set up a huge score for us. He'd found a buyer who wanted four ounces of pure dope. But we didn't *have* four ounces of dope.

"Do your parents have sugar?"

"I'm sure they do."

"Are they home?"

I grabbed some balloons and a funnel and we drove to Dennis's parents' house. Dennis was from an upper-middle-class family. They had a nice house with nice furniture. The walls were covered with pictures of family picnics and graduation ceremonies. Dennis was only a couple of years removed from being the cute, kind high school student holding the family dog in a picture on the wall. I grabbed a box of sugar, mixed it with lactose powder, and poured out four cartoonishly huge balloons.

"How much are we getting?"

"Fifteen hundred an ounce."

Something about it felt wrong, but the money was too good. We drove to the spot and two dudes were sitting in a car. The bad feeling came back.

I said, "I don't like this."

Dennis looked hurt. "He's a righteous dude." He was put out that I dared question his judgment. He was proud of the deal.

When we got in the other car to do the deal, I slid behind the driver. The scene was tense. Tense as fuck. Three of us in that car were gripping hard, something Dennis didn't register. He was smiling. The guy behind the wheel wouldn't look at me.

"Do you have the drugs?" The dude directed the question to me. I didn't say anything. I had no expression on my face. I just looked forward. Dennis seemed confused by my demeanor. He handed the man the balloons. The driver turned to me and shoved a wad of money in my direction. The second he looked at me, I knew he knew I knew he was a cop. He gestured again with the money. I didn't move.

"Take it."

Dennis said, "Danny, take the money." It was too late to stop this train. Dennis was using names. It wasn't like it would have been too hard to figure out who I was, but the whole situation was fucked. Still, I didn't move. Frustrated, Dennis grabbed the money. My mind was churning through a hundred calculations on how fucked up this was.

When we got out, Dennis was upset. I think he expected me to be grateful or impressed by the size of the deal. "What was that all about?"

"Your guy's a narc, Dennis. That was a setup."

"No, trust me, trust me. He's a righteous dude."

I had Dennis drop me off at Johnny's, a diner on the corner of Magnolia and Laurel Canyon. There was a waitress there who was a friend of mine. From grilling her about the joint while deciding whether to rob the place, I knew the owner kept a ton of cash in a big safe in the office. Now I handed her my half of the deal. "I need you to switch this money for me." She looked at the roll in shock. Three thousand dollars was a ton of money in 1965.

"Danny, I don't know if I can."

I knew she had access to the safe. "Please, I really need you to do this."

She disappeared into the back. When she returned, she handed me a manila envelope. "Don't tell anyone I did this."

"You're an angel."

"Tell me something I don't know."

She asked me to stay and have something to eat, but I had things to do. A friend picked me up and we went by the motel, where I grabbed the guns and four thousand dollars I had stashed there. I took it all to my parents' house, where years earlier I'd dug a hole near the fountain in the backyard as a stash spot, and buried the lot: the money, the shotgun, the machine gun, and the hand grenade.

I didn't know what to do. I could've split town—certainly the neighborhood. Just hit the road to lie low somewhere. If a bust was coming, I certainly didn't want it to go down at my parents' house, so I went back to the motel. I was exhausted, burnt-out from running and gunning. My body was tired, and my soul was sick. Dennis pulled up. The second he did, cars flew into the parking lot from all directions. Federal agents with guns drawn screamed, "Get down! Hands on your heads!" Dennis dropped immediately. I rolled under a car. Agents reached under one side to grab me, and I rolled to the other. Back and forth. Feet kicked at me.

I yelled, "Come and get me, motherfuckers!"

Finally, an agent kneeled right next to me and stuck his gun at my face. "I got you, motherfucker."

"Yeah, you got me." Two agents pulled me from under the car and beat the shit out of me.

"Where's my money, motherfucker?" The agent who had been sitting in the front of the car when the deal went down was in my face.

"It's in my pocket."

He rifled through my pocket and found five hundred dollars I'd kept. But when he saw the denominations, he knew it wasn't his money. His case was in danger. "Where's my money?" he yelled.

I was thrown in the back of a brand-new blue Buick Riviera with beige carpet. I remember it was beige because I bled all over it. They beat my ass all the way to the Federal Building downtown.

Each punch was followed by another. "Where's my money?"

For years, I had nightmares in which that agent screamed at me, demanding to know where his money was. I'd wake up in the pen yelling, "Your mom has it, bitch!"

Chapter 3

YOUNG MEN AND FIRE

1965

The Feds were in a bind. They didn't have the deal money. I hadn't touched the drugs or the money in the car when the deal went down. And when they tested the balloons, the stuff came back as pure granulated sugar. To cover their asses, the Feds kicked me back to the police department. If this had happened today, they wouldn't have had a case. There are laws against "silver platter" busts where the Feds hand a case under their jurisdiction to the state. They tried to explain this away by saying local law enforcement agents were in on the bust, even though that wasn't the case.

So I was back in LA County Jail. Dennis was, too, but we were kept apart. One day, the guard came in and said, "Trejo, you have visitors, and they're fine!" I went into the visiting area and saw two women. They were stunning and dressed in killer style. It was my birth mother, Dolores Rivera King, and my sister, Dyhan. I hadn't seen them since I was three and had an accident in a tub we used as a *barrio* swimming pool in my mother's backyard. The way my sister remembers it, it was fairly innocent—I fell and sprained my arm. But when my father heard about the accident, he went crazy. He threatened my mother's husband, told my mother he'd kill her if she ever tried to see me again, and took me to Burbank to live with my grandparents.

My dad had bad-mouthed my birth mom so much when I was a little kid, I truly believed she was a monster. The fact that she had an affair with

26

my father while she was married to a man who was off fighting the Second World War condemned her in my whole family's eyes. Back then, people didn't understand that when you shame the parent, you shame the child. Over time, it was easiest to just stop thinking about her. But now she was in LA County Jail, visiting me.

My birth mother and Dyhan said they'd read about my crime in the paper. My sister was impressed. She said, "I didn't know I had a brother who was a gangster!"

I know this is hard to believe, but my mother was beautiful, and she looked just like me. It was like looking in a mirror. They were the women in my life who hadn't been in my life. But we didn't get into any of that— we didn't talk about the past, what happened, what was lost. I didn't find out that my father had threatened my mother to stay away from me until Dyhan told me years later. That day in County, I was just happy to see them. Having people care about me and visit me in jail meant everything. It gave me hope.

After I said goodbye, I headed back to my cell through a wave of catcalls about how hot my visitors were.

The case had been thrown out of court twice already. The DA only had three shots to secure a conviction of Dennis and me, or our case had to be dropped. The first two times we were going to trial I passed Dennis on my way to the attorney's room. He was heading out as I was heading in. I said, "Keep it together. We got this beat. Hold tough, holmes."

He nodded and made a fist.

The third time I went to the attorney's room, I didn't pass Dennis. I knew what that meant. He'd flipped.

The day of the trial came, and I was brought into court cuffed. They stood me next to Dennis and I looked down at his hands. No cuffs.

He said, "Danny, I have to plead guilty to bunko sales. They said they'd only give you sixty days if I plead guilty."

"Dennis, we have this thing beat. This is their last chance to get us or the case gets thrown out forever. Don't listen to them. They can't promise you shit, Dennis. I can't get sixty days. I violated parole. Don't you fucking get it? Fuck these motherfuckers."

He couldn't look at me. "Danny, either you plead guilty with me, or I'm going to testify that you sold heroin to an undercover police officer."

Their case, which had been so leaky, was now airtight. "I'll get you, Dennis."

"Danny, please understand. You know what they'll do to me in there. You know I can't handle time."

I thought of all his showboating in front of broads about how we'd "hold court in the streets." His tough talk and his "I'm with Trejo" shit. But then I remembered what I had told him about what happened to pretty boys like him in prison, how deeply that had scared him. We had it beat, but he was rightfully terrified, the way 99.9 percent of people are when they are faced with hard time. He didn't grow up with prison as an expected outcome and an uncle who groomed him to succeed there. For those who hadn't grown up going to juvie and knowing the system, going to prison was like going to Indonesia, and guys like Dennis knew nothing of Indonesia.

I may have caused my own downfall, but I was still furious. I wasn't thinking that I was stealing, cheating, dealing, and otherwise living a life of crime. I was just pissed Dennis had pulled us into this deal, didn't have the balls and sense to try and fight it, and was snitching on me.

The judge ordered the bailiff to remove my cuffs for the proceedings.

"But Your Honor—" said the bailiff. He'd seen Dennis and me having a heated conversation and wasn't sure I should be unleashed.

"Don't contradict me, son. Remove the defendant's handcuffs!" As soon as he did, I went after Dennis.

I was sentenced to ten years.

I wasn't sent directly to Soledad. I was lucky. At Chino, in the Guidance Center, the classification committee saw my past history with the Ding Crew and assigned me to a Conservation Camp. I was going to get to fight fires again.

The Conservation Camps were part of a program set up by the California Department of Forestry and Fire Protection to give youth offenders a chance to do meaningful work—fighting fires while serving their sentences. During my first three-year stretch, back when I'd maimed a sailor in tenth grade, I'd been sent to Camp Glenn Rockey in San Dimas. It sits high on a mountain overlooking the Pomona Valley. There are summer camps in the area, and to us kids from the city, that's kind of what Glenn Rockey felt like. There were pine trees, a fence, cabins with cells for lockdown, and a Smokey

Bear watchtower for the guards. To me, after Eastlake, Camp Glenn Rockey felt free.

In November 1961 a fire started in Stone Canyon above Bel Air off Mulholland Drive. Wind gusts of a hundred miles an hour and dry conditions made it spread faster than anything the fire department had ever seen. The crews were ranked from 51 to 55, with 55, the crew I was on, being made up of the most incorrigible juvenile offenders. They called us the Ding Crew. We were the bad seeds of the bad seeds.

Firefighting at night was terrifying. It wasn't the fire itself that scared us. The burning underbrush unleashed huge boulders that we could hear crashing downhill. We'd be trying to catch a few winks of sleep, hear a massive rumbling, and know that a boulder the size of a car was hurtling toward us, but we wouldn't know from where. I was fascinated by how the fire had a life of its own. It made up its own rules. The fire didn't just burn aboveground—it was burning through root systems, too. Trees a hundred meters from each other exploded in flames. I saw a fire catch a deer running downhill, and fires are slower on the downhill. One time we were by a grassy area we'd saved and a rabbit that was on fire ran across the break, spreading the fire to the side we'd just spared.

A juvenile crew is something to behold. We had insane amounts of energy, in part because we competed with each other. We were serious about it, but it was a game at the same time. We could clear a hundred and fifty yards of brush in ten minutes. Some of the adult crews watched us and got pissed off. They weren't hardened convicts, just alcoholics and fuckups behind on child support payments.

One of them said to me, "Hey, slow down. You're making people look bad." There we were in the middle of the biggest fire in LA history and that asshole was worried kids were working harder than him. I said, "Fuck your mother, holmes." All of his boys stood up. I said, "We both have a shovel. What are you going to do?"

Gilbert had taught me exactly how to deal with dudes like this. He said, "The first thing you do if someone starts shit with you is say, 'Fuck your mother, now what are you going to do?'" That's the worst thing you can possibly say, and it stuns them. They're expecting some kind of buildup and instead you take it straight to level Z. By saying "Fuck your mother," what you're really saying is "Let's do this. I want *this*. I'm ready." Most guys will back down.

"Let it go, Dave," another firefighter said. Wise man. Dave checked me out like he was weighing his options. He knew I'd fuck him up.

"Ain't worth it," he said.

Mission accomplished.

"Fuck you, pussy."

My guys cheered, then we got back to work. The fire was shifting quickly, and houses were literally exploding in flames. We were clearing the ground above a group of mansions when a woman and a man came running toward us. A Rolls-Royce in front of their house had just caught on fire. "Save our house! Save our house, please!"

These people would fall on their knees in front of us—we felt like superheroes. Little old ladies who would call the cops if they saw us in the streets were bringing us thermoses of soup and sandwiches.

A fire makes everyone human; it's a great equalizer. They weren't rich people to us right then, they were just people who needed help. We got to work. A team of us used Pulaski axes to clear heavier brush. We were followed by a group with shovels, then the third line used heavy-duty McLeod rakes. We cut a firebreak around their house in twenty minutes. It was a blur of sweat, heat, and smoke that burned my eyes. After the fire passed, the woman hugged us and cried. But there was no time to rest; there were more fires to fight. We slept on the ground in shifts, working around the clock.

After the Bel Air–Brentwood Fire and a secondary fire, the Santa Ynez Fire, were put down, the level of damage was unbelievable. From Malibu, Topanga Canyon, and all through the Valley, all the way to Beverly Hills, hundreds of houses were lost. Burt Lancaster and Zsa Zsa Gabor lost their homes. Richard Nixon hosed his rental down to save it before fleeing. Seeing the fear in people and witnessing their loss made me feel like we were closer than I ever imagined.

When the fires were put down, a big dinner was held at the Beverly Hilton to honor the fire crews. The fire chief singled out the Ding Crew from Camp Glenn Rockey for our work. Rich people from Beverly Hills sent bottles of whiskey to our table. The foremen pretended like they didn't see. We were so proud. It might have been the first time any of us were recognized for anything other than being disappointments. Five of the guys from the Ding Crew ended up having careers in forestry.

The most important thing about the youth fire camps was they made us feel like heroes. We would actually joke around and stand like we were Superman with our hands on our hips, saying, "Dun de dun!" Fighting fires was the first real lesson we delinquents got in building self-esteem.

Now that I was back, a court counselor sent me to Jamestown, an adult Conservation Camp, to train. Firefighting is the hardest manual labor imaginable. We were taken through a program of running, push-ups, and pull-ups to get fit. Years later, when I would hear someone bitching on a film set about how hard the work was, I'd think, *Try fighting fires, asshole. Let's see how you feel throwing a shovelful of dirt at an eighty-foot flame and spitting out rocks and dirt.*

From Jamestown I was transferred to Konocti, and then from there to Magalia, where I was stationed when we were sent to fight a massive fire in the Sequoia National Forest.

I loved fighting fires. We were nestled in the bosom of massive, ancient trees, some older than the pyramids of Giza. It felt holy. We share DNA with trees. Trees communicate with each other; they feed their saplings through their root systems; they favor their own; they help other trees around them knowing they might need that help returned later; they clean the air; there is no life without them. I've never lost my love for the forest.

The fire camps were not the same animal factories that the prisons were, but they weren't without their problems. In Magalia there was a guy who thought he was a badass. Jamestown had a boxing program, and I'd won the CDF lightweight and welterweight titles during my first stint there. This guy knew I was a boxing champion and kept talking smack about how he could kick my ass. One day, he made his move and I cut his face open with a dustpan. His friends jumped in, and when it was all over, two of my crew, Sonny Rios and George Velasquez, and I got hauled in.

That was the end of our firefighting careers. We were told we were being transferred to San Quentin. The home to California's death row, San Quentin was the big house in the California prison system. We'd graduated to the Harvard of penitentiaries.

Chapter 4

THE RIGHT NOW

1966

At night, the colossal castle walls of San Quentin glow through the San Francisco fog. It's like it sucks moonlight from the night sky and reflects it back in a luminescent gray. From the San Rafael Bridge it looks like a medieval fortress vibrating from the inside.

Driving down the foggy road, waist-chained and manacled on the Grey Goose—the prison bus—I remembered again what Jhonnie Harris had said to me about San Quentin. He was right; the headlights were the only thing that were going to beat me there.

I'd been to Tracy, Chino, Vacaville, the camps in Jamestown, Konocti, and Magalia, but San Quentin was different. By the time I got there, San Quentin had a one-hundred-year history of being a place where hopes and dreams about the future die. Since it was night, we entered through the main gate.

I was with my two friends from Camp, Sonny Rios and George Velasquez. The bus pulled into R&R (Receiving and Release). We shuffled in, and they took the waist chains and the shackles off.

"Everyone strip!"

And we did. One of the earliest rules Gilbert had taught me, before I went to juvie, was that when they say, "Strip! Grab your dick! Pull up your balls. Bend over! Spread 'em," you don't look around, you don't hesitate, you just do whatever you're told. Gilbert taught me to act like I'd done it a million times, like it bored me. The strip search is one of the earliest op-portunities guys have to see who's going to be a predator and who's going to be prey. The guys who stand there covering themselves with their hands or even pause for a second, they're already telling not only the guards but also the other inmates that they are fish, insecure and scared. The guy who argued back or bucked at the guards' barked orders wasn't the badass. He was the scared motherfucker.

Then came the medical check, which was just a temperature reading, after which we were herded through the clothing room. Trustees handed us boxers, shirts, shorts, pants, and a jacket. If the inmate thought you were legit, he'd give you your size. If he thought you were a lame, he'd hand you something way too big or too small just to fuck with you. How your clothes fit was one of the first indicators, flagging you as a player or a fucking lame, when you hit the general population. The die is cast early.

From Receiving and Release, we entered the Garden of Beauty. The garden, with its manicured trees and delicate rosebushes, was tended by an old trustee serving multiple life sentences for murder. Word was if someone so much as spat in the garden, they'd be dead. We passed the Adminis-trative Segregation Building on our left and stepped into the Main Yard. The Main Yard in San Quentin is perfectly designed—architecturally and psychologically—to fuck your mind.

Across the Yard, on top of the North Block, was Condemned Men's Row, better known as Death Row. On the tall metal chimney above the gas cham-ber there was a light piercing the fog. It was green now, but I already knew that it would turn red when someone was being gassed and everyone had to leave the Yard.

San Quentin is the most Right Now place on Earth that isn't a war zone. If you want to survive, you have no choice but to be in one place, *this very moment*, and only this moment. Will you live or will you die—*today*? First thing you have to do when you get locked up is make peace with the Right Now. It will never be your friend, but you can't let it be your enemy or you'll go insane. Sure, a certain level of insanity helps you survive the pen, but you can't go too far over the edge.

The Right Now was all we had, but the past surrounded us, a distraction and danger. San Quentin is haunted with the ghosts of everyone who has been shanked, beaten, or strangled to death within its walls; the ghosts of every man who ripped up a sheet, wrapped it around his neck, and jumped off a tier; the ghosts of those gassed in the execution chamber. Women, too. Not long before I got there, a woman who murdered her pregnant niece had been executed, along with two male accomplices. Their spirits swirled around me. You can't tell me those souls were at rest. Even in the Right Now, the hopelessness of my future taunted me. San Quentin was every nightmare I'd ever had rolled into one, but if someone asked me what the dream was about, I couldn't say.

The Right Now was so heavy, the dude in front of me couldn't handle it. He suddenly socked the guy standing next to him, knowing it meant he'd be taken away. Wherever he was going, it was anywhere but here.

Until I was assigned a cell, I was held in B Section, where everyone coming to Quentin was put while the prison officials figured out what your status was—if you were a snitch, if you had enemies, if you had special needs—and classified you accordingly; that is, assigned you a prison block. When I came in, mattress and blanket rolled up under my arm, everyone was yelling shit at me. I didn't yell back because I didn't know the play yet. My first night there, a kite (a message on a little piece of paper) got shoved into my cell—it was from an old crime partner of mine, Tyrone. Apparently, the kite informed me, a guy I'd burned on the streets in LA was in San Quentin telling everyone I'd ripped him off and he knew I was coming.

I sent a message back to Tyrone: *Don't let me come out of my cell with just my dick in my hand.*

I needed a shank.

That first night in B Section, I stared at the ceiling. The cooling water pipes sounded like little explosions. Then the screaming started. Some men were insane; others were being raped. Then came real explosions. Before disposable razors, men would get the big, old-fashioned kind of shavers and fill them with match heads. They launched these minibombs from their cells, and they landed like M-80s on the concrete below the tiers, echoing through the whole block. Between the screaming, the explosions, and the knowledge of what I'd have to do to make it in Quentin, it felt like a war zone.

Then, for a brief, magical moment, the place fell silent; the screaming stopped; even the water pipes stopped squealing.

I was twenty-one years old.

I said to myself, *Danny, you're going to die here.*

I got one hour of sleep that night.

Violence and death shimmered in the air at San Quentin like the heat distortion above a desert highway. I was sitting in B Section a few days later when I heard a guy screaming. A guard was running after him, his feet pounding the floor, and I heard him yell, "Halt! Halt!" Then he shot the inmate—right there in the hallway of the block, a very loud crack. Everything went quiet.

Sonny and George were in B Section with me. I yelled, "He shot him!" but it came out weirdly high-pitched and weak.

I immediately dropped my voice and said to the *vato* in the cell next to me, "Beto, see that?"

He said, "Fuck you!" Then he mimicked a little girl's voice, "He shot him!"

But by then all of B Section was making fun of me, yelling, "He shot him! Oh my God, he shot him!" like squealing teenagers. I'm lucky I didn't end up with the nickname "He shot him!"

I stayed in B Section about twenty days before I was assigned to South Block, cell C550. The first night there, I again couldn't sleep. While it was less insane than B Section, there were still screams and creepy laughter that punctuated the night. Through the wall between B and C Sections, I heard the muffled explosions of the shaver bombs being launched from the tiers, like a mortar attack on a village in the next valley.

What I remember most about San Quentin was being cold all the time. I could never get warm. And the way the walls were painted made the light in the Yard so bright, even when it was gray—even at night it could hurt your eyes. I'll never forget the smell. San Quentin has a funk to it, a moldy, smoking stank that could never be covered, no matter how much bleach was used to clean it up.

My buddy Tyrone was a good-looking Mexican whose mother had named him after her favorite actor, Tyrone Power. Tyrone was very sensitive to how you pronounced his name. If someone made it sound too Black by putting the emphasis on the first syllable—*TY-rone*—he'd go apeshit on them. Another *vato* from LA, Cookie, had an equally low rage threshold. He was a beautiful Mexican who must have weighed 120 pounds, tops, but he was a stone-cold killer. Because he was so small, Cookie was underestimated and picked on—to the bully's peril. He had stabbed and killed a man who grabbed his ass at a dance. Whether it was an accident or a deliberate fuck-you move on the part of the man didn't matter. It was his last mistake.

In life, you have to know who you are fucking with. If anyone caught Cookie's eyes on the Yard, he'd say, "You want this? Huh, motherfucker?" They'd back off. If they didn't, they'd be dead.

A couple days in, Tyrone, Cookie, and I were approaching the lower yard on Quentin and these two guys fast-stepped around us and stabbed a guy six or seven times. I froze.

"Come on, come on," Tyrone said. "We got to get off the Yard." He dragged me toward the Block.

To see someone used as a pincushion—the initial brutality was shocking. But because there were killings all the time in San Quentin—stabbings, beatings—I got used to it. Fast. It's sick to say, but eventually, when someone got hit on the Yard, it was exciting. Shit jumping off made us all buzz.

Executions were the opposite.

Inmates killing each other was one thing, but it was the government-sanctioned executions that added the heaviest layer to the Right Now of San Quentin. It didn't matter how bad you were, how organized your crew was—La Eme might run the Yard, Nuestra Familia, the Aryan Brotherhood, or the Black Guerrilla Family might fight them for it—but the ultimate predator in San Quentin was always the warden, the guards, the hangman.

The guards said "Dead man walking" when they shuffled the condemned through the Yard for a meeting with their lawyers or whoever. We were supposed to get out of the way and turn our backs as they passed by, not making eye contact with the prisoner. But when the Death Row inmates came through, we'd half twist around to get a look at them. To the world outside, they were infamous. In our world, they were famous. Usually, the condemned man would try to make eye contact and say hello to whoever they could because getting off the Row was like a vacation for them.

We all know the grim reaper is coming for us—but the condemned men in San Quentin *know* know. The day is coming. They'll be given a diaper, and the red light will shine for them, and between that day and this one there is nothing but more of the same. We saw that in their eyes and we felt the doom coming off them like a wolf separated from its pack, left to die alone.

In San Quentin, hopelessness is carved in men's faces. Maybe they didn't get a letter, or a visit, or someone gave them a hard look, or blew them a kiss—whatever the cause, you could see when they were broken.

I remember there was one *vato*, he was all dressed up. He made a mistake of telling everyone he had a broad visiting. Bus after bus came and went with no sign of her. After the last bus unloaded, he couldn't conceal his grief.

Smelling blood, we all went off. "Sancho must be fucking her right, *ese*."

"Sorry, *carnal*, Pedro wouldn't let her come today. Maybe he'll let her come some other week if he ain't fucking her."

The *vato* was broken. He killed himself by jumping off the tier.

One day on the Yard, Ty said a *mayate*—pejorative Spanish slang for a Black prisoner—had come in from Tracy talking about how I'd fucked him over. "This *mayate*, this dude *está mirando corto*." He's looking at you short. It was likely. We fucked a lot of people over in Tracy. It is what it was. Apparently, I'd robbed him and his partner. The other guy was already dead—killed in Tracy—but this one was with us in Quentin.

"Ty," I said. "Get me something." We'd either get shanks from the construction crew or make them from anything metal, usually our bunks. Years later they'd get more creative and melt them down out of anything plastic: cups, shampoo or hair gel bottles, toothbrushes. But the metal shanks of my era were better. Whatever they were made of, they had to be holstered in either paper, cardboard, or plastic and tape so they could be keistered in our only real hiding spot—our assholes. The shank Ty was going to get me was coming from the metal shop. There was a Mexican from Wilmington who'd make little key-like things in the welding shop that could open the light fixture in your cell so you could stash shivs. If the guards didn't find the key, you were good, and the guards weren't looking for keys. The plan was for Ty to get the shiv later in the day and store it in his light socket to give me the next morning.

The stakes are high in prison, they always are. But this was different-level real shit. Some of the guys I rolled with had killed this guy's partner back in Tracy, and he blamed me for the death. Everything in his world—in prison, on the street—was riding on how he dealt with this situation.

It was kill-or-die time.

Ty said, "Until I get it to you, vest yourself." What he meant was that I should armor up—put a magazine down my shorts to protect me from a knife blow. Back then we'd get magazines from the library cart. *National Geographic* was thick, which was important, but its small size made it hard to tuck into your shorts and under your jacket so that it would stay. *Look* and *Life* magazines worked better because they were long. It's amazing how much protection even a thin magazine offers against a shiv.

The next morning, I grabbed a *Look* from my cell to give me a layer of armor while I looked for Tyrone out on the Yard. I tucked it in my shorts, pulled my T-shirt over it, then put my jacket on and buttoned it up. I left my cell, and the second I rounded the corner of my tier to hit the stairway, the brother stepped up and hit me twice in the stomach—*Bam! Bam!* He hit me so hard, it knocked the wind out of me.

Looking down, I saw my jacket was covered with blood. I got light-headed. I thought I was done. From over this dude's shoulder, I saw Ty running up the steps four at a time. Just as the Black dude turned to run, he grunted two sick-sounding animal grunts, *"Uuuuuhng, uuuuuhng,"* and dropped on the stairs. Tyrone was standing behind him holding a shank. He'd got him right in the heart.

I said, "Ty, I've been hit."

"No you haven't."

"I've been hit."

Ty pointed at the man's bloody hand. "The blood on you is his." Ty was in no mood to stand around and talk. "C'mon, Danny. We gotta hit the Yard."

I dumped my bloody jacket and stepped over the man's body, and we fast-stepped it to the Yard just as the alarms sounded and the doors slammed shut.

As soon as we hit the Yard, the gates locked behind us. We were safe.

Ty passed me his jacket.

"Damn, *carnal*, thank God you were there."

"You owe me, holmes. You owe me," said Ty.

"Fuck yeah."

"Can we shower together?"

We burst out laughing at the absurdity of it all, the dark, warped humor of the pen. One time I saw a guy stumble through the Yard desperately trying to pull a knife out of his back that someone had just stuck there, and everyone burst into laughter. It was so surreal. I thought, *This place is fucked up.*

Worst part of it was, I was laughing, too.

I pulled out the magazine. "Thank God for *Look* magazine."

Ty looked at me real serious. Then, pitching his voice real high, like a teenaged girl's, he squealed, "I've been HIIIIIIIT."

We laughed so hard we almost pissed our pants.

A man was dead on the stairwell around the corner from my cell and I didn't care. It was him or me, and he had brought it on. Enough time in prison and it starts to shape your mind—the violence, the will to survive, what's funny, and the value of one man's life.

The guy who had the heroin bag in Quentin was Richard Berry, the heroin dealer I knew from the Valley. The same guy Dennis and I had gone to with the guns after Dennis wrecked his car in that park in North Hollywood. Richard was a stone-cold junkie. A small jacket hung on the man like an extra large. But he was doing good inside. He was the richest guy in Quentin.

Ty and I started working for Richard collecting debts. Richard said, "Danny, some guys owe me money, these Samoans." I found them on the Yard and went up to them with Ty, Cookie, and Froggy, another *vato* from LA, on my back. I sat down across from a guy who was as big as a house. I said very properly, very politely, "Excuse me. Hi, hello. I want you to write your family and tell them if they don't send money by Tuesday, you're going to die."

His mouth hung open.

"Yeah," I continued, "you owe Richard Berry some money, and that's my money, and I want my money." Ty, Cookie, and Froggy stepped closer. "If you don't have it by next week, we're going to have to charge you interest, and I don't want to charge you interest."

He said, "Okay, okay." Two days later, the Samoans approached me. "Danny, we don't have any cash, but we have cigarettes—we got nineteen cartons—will you take that?"

Richard was psyched. Cigarettes were as good or better than money. In return for my work, Richard cut me off a lot of heroin. I got to use as much as I wanted and sell the rest. The arrangement reminded me of when Dennis and I had traded guns to Richard for heroin right after we'd hit that tree in North Hollywood Park. It got my wheels turning. I asked Richard how he got busted and he said he'd been raided. I put two and two together. I was pretty sure I wasn't the only one Dennis had rolled over on.

I settled into San Quentin, working for Richard and boxing. When I came to San Quentin I already had a reputation as a boxer. I'd been boxing since I was eight years old—my uncle Gilbert taught me how. Around the same time, Gilbert was training for the Golden Gloves, so he used me as his sparring partner. He was fourteen, six years older than me, but it didn't stop him from going at me hard. He used to throw rocks in my face when I wasn't looking to sharpen my reflexes. If I didn't move my head in time, I'd get hit with these big old rocks. He told me he was doing it to help me get faster, but he was probably just fucking with me. I had knots on my head from the rocks that hit me, but I got real good at slipping punches.

Gilbert was a great boxer, probably good enough to have gone pro later. He was the boxing champ in the Army and in prison. But I may have been better. A couple of years into boxing with Gilbert I learned how to not just avoid getting hit, I learned how to hit back. I learned how to throw lightning-fast jabs with a magazine under my armpit and how to keep it from falling when I set up to throw the jab again. I kept my punches tight, straight, and fast. By ten I could throw a three-punch combination: jab, right hand, hook—the combination Floyd Mayweather uses so beautifully. In the ring, I was a machine. That was my style—not to get hit. But if I did, it was alright. I had an iron chin. It didn't matter what came my way. I was undefeatable. Even the dudes in the pen who could fight on the street couldn't touch me in the ring. They weren't trained boxers.

What Gilbert was teaching me was incredibly valuable. He said, "When you know you can beat anyone with your fists, it's going to change the way you deal with everything. It gives you confidence, like carrying a piece."

He was right.

I had boxed in every institution I had ever been in, from juvie to Jamestown, so by the time I got to San Quentin I had a reputation, especially among the Mexicans. The word was, "Oh, fuck yeah! We got a champ."

They had fights every month, so I started training in the gym, where they had a ring and heavy bags. The guards took notice of me, and then I had status and privileges. They let the fighters go to breakfast early so we could head out to do roadwork on the track.

There were plenty of fighters who had no formal training. I could tell just by talking to someone how he'd be in the ring. How confident he was, how he held his body, if he got heated easily, all these things told me how knowledgeable he was about fighting. I put this knowledge to use on the streets, too. If I got into an argument with someone, I could tell if he could fight just by how he stood. Depending on how he was standing, I knew which arm he'd use to throw a punch and whether he'd be off-balance or not. If his legs were squared up with his shoulders, he was telling me he was going to fall. I knew how to read bodies and body language. I knew what to do and how fast I could do it because I'd done it so many times that it was a reflex.

Some guys did their time reading, playing chess, running the track, or playing pinochle. Each of these was an escape to another world—there were four guys at SQ who would play pinochle for a whole day, then leave the cards so they could return to them the next. The guys who didn't have something like that went crazy. For me, it was boxing. Whenever I was boxing, I wasn't in the penitentiary. My mind was in another world. And it did more than pass the time. Like the firefighting I'd done in juvie and afterward at the adult Conservation Camps, it felt important.

My first competition was a title fight. Even in the joint, when they announced my name, I felt like I was a star. Everyone would be bonaroo—all decked out—like it was a fight in Vegas. After all the roadwork, all the sparring, I was excited. I knew I was going to show everyone in that penitentiary just what I could do. When you know you've put in the work, when you know you did three miles of track work instead of two, you are filled with confidence. Every time I stepped in a ring I was representing my people, and I was going to make them proud.

When I climbed into the ring, it was electric. Everybody was cheering like I was a celebrity. They knew who I was. They were expecting something, and I was going to deliver.

The only fight I ever lost was back in Jamestown, and it was because I threw it. I didn't have any money on my books when I got there, and I needed it. Chino Sainz came up to me and said, "We have this fight for you."

I'd just arrived, but I was Gilbert's nephew, so everyone already knew I could fight. I didn't have time to put in proper training, so I said, "Put some money on the other guy." Everyone who knew me put money on him, I made a cut, and we all did pretty well that day. After that I became champion of Jamestown and never lost again.

A fight in San Quentin was a war. The gym was in an enormous metal-and-cement warehouse—it could fit most of the prison population. It was the 60s, and the race wars and the gang wars were heating up. The boxing matches were a way of establishing and claiming racial superiority in the joint. But even when I was fighting another Mexican, the Syndicate bet on me because they knew I wasn't going to lose.

The inmates sat on chairs that were all locked together so they couldn't pick them up if a fight broke out, but there actually weren't many riots at the events. We segregated ourselves to keep the peace because we knew if we fucked up they'd take boxing away from us, and nobody wanted that.

The guy I was fighting was a roundhouse slugger, so I just got him with jabs, jabs, jabs. Maybe he could fight on the streets, but in a ring, he wasn't shit. I smoked him.

Moments like that, my life in prison felt just as full as it ever had on the outside. But then there were moments when I feared prison was turning me into someone I didn't recognize. Playing dominoes at a table on the Main Yard, I had picked four fives. In dominoes, that's like getting a royal flush in poker. Even better, there was big money on the table. I couldn't wait to play them. It was a Black guy's turn. Only when heavy gambling was going down would whites, Blacks, and Mexicans play against each other. This guy was thinking too long, but I kept my cool because I knew I was about to blow everyone's mind with what I had in my hand. A lot of money was flowing. The man finally moved, and it was my time to hit it. More money came onto the table. I didn't notice a dude roll up because there were so many people watching. Then: *bam bam bam bam*. The dude hit a man who was leaning over the table next to the Black guy three times in the back and once in the neck. He must have severed a major artery because blood was squirting everywhere. I instinctively covered my face and got blood on my sleeve and hand.

Ty grabbed me. "What you doing, *carnal*? We've got to step."

I held up the dominoes. "No, no! Keep playing!"

"Who gives a fuck?"

"I have a run of fives."

Ty wasn't impressed. "We got to go."

I moved with everyone else. We had to get inside before they shut down the Yard and we were all stuck outside.

When I got back to my cell, I was in a rage. I was holding on to the blood-soaked dominoes so hard they almost cut my hand. I thought, *What kind of animal have I become? What kind of* animal *have I become?*

As far as the prison system was concerned, what I had become was an "Institutional Convenience," which meant "Do whatever the hell you want with him because he's too much trouble." While some of the guards liked me because I was a boxer and ran protection rackets, I was simply doing too much business far too often for the authorities to continue to look the other way. The fact that I handled the heroin bag for Richard was common knowledge and something any one of a number of snitches might have told the guards. Another factor was race. Whenever a group of guys got too organized, the bulls would ship them off to other institutions.

Whatever the reason, I was sent off to Folsom. The ink on my tattoo—a huge, hot *charra* in a sombrero sprawled across my chest—was barely dry. *Charras* are the Mexican women who fought with Pancho Villa. They carried rifles and dynamite; they fought alongside the men. Mine was inked by Harry "Super Jew" Ross, a bad motherfucker from my hometown of Pacoima, who became a world-famous tattoo artist later in life. Mine was his first. Harry had started it in Susanville back in '65. I went big because I thought I was in for ten years. If I'd known it was only going to be four, maybe I would have gotten something less massive, like a puppy. Other guys were getting tattoos of Aztec warriors, but I didn't want a dude. Harry used three E guitar strings run through a melted-down toothbrush, dipping them in India ink or melted-down chess pieces. He did the outline in Susanville, but after that I cut that dude's face in Magalia and got shipped off to San Quentin. When Harry got to San Quentin, he did the shading, but then I went to Folsom. Harry said, "Don't touch your tattoo—wait till I get there." Harry showed up at Folsom and had nearly finished shading it on the Yard when I got sent to Soledad.

Chapter 5

HELP

1968

Prison is a waste of the best years in a person's life, but when I arrived in Soledad I wasn't there to do my time and get home. Since I assumed I'd always be there, I treated it like my job.

I was resourceful, and resources in prison are traded in different currencies—food, drugs, whatever.

Back in '61 in LA County I saw the "whatever" of this stretched beyond belief. By then every type of lockup was home to me. I'd been locked up so many times, I was more used to being inside than out. While I was waiting to get shipped out to Tracy, there was a greasy, dirty, scrawny white boy in County. He was so poor, he didn't have a belt, and instead used a piece of string to keep his pants up.

The dude was going to get jumped by the Blacks, so he came to us for protection. The problem was he didn't have any money. I felt sorry for him. It was clear the only shower the man was ever going to have was the one he was going to get in jail. There were three in our cell—Johnny Ronnie, Tacho, and me—so we told the dude he could clean up for us and we'd keep an eye out for him. He couldn't sleep in our cell, but we let him sleep just outside so people knew he had eyes on him.

A couple of days later the guy told me he had hypnotic powers and he could get us high. We weren't doing anything, so we said, "Why not give it a shot?"

44

It was like a guided meditation. He talked us through the whole thing, rolling a joint, sparking it up, taking a deep hit, and the three of us felt super high. The man said, "Your body already remembers. It knows what to do. It anticipates getting high, and that's how it works."

That got my wheels turning. The next day I said to the dude, "If you can do that for weed, can you get us high on heroin?"

He said he could, but we'd have to really focus for it to work. I grabbed Tacho and Johnny Ronnie, and the dude sat us down and told us to close our eyes. For fifteen minutes, in great detail, he walked us through the process of copping the dope, finding a place to fix, cooking the heroin in a spoon, drawing it into a needle, and sticking it in our veins.

Even before I fake-fixed, I could taste it in my mouth. Any junkie knows what that is like. By the time he described it hitting my bloodstream, I felt the warmth flowing through my body.

If that white boy wasn't a career criminal, he could have been a professional hypnotist, someone who went to high schools and state fairs and got people to come onstage and act like cats and stuff.

But he was, in fact, a career criminal. He was Charles Manson.

Inside, Manson worked alone. The elaborately constructed social structure we Mexicans had was something denied him, even by his fellow white prisoners. Men fight to the death in prison over the gang they're in, but the different ethnic groups also cooperate with each other more than people think. It's the way we keep order. If someone fucks up and owes a debt or fucks with people and causes problems, it is up to their gang to regulate them. Prison gang life eluded Charles Manson, and even if he could have fallen into it, he sure as shit wouldn't have been a leader. It was only after he got out that he was able to create the social structure he wanted by finding a bunch of lost hippies in Haight-Ashbury and making them into a "Family." If Manson had tried to pull his game in East LA, he'd never have been at the helm of shit.

I was only in Soledad for a couple of days before I started my play. For that, I needed help from the Black inmates. I had a deal with a few of them that if they helped me out, I'd kick them back money.

A scenario might play out like this. It's lunchtime and I see there are new inmates in the chow hall. The guards direct the new guys to go this way or that, sometimes intentionally sending them in the wrong direction. A young guy might be sent over to a table full of guys of a different race, and I'll know he's a fish because he's already fucked up by listening to the guards instead of going with his own.

I approach this person and say, "What's up, holmes? You alright?" He might confess that he's alright, but afraid, unsure of the ropes, where to go, and what to do, or he might pretend he has everything under control and can handle himself.

"Fuck this, I'm good."

Reading fear is perhaps my greatest gift. And in prison, fear is everywhere. "You sure? Because you seem a little unsure."

I let him do his thing and that night, in the showers, I clear the joint out. Then I send four of the biggest, baddest-looking motherfuckers into the showers with full-on erections to surround him. Whatever the hell he's told himself about how things might go down and how much control he'll have goes out the window at that point. It's a recalculation as terrifying as it sounds.

This is where I step in. I look over the four and say, "What's up?"

They stare back at me, and we have a standoff that's been prearranged and rehearsed. Acting 101. From the looks on their faces, they appear to be weighing the costs of what's going down. Finally, they appear to relent. All the inmate knows for sure is that I just saved him from the most terrifying situation he's ever been in. Now he's of a different mindset—now that he knows the consequences of not paying, the only question that remains is how much I can milk him for on a monthly basis. Am I scamming him or doing him a favor? The truth is, whether it came from me or someone else, this is what was awaiting him. He needs structure and protection or he's never going to survive.

This is the world I was in. And, again, I was doing it well. Too well. I would cruise up and down the main hallway (we called it "Broadway") doing deals, flagrantly flouting the rules. I ran into an old-timer who said, "Danny, you remind me of me thirty years ago. Just keep going, and you'll be in here when you're old, just like me."

I had clean underwear, clean socks, custom-made boots. Harry "Super Jew" Ross had made it to Soledad and finished my *charra* tattoo. I was wearing too much starch on my clothes, they were pressed too nice, I was too "bonaroo." My cell was spotless. I was seen on the Mainline doing too much business. As far as they were concerned, I was in too many places far too often. I was calling shots.

They pulled what they call an *arrastre*, an extraction. When the guard asked for my ID, I said, "Fuck, man. C'mon."

"You got too much of a good thing going here, Trejo." They pulled me off the Mainline and transferred me to North, another part of the prison for inmates who had recently transitioned from Youth Authority. It housed a bunch of young, dumb fucks who thought they were bad. They couldn't wait to put in work and get noticed by the Syndicate or the emerging Black Guerrilla Family or whatever prison gang they hoped to be brought into. I was only twenty-four, but compared to the eighteen- and nineteen-year-olds in North, I was an OG with status. I'd already been to Chino, Jamestown, Folsom, and San Quentin. My résumé was beyond question. But getting transferred meant I'd lost my bags and would have to start over again.

It took me half an hour to put my stamp down.

In the intake line, a kid named O'Connor came up to me and asked if I could help him with some brothers who tried to rape him in Tracy.

"Do you draw?"

"Every month. My friends do, too."

"Can you get a shank?"

O'Connor nodded. I was shooting dope and using pills every day at that point and hadn't had a fix in almost twenty hours. I was kicking, cold, and felt sick to my stomach, but I thought, *Fuck it, I have to earn. I'll start here.*

"Follow me," I said. I knew in a new environment I had to immediately establish who I was and let everyone know the rumors were true—I was the Mexican not to fuck with.

As soon as we entered Lassen A, I did a quick scan.

"That them?"

I nodded toward four Black inmates standing on a set of stairs across the tier.

O'Connor said, "Yeah."

"Go get it now." I wasn't going into this empty-handed.

O'Connor had a friend create a distraction for the guard. The kid went to the door and started pointing and screaming like he was nuts. The guard pulled him away and O'Connor took off running to Lassen B, the adjacent cell block. I squatted in front of O'Connor's cell on the first tier and took in the scene. Everyone went back to what they were doing, but they were aware something was brewing. There were Mexicans up on the second tier talking, dudes at tables playing cards, but everyone was on alert. The four brothers, who'd seen me with their target O'Connor, were mad-dogging me. Their leader was a thin, muscular punk.

O'Connor came running back.

"Did you get it?"

He nodded and pulled up his shirt. Two swords were tucked in his pants. That meant a lot. O'Connor was pretty. He was always going to be prey, but not only was he willing to pay me for protection, he was willing to put in work.

I said, "Turn around and let them see you pass me one."

He handed me a screwdriver shaved down to a pick. They stopped glaring as soon as they saw O'Connor hand me that sword.

"Stay behind me and don't do shit till I tell you."

I tucked the shank in my pants and made a beeline to the stairs. Three of the dudes immediately stepped back. Big mistake. You never take a step back. I went straight for the leader.

"You know this man?" I was in his face, close enough to make him feel trapped, far enough away to pull my piece and stick him.

"Yeah, we know him from Tracy."

His mind was racing; he was scared. He didn't know what move to make or if he could make one at all. In a split second, his expression went from cocky, dismissive, smirky, and hard, to one that said *I might die here.*

There are two kinds of people in the pen: predator and prey. You wake up and choose which one you're going to be every day. This man was a predator. He was a rapist who picked easy targets, probably had since his days in juvenile hall. He did in Tracy, for sure. He woke up that morning and decided he was a predator. But so did I.

It was his move. Would he fight? Probably not. People don't fight in prisons like they show in the movies; you don't square off and throw fists. If you do, you both get in trouble. Even though I'd been a boxer since I was eight,

I'd much rather stab you three times, drop the shank, and walk away. You can block a punch, but you can't block a knife.

"You don't know him anymore, understand?" I wasn't asking a question; I was making a statement.

He nodded, but his eyes were darting all over like pinballs. Everyone on the tier was watching. No one except him and his buddies had seen O'Connor slip me a shank.

"If I see you behind my back or his, I'll kill you."

He had two choices: he could throw down and make it happen, which was unlikely since he knew I had a sharp-as-fuck six-inch screwdriver, or he could back down. He backed down. That decision would stay with him for the rest of his time in the system. It would also be known on the streets. Nothing that goes down inside prison walls isn't known on the streets. He would always be the brother who backed down. Carrying that reputation is the kind of thing that might get him killed down the line, in or outside.

There was a white guard in North named Morris who I think liked that I looked out for a vulnerable white inmate. That night on his rounds he was walking by my cell and stopped. I sprang awake. He said, "That was a good move, Trejo," and moved on.

In those years, the white inmates weren't as organized as they soon became. Mexicans and Blacks had their own systems that any new Mexican or Black inmate, scared or not, would have to fall into line with. Also, in the mid-60s, because of the changing social attitudes, there was pressure on the judicial system to start punishing white kids the same way they had always punished everyone else. With the increase in white convictions, there were a lot of white inmates whose first arrest sent them to prison. They didn't have the "benefit" of learning the ropes at juvenile hall and YTS. These guys arrived at institutions where they had no connections, were outnumbered and needed protection, and that combination made for great customers. And I think a lot of the guards, who were predominantly white, of course, were happy that someone was looking out for these guys.

A couple of days later, O'Connor got rolled up and sent to Vacaville. The guards had studied his jacket and seen that he'd been victim of too many rape attempts. All the pretty boys get sent to Vacaville at some point. Nowhere in the California prison system was safe, but Vacaville was safer than Soledad or San Quentin.

After O'Connor split, I requested that the guards send me back to Central. Instead, Lieutenant Mesro and Captain Rogers called me into their office.

"Trejo, we want you to stay."

"I don't think so."

"We're not asking."

"There are too many young dumbfucks here."

"That's why we want you to stay. We think you could help bring some order."

Mesro sweetened the offer by telling me I could run the boxing gym. I liked the idea. Besides the sixteen dollars a month the gig paid, I particularly liked the fact the gym was next to the loading dock—I'd have first dibs on everything that came into the prison, and I could stash my take in the gym.

Captain Rogers stood.

"Why don't you go back to your cell and have a think on it?"

When I got back to my cell, I found a half pint of whiskey sitting on my bunk. I'm not saying it was deliberately left there for me, but I'm not saying it wasn't.

I took the job.

The guards were glad that they had a bully slayer back in North, but I came by it honestly. My uncle hated bullies more than anyone. Gilbert was as bad as they came, but he used to always say, "Fuck bullies." If it was mutual combat with guys who could handle themselves, all bets were off. But he would never punch down or pick on weak, defenseless people. Especially in prison, where there were innocent people everywhere.

The first time I was doing a real stretch in Eastlake, I got busted for something and was thrown in the hole. I was classified in G&H, which meant I was in the middle age group that was locked up. In with me was a little blond boy of about ten who I swear to God had a streak of dyed blue hair. He was classified as T&V, one of the youngest age groups. This kid started talking to me and I thought, *My God, this youngster is a little girl.* I didn't think it in a critical way—he was truly a little girl. That moment is when I first realized that people are who they are. That there are people among us who don't fit into any box and it's not a conscious decision they make, it just is.

This kid, I'll call him Charlie, was struggling in lockup. I asked what he was in for, and he said he was always in trouble. His parents were divorcing, and they didn't know what to do with him because he was different. I thought, *My God, they stuck this little kid in this hellhole simply because he's gay.* There were all kinds of kids who were sent to juvie simply because their parents were fighting over custody or they had been molested or any number of things that weren't their fault. Juvie was full of kids who were on a path to being career criminals, and these innocent victims of the system were at their mercy.

When I got released back onto the Yard, I saw some older Mexican boys fucking with Charlie. I whistled to them and pointed at Charlie. "He's mine," I said. Even in juvenile hall, saying someone was yours meant a lot. It meant you were willing to do what you had to if someone challenged you and what was yours.

They said, "He's yours?"

I nodded.

"Alright, then, holmes."

Word got around that Charlie was protected. Maybe in that instance I saved a kid from a life-altering event that would have destroyed him. But there were too many Charlies and not enough guys willing to stick their necks out to protect them. I had always been that person for my friends on the outside when I was young: Timmy Sanchez, Mike Schwartz, and Rudy Imomota come to mind. But the stakes inside were so much higher than just an ass whipping in a park. Charlie was the first person who really opened my heart to the plight of innocents in the animal factory, but he certainly wasn't the last.

After I was processed in Chino and classified to be sent to Jamestown in '65, I was sent to Vacaville on my way there. I was twenty-one. When I first got to Vacaville, I was wearing whites. Whites are what you travel in. They make them with a target on the back in case you run. Because I was going to be there for a few days, I got processed and was given a set of greens to change into.

I hit the Yard and found a heavy bag. It had been a while since I'd boxed, but it came back fast. Hitting a heavy bag serves two purposes: it's good to get the training in, but it also shows everyone around what you can do with your fists.

A huge white guy sat down and watched me. He had the meanest expression on his face. This guy didn't weigh a pound less than 325 and it was all muscle. He was a specimen. I hit the bag harder. Faster. Nothing registered on the man's face. I hit it harder and harder. I didn't know what the fuck he wanted with me.

Beat, I gave up and started walking away when the tiniest, most childlike voice stopped me. "Can you teach me to do that?"

I looked back. It was the man. I was stunned by the disconnect between his voice and the size of his body.

"Please, can you teach me to do that?"

"Sure, buddy. But I'm in whites. I'm only going to be here for a few days."

"No, no," he said, "you're in greens." He pointed to my clothes.

"I just put these on to hit the Yard." I was intrigued. "What are you here for?"

He got a sad look on his face. It was clear he was remembering something painful. "This man kept calling me names and hitting me, and he wouldn't stop, and I asked him to stop, and he wouldn't so I hit him, and I hit him, and he ended up dead. I didn't mean to kill him. I got Life."

This was some Lennie from *Of Mice and Men* stuff. This huge, innocent child trapped in the body of a monstrously powerful man was just someone who'd been bullied one too many times. He was clearly developmentally disabled. I wondered about his family, his life, how he must have been endlessly teased and tormented. But without even knowing the details behind the crime that put him in prison for the rest of his life, I knew the story. I could almost see the asshole who'd pushed him too far. The outer shell I wore inside prison was always strong, but this man cracked it. It made me think about the cruelty of the universe on the gentlest of creatures. I thought of a Pekinese my aunt Sharon had. She'd dropped it off at my grandmother's house and asked me to look after it. I fed it with Bozoo, Prince, and Butch, the big, tough dogs my family kept. The poor little thing tried to eat and the big dogs bared their teeth and snapped at it. It looked at me with these terrified little eyes and I broke. I grabbed the three big dogs, pulled them away, tied them up, and made a new bowl for Sharon's dog.

"C'mon, eat." She was so happy. I said, "Hurry up before Gilbert sees what I'm doing."

"I'm sorry; I can teach you, holmes," I said to the man now.

The man looked like he was going to cry. "I'm losing my friend," he said.

"I'll always be your friend, buddy. I might not be here, but we'll always be friends."

"Thanks, pal." He wandered off and I changed back into my whites. I've thought about that man for fifty-five years. I've thought about Charlie for almost sixty.

For the guards, there was huge value to having someone like me, someone who would stand up for the vulnerable. It helped regulate the prison. It also ensured that the people under protection would not try and do stupid shit on their own. Once you were protected, you couldn't act bad or start shit, or you'd be cut loose.

I settled into life in North. I ran the gym, the heroin bag, and my protection racket. I had good money coming in. I was sending money to my mom on the outside. I got to spar every day. A guy I was protecting, Schmitty, ran the laundry room. For a pack of cigarettes, I'd get inmates clean socks and underwear and not the shit-stained things they handed out. That year, North had champions in every weight class. I could have taken the welterweight title as well as the lightweight, but I let a buddy named Bobby Olivarez have that shot. The men I protected cleaned my cell, shined my custom-made boots, pressed and starched my clothes. The walls of my cell were waxed; the concrete floor was covered in polyurethane until it shone like glass. Unlike Central, in North the guards didn't care if I was bonaroo because I was keeping things in order.

On the outside this would all be called extortion; on the inside, it was survival. The relationship worked two ways: I had eyes on their backs; they had eyes on mine. I could die just as easily as they could.

Then came Cinco de Mayo. The riot went down, and I found myself in solitary facing capital charges. The term *capital charges* is taken from the Latin for head, *caput*. Because the prisoner can lose his head.

"They're going to top us, Danny. They're going to kill us good." Henry kept saying that over and over.

It was August of 1968, and we were in X Wing. If we were cool, the guard would put the radio on. One day he put on the Beatles' new, hit single, "Hey Jude." We were all hearing it for the first time, and you could hear a pin drop, it was so beautiful. When it got to the part where Paul McCartney starts singing, "Ooooahhh Judee Judee Judee Judee Judee Jooooood!" everything blew up. In that moment it was easy to see

how Manson became obsessed with the *White Album* and why crazy people thought the Beatles were speaking specifically to them. The song spoke
right to us, not because it was specific but because it had a deeper impact
on the soul—sometimes that was a dark impact, the musical equivalent of
a prison riot.

There was a homosexual in solitary with us named Bambi. Bambi's cell
was across from mine. Bambi was known for the pornographic letters she
wrote—we would use them to jack off. We called them love letters.

"Bambi," I said, "write me a love letter."

A box of cornflakes on a fishing line slid across the tier to my cell door.
There was just enough space to squeeze it under. I found the letter tucked
inside with a comic book that had been used as a weight. I glanced at it, then
turned my attention to the love letter. Bambi had written a graphic descrip-
tion of sex. It was *dirty* dirty—it didn't sit right with me. So instead I turned
my attention to the comic. It was one of those small pamphlets with Chris-
tian themes that floated around the prison. This one was called "Joe's Woes."
It was about a guy named Joe who had an alcohol problem. Joe couldn't get
on top of his problem and was resistant to the idea that there was a spiritual
solution.

And it all came back. What that man had said to me nine years earlier at a
twelve-step meeting I'd crashed by accident when I was fifteen. There were
twelve of us. We were looking for a party at Bonnie Whipple's house off Van
Nuys Boulevard. My friend Julian was in love with her. We drove up Van
Nuys and near Lev Street we saw a house with a bunch of cars parked outside. I figured that's where the party must be. I pulled a wooden crate with
two bottles of wine, a case of beer, a half-pint of whiskey, a .38 snub-nosed
revolver, and a tire iron (for good measure) out of the trunk of the Chevy
and told my crew to stay together.

Back then, house parties were where you'd go to find women and to fight.
A lot of times guys didn't like a bunch of dudes from another part of the Valley showing up at their party and they would challenge you. When you came
through the door, they either rushed you or fell back. Steps backward meant
the same out there as they did in the joint.

I opened the door and burst in, wondering which of the two reactions I
was going to get. To my surprise, everyone in the room was old. On the wall
was a big sign that read "We Care."

We'd bum-rushed the Friday-night meeting of the We Care group, part of a twelve-step program that helps people recover from alcoholism. Immediately, an older guy stepped toward me with a cup of coffee in his hand. He smiled. "What's your name?"

"Danny." I didn't have time to think. He was so calm and friendly I was taken by surprise. I was immediately honest in a way I'd never been with adults or the cops.

"Danny, why don't you put that stuff down outside and stay for the meeting?"

I looked around. My friends had all been surrounded by people like this man—smiling older men and women who all had coffee cups in one hand and cigarettes in the other.

"We made a mistake."

He nodded to the crate of alcohol. "You may think you made a mistake, Danny, but if you continue with that stuff, the only three destinations waiting for you are jails, institutions, or death. I'm serious."

I know this sounds corny, but what he said cursed me. It cursed me with a knowledge about drug and alcohol abuse that is universal, true, and carved in marble in the desert somewhere, like an ancient proverb. After that day and before I got sober, anytime I got pulled over by cops and sat there cussing myself, wondering how bad it was going to be, the lights on the patrol car would taunt me. They'd flash in a way that seemed to chant, *Jails, institutions, death. Jails, institutions, death.*

Once you know where drugs and alcohol will take you, you can never enjoy them the same way again, but I was nowhere close to ready to hear it at that time. I had more crimes to pull, more stints in prison to endure.

"I got to go."

I called my boys and we left. Julian said to me, "Are we going to look for Bonnie's house?"

"No, let's get the fuck out of here."

I didn't want to party anywhere near the We Care group.

The guy at that meeting had seen the future. In 1968, after the riot at Soledad, I was in jail, I'd been in institutions, and now I was looking at death. I thought of what I'd heard in those meetings with Frank in YTS. They were always saying to find a God to believe in, a God of your own understanding, just something bigger than you, a power greater than yourself. I struggled with that. I had always been blessed with faith in something bigger in the universe, but formal religion had been hard for me. I saw all those old Mexican ladies praying to God and giving everything they had to charity, but their lives were still so hard.

Those were the meetings where I first met Jhonnie Harris, the ex-con. I asked him, "What are you going to teach me, old man?" and he said, "Nothing. I'm going to give you a preview of the coming attractions, punk." He asked me what I wanted out of the program, and I said I wanted to get out of my cell and see women. That's when he looked me over and said, "Danny, the only thing that's going to beat you to San Quentin are the lights on the bus." And he was right.

Jhonnie had been a famous barber in San Quentin, which, other than the captain's clerk, was one of the most respected positions you could hold. Anyone who has control of an open razor in a prison has to be trusted and respected. That's the way it works in our world. Jhonnie was one of the guys who you could say was handsome—only problem is there's no such thing as handsome in the pen: handsome was pretty. Jhonnie was manly; he wore a nice sport jacket and a tie with a beautiful knot. That right there impressed me. The fact that he'd been in San Quentin impressed me more. When he started talking you knew he was who he said he was, and you knew that he didn't take too many steps backward.

When it came to finding a higher power, Jhonnie had said, "Danny, you've got to find something to believe in other than yourself. And you don't even believe in yourself. I hope you find God, be it through 'Good Orderly Direction' or 'The power of the group', whatever it is, I pray you find Him now."

But the God I kept coming back to, the God of my understanding, was the God I'd been raised with. The God of my grandmother's Bible. That God was punishing, the God that said we'd all been born of sin. The God behind my grandmother saying, *"¡Te castigó Dios!"* anytime I tripped and fell. I'd never suggest to anyone this conception of God isn't right, or my understanding is the last word on the subject, but it's where my mind went. More importantly, it's where my heart went.

On the wall of my cell, in shit, someone had written *Fuck God*. No doubt they wrote it in a moment of utter despair when they felt God had abandoned them in that pit. I didn't feel that way. Everything that had happened to me was the result of decisions and choices I made. I always had good information I chose to ignore. Even my father's constant anger at me came from his being terrified of and disappointed by the choices I was making. He was powerless over me.

I was more scared than I'd ever been, stuck in the limbo of not knowing whether they were going to prosecute me, and if I were prosecuted, if I'd be executed as well. We all know we're going to die, but if you are sitting in a cell looking at the death penalty, you can see the grim reaper sitting right next to you, laughing. He's laughing because you will never see your loved ones again, you will never hug your cousins, you will never meet the children you will not have, you will never feel the sun on your face except in waist chains with two bulls on either side of you, pulling you in chains. It is quite simply the end of hopes and dreams.

I've always liked that saying, "If you're going to pray, why worry? And if you're going to worry, why pray?" So was I going to stay scared, or was I going to pray? The choice was mine. I was that Mexican you feared. I had achieved that. But now I was up against something stronger than me. A power greater than myself. I said to God out loud, "God, if You're there, me, Henry, and Ray will be alright. If You're not, we're fucked."

Faith shoves fear out of the room. There's no room for fear if you fill your soul with faith. Immediately, a calm came over me. All this terrible weight I didn't even know I had been carrying left me. I felt exhausted, but in a good way. I relaxed and decided to let God carry the weight.

I prayed, "God, if You allow me to die with dignity, I will say Your name every day and do everything I can to help my fellow man." I wasn't asking God to make me a movie star or let me travel the world or get into restaurants or have friends everywhere. I was asking God to allow me to die with dignity.

I was taught that God answers every prayer, even if His answer is "No." The only prayer that had stuck with me my whole life, the prayer that hit me like a rock in the chest when I learned it in catechism, was the Prayer of St. Francis: "Let me not seek to be consoled as to console." In that cell, I asked God for help and His answer was "Help." I understood: Help *others*. That's what people used to say in those meetings I went to. "You can't keep grace unless you give it away," they said. "You have to be of service to others;

even if they don't get it, you will." I assumed my answer from God was just to help my fellow inmates, 'cause I figured I was dead in five years.

In that cell God killed the old me, made a new Danny Trejo, and said, "Now let's see what you do with him."

The weeks that followed were the miracle. God worked His magic. The whole prosecution was vague as fuck—Lieutenant Gibbons couldn't say for sure who it was that threw the rock. When inmates were questioned, they said, "Mickey Mouse did it," or "Popeye did it." The coach of the junior college team wanted to do his testimony remotely—this was long before Zoom, and that didn't fly. And the third baseman couldn't be found. The district attorney decided not to move forward because they didn't feel they'd have enough to prosecute.

When I went into the hole, I was shooting three or four grams of heroin a day. I was doing ten, fifteen pills a day. I was drinking every day. Any kick off heroin with no access to methadone is brutal, and in prison there was no access to methadone. Since I'd been given pills in the beginning of my time in the hole, around Cinco de Mayo, and it took me a few months to get clean of them, August 23 is the day I chose as my sobriety date. In reality it might have been a few days before that, but it felt clean to me. I was released from the hole back into the general population on August 28, 1968. If a fortune-teller with a crystal ball had told me the exact journey I'd take in the next fifty-one years, I would have said, "Fuck you. You're nuts."

Chapter 6

ZIP-A-DEE-DOO-DAH

1968

I was back in North, but things had changed. When I came out of the hole Lieutenant Mesro and Captain Rogers put me right back running the gym, but I gave up the heroin bag. I really wanted the money, but I knew I wouldn't be honoring my agreement with God if I kept dealing drugs, even if I'd stopped using. But I kept making money running protection rackets.

Then the guards came to me with a proposition. They wanted to create a position for me as an "Inmate Social Catalyst," as they called it. I had no idea what *catalyst* meant. "It helps things change," said Morris, "and it pays eighteen dollars a month."

Things were moving fast.

A guy I knew who arranged twelve-step meetings for prisoners told me the group was in danger of losing their accreditation if they didn't get more inmates to attend meetings. This is where the rubber met the road. I had promised I would say God's name every day and help my fellow man, and I'd sworn to be clean and sober. Was I serious or not?

"I'll come," I said, "as long as you make me president."

The man laughed. "We don't have 'presidents,' Danny, but we have the position of chairman, and if you help me keep our accreditation, I'll make you chairman, gladly."

I accepted. I made eight guys I was protecting attend the next meeting. After attending meetings for a few weeks, three of them decided to stay on because they realized they needed it. I know a couple of them managed to stay sober for as long as I had before they passed of natural causes. These were the first people I helped toward recovery, even though the only reason I brought them was because I knew they were going to lose their accreditation if they didn't get asses in the seats, and I really wanted to attend meetings and become chairman. When I saw the change over the course of even a few months in those three guys, it made me realize how much I was changing. They say in recovery, "Sometimes you can see the change in others better than you can see it in yourself."

The miracles were happening everywhere. I'd made the decision to be clean and sober, and people immediately started coming to me for help. There was one dude who couldn't stop sniffing glue. He came to me and begged me for help. He was so desperate to get clean, he and I worked out a deal where he'd be on lockdown in his cell and could only come out for showers and chow. I paid three dudes to keep eyes on him, and everyone in the block knew they couldn't sell or slip him drugs or they'd be in shit with me.

I wasn't just providing prison protection, I was doing something that felt important. By simply keeping my promise to God, I saw people changing around me. Maybe these opportunities had been there all along. I know that me being so visibly involved in recovery made it okay for others to join in. Because I was older and had been in Folsom and San Quentin, I was respected. People who would have blown off going to meetings came around because they thought, *If it's cool for Trejo, it must be cool for me.*

The meetings grew. An old-timer came in from the town to attend meetings in the prison as part of a program called H&I, Hospitals and Institutions. The old guy—I'll call him Sam—was severely sick. His diabetes had already claimed a leg and most of his fingers. A man named Larry used to bring him in a special van that could accommodate Sam's wheelchair.

One night, after the meeting, Sam heard me bitching about something and said, "Danny, why don't you try singing 'Zip-a-Dee-Doo-Dah' every morning when you wake up?" I knew the song, but so what?

"Sam, why the fuck would I sing 'Zip-a-Dee-Doo-Dah?'" I asked.

"Sing 'Zip-a-Dee-Doo-Dah' and jump up and down on your bunk every morning."

"Listen, Sam," I said, "I appreciate you coming down and all that, but I'm still in prison. I know what I'm going to be doing next Wednesday, you understand? I'm on lockdown. I'm a prisoner."

"Danny," he said, "do you know how much I would give to be able to jump up and down again on a bunk or a bed?" He pointed to his stump. "I have dreams of walking and hopping up and down. I'll never be able to until I'm in heaven."

I got what he was saying, but there was no way in hell I was going to do it.

And yet . . . the next morning, I was brushing my teeth, and I found myself singing, "Zip-a-dee-doo-dah, zip-a-dee-ay! / My, oh, my, what a wonderful day. / Plenty of sunshine headin' my way . . ." Immediately, I had a smile on my face. I started laughing. I was transformed. My mind was filled with happy thoughts. I was starting my day on a positive note. I thought about what an outside speaker had said at a meeting: "Have a good day, which becomes a great month, which becomes a great year, which becomes a great life."

Gilbert had always told me to believe that I was where I was supposed to be. You can't survive prison by looking at birds and mountains and wishing you were someplace else. You can't wait for letters and visits. That'll kill you.

I had thrived in prison following Gilbert's rules, but through the meetings and what was shared, I learned I didn't have to be a slave to my circumstances. I could look beyond the prison walls from within the prison walls by changing who I was. Letting go of drugs was getting a gorilla off my back. I could face any scenario without turning to chemicals to protect my soul. Taking it day by day, I didn't need to feel guilt and regret and anger for the past. I didn't need to fear the future. Those things were outside of me and I could just be.

I kept singing the song, sometimes to myself, sometimes out loud. I came out on the Yard singing, "Mister Bluebird's on my shoulder. / It's the truth, it's 'actch'll.' / Ev'rything is 'satisfactch'll,'" and crossed paths with Joe Rodriguez. He must have thought I was crazy. Joe said, "You alright, holmes?"

"Yeah, Joe. I'm more than alright."

Singing "Zip-a-Dee-Doo-Dah" was my first real attempt at morning prayer and meditation. It took me out of myself. Even when I was a child, I'd wake up with a hundred pounds of dread and anxiety on my chest. Except on the days that Gilbert would wake me up to go fishing. On those days, my life became a great adventure. I have a friend named Chris Davis who says,

"Have a nice day. That is, of course, unless you've already gone ahead and made other plans." It cracks me up every time because it's so true. At night my subconscious churned through so much unresolved mayhem, and it couldn't wait to kick my ass in the morning. I'd wake up and my first thought would be *I'm fucked*. "Zip-a-Dee-Doo-Dah" washed that away. It taught me that even in prison I could be free.

My work as an "Inmate Social Catalyst" was becoming fruitful. There was an inmate in North who'd been written up twice for tattooing. He asked me as the liaison what he should do. "If you get written up one more time, holmes, you're going to the hole. How much do you get for a tattoo?"

"Six cartons."

"Then you should give two of those cartons to two dudes you have standing lookout so you'll get a heads-up when the guards are doing their rounds."

When I met with Mesro and Rogers, they asked me how things were going. As an example of how helpful I was being, I mentioned that inmates had asked for my advice on how to get away with shit and that I told them to pay other inmates to be on the lookout so they wouldn't get busted.

The guards contemplated this for a second. They weren't mad. They knew snitching wasn't part of our deal. Stuff was going to go down in the facility and they wanted some order to it. "That's a smooth play, Trejo," one said.

On August 23, 1969, almost exactly one year after I'd been cut loose from the hole, on the first anniversary of my sobriety date, I was released from Soledad.

I was given a "Please Don't Rain on Me" suit, two hundred dollars, and a Greyhound bus ticket to San Fernando.

Part Two

THE RIGHT MAN FOR THE JOB

Chapter 7

CLEAN, SOBER,
AND SCARED

1969

The cocoa-brown Chevy pulled a U-turn. A girl in the back seat was high as fuck and wearing a miniskirt with a little dash of red panty flashing. I know this because she called me over. I'd been locked up for four years. When I stepped up to the car, I got a massive whiff of marijuana, perfume, and hair spray. She'd already hit a triple. She was so beautiful, I wondered if she was real or something out of my imagination.

"I know you, Danny Trejo." She stretched out my name and made it sound sexy. "You know my older brother."

Too many people in the San Fernando Valley knew me for all the wrong reasons.

"Yeah, I'm Danny Trejo."

"I want you to come party with me and my girlfriends." She put her face into the sunlight and smiled. A big red pill was stuck to her chin. I recognized it as Seconal. It matched her panties. She was too high to notice. I wanted to suck that red devil right off her face.

I had been in town for minutes and already I was facing a beautiful, mini-skirt-wearing, metallic-red-pantied angel sent by the devil.

"I gotta go."

"Fuck. Don't go."

Getting out of prison in 1969, it felt like the world had skipped a few decades since I went in. The summer of love had happened; the Vietnam War was at its height. Everyone dressed differently. The music was different. Women cussed and had casual sex. It hadn't been like that back in '65. Back then, the only broads who did those things were hookers and gangsters. Now it seemed like everyone was game. It took the dirtiness out of it, and I liked dirtiness.

I found a pay phone and called Frank Russo. If anyone could keep me sober, it was Frank. I told him I'd just been released from Soledad, I was at the bus station, and that a woman with red panties and a Seconal on her chin wanted me to party with her.

"Don't move, Danny. I'm coming to get you." He was about to hang up when he said, "Talk to Sherry till I get there," and handed the phone to his wife. He knew he had to keep me on the phone or he might lose me for another ten years. If Frank hadn't been home to answer his phone that day, I'd either be in jail or dead.

My parole officer had set me up to live in a halfway house, but a drug addict had just died there, so they decided they didn't want more drug addicts, even if they'd been clean for a year. Instead, Frank dropped me off at my parents' house. My mother—the stepmother who had raised me since I was three—answered the door. "*Mijo*, you're home." She didn't sound too excited, and she didn't open the screen door, a detail not lost on me. I could see the profile of my father watching the news in the living room. "Where are you staying?"

"Hey, Mom. My parole plans fell through. I was thinking maybe I'd stay here until I get my feet on the ground."

She paused for a long time, then looked back at my father. "Dan, Danny wants to know if he can stay here for a few days."

Without turning, he said, "Tell him yeah."

"Well, come in."

I stepped into the living room and said hello to my father. He didn't take his eyes off the television. The tension was thick.

But it had always been like that with my father and my stepmother.

My birth mom and dad, Dolores Rivera King and Dionisio Trejo, met in a dance hall in Highland Park in 1943. She was married to another man, but he was off fighting the war in the Pacific. My parents were zoot suiters—the men wore flashy suits with pegged trousers with broad-shouldered jackets, and the women wore flared skirts and had bouffants. My father was a *pachuco*, the kind of zoot suiter who threw down. If someone gave him shit, he gave it back times five.

I was born on May 16, 1944, in Maywood, California. I would've been born in East LA, but my mother was turned away from the hospital. They needed the beds for soldiers.

After I was born, my mother and father were at a bar and a man grabbed my mom's ass. My father stabbed him. To escape the police, my dad scooped up my mother, my mother's older children, and me and drove to San Antonio, Texas.

About a year later, we returned to LA. My dad knew he had to face the law. He begged my grandmother to pay for an attorney to represent him and promised that if she did, he'd never go back to jail for the rest of his life. He was a man of his word. He spent the next thirty-four years of his life working construction and earning a steady paycheck. After he banned my birth mother from our lives, he married my stepmom, who was the "mom" I grew up with. He expected her to take care of me and raise me as her own.

I think a big part of why I disappointed my father so deeply was that he figured if he could get arrested once and then clean up his act for good, why couldn't I? He saw me as a failure and a disappointment. I could do no right.

Ever since I was a kid, when my dad got drunk, I was the target of his anger. One time out at Tujunga Canyon, where we used to go for family barbecues, my dad got mad at me and locked me in his car. It was over a hundred degrees that day. He told everyone to leave me be. I think my aunts wanted to help, but they were too scared to get involved. So everyone continued picnicking and drinking while I watched from the oven of the hot car.

I leaned back against the seat, then curled on the floor. I started falling asleep or passing out, I didn't know which; all I knew was I was losing consciousness, but I fought it hard because I didn't want my dad to think he'd won. My uncle Gilbert finally opened the door and pulled me out. My dad was yelling at him about it, and Gilbert told him to lighten up. That was the only time I saw them fight. Gilbert was the only person who wasn't scared of my father. They were giving it to each other pretty good until my dad body-slammed Gilbert into a car. He'd already hit me, so I stayed on the ground pretending I was knocked out. When my dad wandered off, huffing and cussing, Gilbert gave me a wink. He had my back.

A few weeks later, my grandfather was screaming at Gilbert and me about being fuckups, saying he was going to kill us. I don't remember what it was about, but on any given day he could have found a hundred legitimate reasons. I knew any minute he was going to reach over and slap the shit out of me. I was so scared I literally puckered my asshole not to shit myself from the beating that was coming. My dad was a scary dude, but even he and my uncles were terrified of my grandpa. I looked out of the corner of my eye and saw Gilbert nodding off. He was still on his feet but fully asleep. My grandpa got so angry, he grabbed his head in both hands and let out a strange noise, almost like an injured animal's cry, then disappeared into his bedroom. The whole time Gilbert was stooped over, drooling. When he came to, he had no idea what had gone down.

"Did he hit us, holmes?"

That was a huge moment in my life. I realized Gilbert had a secret way to check out when things got hot. At the time I didn't know it was heroin, I just knew I wanted the same escape hatch.

A few days after that Gilbert was arrested for something and when he returned from a three-day stretch in County he ran straight from the car into my grandfather's bedroom and then into the bathroom. I followed him there and found him with a belt around his arm and the big glass syringe my grandpa used for his diabetes. I knew what it was because I'd seen my grandma inject him with insulin every morning. I got in big trouble for using it as a squirt gun one time.

"Let me have some or I'll tell Grandpa you're using his thing," I said.

"I can't do that to you."

"I swear I'll tell."

Gilbert told me to hold the belt. He held the needle to his forearm and when it registered it was like a little bomb went off—an explosion of cloudy blood filled the glass tube. He told me to let go. Instantly, I saw a whole change came over him—he was back to being that guy who could go to sleep in front of a dragon.

Gilbert helped me tie off with the belt and gave me a fix. It was better than anything I'd ever felt, a euphoria stronger than words can describe. Anything I was stressing over went away. I didn't have to worry about school. I didn't have to worry about parents. It was *all* gone and replaced with a feeling of joy I never thought possible.

I woke up soaking wet in my grandma's front yard to Gilbert slapping my cheeks. Later, Gilbert told me I had OD'd and he had stuck me under a cold shower. I heard music coming from down the street. It was the ice cream truck.

Gilbert pulled some money out of his pocket and said, "Buy us two big sticks, one for you and one for me."

I grabbed the dollar, pulled myself off the ground, and bought us ice cream.

I was twelve.

Heroin could magically take away whatever was bothering me, even if I didn't know it was bothering me. It felt like a warm blanket, and I thought, *Thank you, warm blanket.* It protected me from my father's rage, my grandfather's rage, and then my own. But pretty soon that warm blanket started strangling me.

Now, thirteen years later, I walked past my silent father and into my room, the room I'd had as a kid, the room where I was first arrested. I'd been away for almost five years and had hoped to come home to a warm reception, but their response was so cold and distant I wanted to scream. I took off my "Please Don't Rain on Me" suit and looked at myself in the mirror. I'd changed a lot since I was last home. Couldn't they see it? Weight lifting in the pen had added a lot of bulk. There were new lines on my face. I was an old twenty-five. I took off my shirt; Harry "Super Jew" Ross's *charra* looked back at me. In the mirror I saw a killer, a shot-caller, a predator, but I felt like a little kid who had just been slapped in public. My own parents didn't want me home.

I hated myself and my situation. I wondered if it was a mistake to have even left prison. A few days earlier, as my release date neared, all kinds of crazy shit had swirled through my brain: Could I handle the outside world? Had it changed too much for me? Would parole officers make me jump through too many hoops? Would cops always target me on the outside?

Bare-chested, I went back into the living room and sat on an ottoman across from my father. He tensed up. My father hated tattoos, always had, and now I had one that screamed I'd just been released from San Quentin, Folsom, and Soledad.

My father and I sat quietly for what seemed like a long time. It was a quiet I recognized from prison—the kind of quiet that descends right before a riot.

"Can I get you cookies and milk?" My mom said it like she was June Cleaver in *Leave It to Beaver*. I had to get out of there. It was all I could do to eat my mother's snack. I laugh thinking back on it now. My dad and I were two of the angriest, most pent-up, rage-filled motherfuckers ever to dip cookies in glasses of milk. I called Frank. He was expecting the call. He knew it wasn't going to go the way I hoped when I got home. He picked me up.

"We're going to a meeting."

I knew that was coming, but I couldn't help wishing he'd said, *Let's go find that cocoa-brown Chevy and the girl with the bright red panties.*

When I got in Frank's car, I told him my father hadn't looked me in the eye once since I got home. He said, "Danny, look at it from their perspective. Your parents are working their hardest to be good, law-abiding Republicans, and you're fucking up their program." Back then, *Republicans* was our catchall term for white, conservative people.

Frank brought me to a meeting in Reseda. The room was full of a bunch of sober cowboys chewing tobacco and spitting into cups. I immediately hated it, hated everyone there. I sure as hell wasn't a cowboy. I scowled at Frank.

"It'll get better," he whispered.

At the end of the meeting a young woman about twenty or so asked me to give her my hand.

I was confused. "What for?" I asked. I hadn't touched a woman in a long time. I hadn't even hugged my mom when I got home.

"For the prayer," she said.

I took her hand in my left hand and a young guy's in my right. Frank was looking at me from across the circle, smiling like, "See? I told you this would get better."

After the meeting, we took that girl and her friend out to Du-par's on Ventura—that was *the* spot. It felt good to drink real coffee out of a real coffee cup, to laugh, and to drive around afterward.

After Du-par's we went to Reseda Park. I wandered away from Frank and the girls to take a piss in the dark. I aimed my pee at a duck that had wandered too close to me, and he looked at me so angrily I laughed out loud. I heard Frank and the girls talking in the distance and I realized I was happy. I was free. I had an epiphany. I realized I needed the program of recovery. I conceded to my innermost self that without meetings my life was unmanageable and I needed to do what Jhonnie Harris had told me years earlier when he'd said, "Join us, Danny." I needed sobriety not just to get out of the hole or look good for a parole board; I needed it for my life to make sense.

The next morning I woke up back in my childhood bedroom, again feeling lost. I knew I wanted sobriety and fellowship, and I knew I had a lot of work to do to get my life together, but I didn't know where to start.

My family had lived in Pacoima, a neighborhood in the northern San Fernando Valley of LA, since the 50s, when it was exactly like *La Bamba,* the movie about Ritchie Valens, who came from Pacoima and shot to fame during the same period.

Back then, Pacoima was blue-collar but evenly mixed between Blacks, whites, and Mexicans. The city was segregated along San Fernando Road, with Blacks on one side in the projects and Mexicans and whites on the other. People lived in poverty. Pacoima in the 50s was known as the murder capital of Los Angeles. A lot of people worked on farms, and a lot of families lived in garages behind other homes, sharing a bathroom and running extension cords to get power.

Now more Latinos had moved in, and most of the Blacks had moved out. Pacoima had more sidewalks and paved streets and a commercial strip along Van Nuys Boulevard, but most of the houses were old and in disrepair. Compared to a lot of families, we had a lot. Some friends of mine came from nothing. When I was in juvenile hall, there were kids from my neighborhood for whom it was like a resort. Juvenile hall was the first place a lot of those kids had ever had a decent meal. A kid named Gabbie from Clanton in East LA said, "Real butter, Danny. They have *real* butter. And milk!" Gabbie was *poor* poor; we were working poor. With my dad consistently doing construction and my mother being obsessive about cooking and keeping a clean house, we always had the basic necessities, but behind closed doors our house was like an icebox. The only time I enjoyed living with my mom and my dad was when my uncle Bill was arrested and his daughters, my cousins Sharon, Yolanda, and Lynn, moved in with us when I was starting junior high. There was safety in numbers.

Not knowing what to do with myself, I went out on the street. I trusted God. He had pulled me out of the deepest pit when I asked for His help. But it had been easier to lean on God in prison. What would I do now that I was out?

Across the street, I saw an old lady, Mrs. Sanchez, dragging two big trash cans from her backyard. I ran toward her.

She about fell over backward. *"¡No me robes! No me robes!"*

I said, "*¡Cállate!* I ain't going to rob you! I want to help you. Give me the trash cans."

The problem wasn't that she didn't know me. The problem was she did. I'd grown up on that block. I'd probably robbed her garage before. I'm sure I scared her. I was desperate, I looked dangerous, and everyone knew where I had been for almost the last five years. "I'm sorry. I just want to help you."

I grabbed the trash cans and dragged them toward the street. They were definitely too heavy for a lady her age.

She said, "Since they tore up the alley for construction, I have to take them out to the front of the house."

She was grateful, but she never took her eyes off me for a second. It was only a small act, and a highly confusing one for her, but it made me feel a hell of a lot better.

Chapter 8

FAMILIAR FACES

1969

Frank Carlisi and Frank Russo came to the rescue yet again. I returned to my old job sanding and painting cars at Carlisi's, the one I'd sustained only for twenty-nine days when I was out in '65. Frank made sure I hit meetings with him every day.

While I was away, Frank had teamed up with a judge, the Honorable Charles Hughes, to start a rehab program as an alternative to juvie for kids who were up on drug charges. Judge Hughes was forward-thinking. He saw that 75 percent of the cases coming through his court were drug-related, a problem he didn't believe "iron bar therapy," could cure. Recovery in Freedom (R.I.F.) had meetings every day, and Frank thought I could be a positive influence on the young people. The kids he was talking about were nineteen and twenty. Even though I was only twenty-five, my stint in prison definitely made me an elder statesman to them.

R.I.F. was in the Valley—in Reseda—on the second story of a building above a flower shop. The first day I walked in, the kids all took one look at me, all tattooed out, and were intrigued. Then we started talking, and when I started sharing about the pen, I could tell many of them who were facing court dates wanted to know everything about prison—especially how to avoid going there.

I made it simple. "Do what the judge tells you to do," I said. Doing what any person in authority instructed them to do, whether it was a teacher, their parents, a cop, or a judge, was something they, as rebellious teenagers, were hardwired not to do. But they listened with opened ears when hearing the exact same advice from me, someone with experience, someone who'd been deep in the system.

After the meeting they gathered around me like a flock around its shepherd. When we left Frank said, "Danny, these kids are impressed with your tattoos. Don't start thinking you're the Messiah."

But he was right that I could help them. They related to me—not the armed robberies I'd committed but the driving down Van Nuys and Ventura and drinking and doing heroin and fighting. Most of them were staring at prison sentences if they fucked up this chance. I gave them an overview of prison life, and I gave it to them straight. I never said it to clown them or diminish them—I just gave them a few previews of coming attractions. None of which were very attractive.

"In prison," I told them, "you are either going to be a girl or a killer. That's all, but don't think that it's that simple. It's easy for a kid like me, who grew up in the ghetto, to be a killer, but you grew up in Reseda. You don't want to be either a girl or a killer. Can you spiritually live with either of those options?" I told them the words that had stuck with me ever since I crashed the We Care meeting in '59. "If you continue with that stuff you are going to die, go insane, or go to jail." The second part was especially true in 1969 because a lot of kids were doing incredible amounts of acid that was frying their brains. Drugs had changed from when I was using.

The fact that I'd done all those years in prison meant a lot to them. They took what I had to say seriously. I was beginning to understand that even if you've done terrible things, sharing with others, having them witness how you've been able to turn yourself around, helps them see that they can do it for themselves.

Jhonnie had said to me in YTS, "Danny, why don't you give yourself a break and get off the hamster wheel you're on?" I couldn't hear what Jhonnie was trying to tell me then, but I sure as hell was hoping the kids at R.I.F. could hear it from me now.

Frank and I stayed busy. We worked, went to meetings, collected food for a food bank, and carried socks and thermal underwear around in our trunks for homeless people we'd find on the streets. It felt good to be a helper and not a taker.

I was at Carlisi's one day when my uncle Gilbert dropped by. He'd been out of Folsom for only about a week, and I knew he'd be coming around. He pulled up in a black Lincoln Continental. He was wearing a black fedora, a long black topcoat, a silk shirt, and black bolero pants. He had on four-hundred-dollar shoes and that was just for the left one. He always did look like a movie star.

I walked in from the back in coveralls covered in dirt, looking like an escaped Vietcong.

He looked at me with genuine pity. "Danny, what are you doing?"

"Working."

"This? This is chump money. Come back and work with me, like old times." He put two quarter ounces of heroin and a thousand dollars in cash on the counter.

Like old times.

I had worshipped Gilbert since I was a kid. He'd been my role model, and I'd followed in his footsteps ever since he'd let me. The first time Gilbert took notice of me I found him sitting on the bed at my grandparents' house with a big glass bowl on his lap. He told me to come closer. I watched him sift through a bunch of leaves and take out what I discovered later were stems and seeds. I had no idea it was marijuana; I was just thrilled that Gilbert knew I was alive and was paying attention to me. He was only thirteen, but he already had movie star looks. Tall, handsome, with a smile like nothing you'd ever seen. He lived, slept, and ate with the men. To me, he was a man.

"I need your help. Come on."

Gilbert checked on my grandpa. He was taking a nap. We climbed into his '38 Chevy and Gilbert handed me a bag.

"Every time a new song comes on the radio, I want you to count it."

Back in 1951, songs were all the same length—a little less than three minutes. The hits were songs like "Jezebel" by Frankie Laine and "Too Young" by Nat King Cole. I couldn't have been happier. I was with my hero. We took off down East Palm to San Fernando Road.

Every couple of songs, Gilbert would stop, ask me to hand him the bag that was filled with what I thought were cigarettes, and tell me to wait. We went to three different places and then headed home. When we pulled into the driveway, Gilbert asked, "How many?"

"How many what?"

"Songs, *tonto*!" He said it with a laugh.

"Thirteen."

He smiled and rubbed my head. Inside his room, Grandpa was still snoring away.

Gilbert leaned down and put his hands on my shoulders. "Good job."

I was proud as fuck. It was an adventure. Most importantly, it was an adventure with Gilbert. I was seven, and I'd just completed my first drug deal.

About a year later, the family had moved to Penrose when the state claimed my grandma's house by eminent domain to make the Garden Freeway. I was running through the house wearing a cowboy hat and shooting a cap gun.

Bam. Bam. Bam.

"*¡Cállate, cochino!*"

My grandma told me to go out back with Gilbert and his friends. "They're reading the Bible," she said.

They had a Bible, that was true, but they weren't reading it. They had Grandma's fancy Bible. It was red with gold-leafed pages. Any Mexican family knows the Bible I'm talking about. It was the fanciest object in any Mexican household and sold for twenty-two dollars on a payment plan spread out over five years. I was shocked she let it out of the house, but by that point Gilbert was getting in so much trouble, she was probably overjoyed he wanted to read the good word.

Gilbert, Charlie Diaz, Bobby Ortega, and another dude had the Bible open to a picture of Jesus on the cross. On the table next to it was a big pile of what looked like tea. My first thought was that it was Yerba Buena, a tea my grandmother would make.

I pointed to the pile of leaves and said, "Yerba Buena," and Charlie said, "You're right, it is good weed."

Turns out, Gilbert and his friends were using the fake Bible study as a decoy while they separated the stems and seeds from the bud.

Back then, there was no such thing as proper rolling paper, not that we knew of. Gilbert used butcher paper and stuck the whole thing in his mouth to get it to hold tight.

"Let's get Danny Boy loaded!"

They all thought that was a great idea, so Gilbert lit one end of the wet joint.

I couldn't get a pull, so Gilbert took a hit himself and blew the smoke into a paper bag and let me huff it through a hole. That worked well. Really, really well.

I huffed while the older boys whooped and hollered, urging me on.

When I went back inside, I was flying. I was jumping off the furniture, spinning in circles. Grandma got mad at me for clowning again. I laughed like crazy and she kicked me out of the room. My poor *abuelita* had no clue. It was the first time I got high and far from the last.

Seven years later Gilbert and I had a business going. Gilbert was twenty years old and had just gotten back from the military. He'd been a paratrooper for two years. He didn't waste time hitting the streets. On Saturdays we liked to get an early start. I went by his house and my grandma, his mother, would make us breakfast of chorizo and eggs. Then we'd head downtown to Temple Street to our dealer Chuey's place to pick up the heroin we'd sell that day in Sun Valley Park.

Chuey's picture belonged with Richard Berry's in the dictionary, next to the definition of *heroin addict*, but he lived with his wife and kids in a tidy, homey house. We got the heroin and headed back to the Valley.

Filling balloons is part of the job. You get a funnel, put a balloon over the spout, and tap the white-beige powder into the balloon. We made thirty, forty, or sixty balloons and headed to Sun Valley Park. Gilbert stood in one part of the park and did the deal, while I stood across the park. As soon as Gilbert had the money, he signaled how many balloons to give the customer by holding up his fingers. By the time they came over to me, I had the exact number in my mouth ready for them.

My mother was cold, my father was disappointed in me, and I was watching the perfect TV parents in *The Adventures of Ozzie and Harriet* and *My Three Sons*, sniffing glue to deal with the emptiness, when my uncle, coolest dude in the world, found time for me.

Can I go with you?

Sure!

So what if he was going to drop off a half ounce of heroin? Whatever Gilbert did, I followed. I was true to him and would have done anything for his approval. If he'd played football, I would have been an athlete. It just so happened he was a drug-dealing gangster.

But Gilbert wasn't just my guide into the world of drugs. He was my guide in all things. One morning before he'd gone into the military, when I was eight years old, Gilbert woke me up early.

"Let's go fishing," he said.

We went into the backyard, dug up earthworms and night crawlers, and put them in a coffee tin with holes poked in the lid.

We walked along Glenoaks Boulevard to Hansen Dam. It was five miles, but it didn't seem that far with Gilbert. Glenoaks Boulevard was desolate north of Pacoima, all fields and dirt lots. Gilbert took the opportunity to give me notes on how I walked. "Men walk like this," he said, and showed me. I was an eager student.

We crossed a field with tall grass. Gilbert laid down the fishing rods and said, "I gotta piss." I thought I'd do the same, so I pulled down my pants and squatted.

Gilbert looked confused. "What you doing? You gotta shit?"

"No. I just have to pee."

I'd grown up surrounded by my aunts and girl cousins, and all of them peed sitting down. I didn't know how my dad peed because he was in and out and always mad and him pissing was something I'd never seen. Peeing sitting down was normal to me but not to Gilbert.

He shoved me hard into the dirt. "Boys piss standing up, fool!"

I jumped up screaming. "I was joking!" I still remember the pee on my pants when I tried to pull them up. I was so ashamed; my uncle, my hero, was looking at me with disgust like I was one of the sissies the men in my family made fun of.

In that dirt lot, I went from Shirley Temple to John Wayne in an instant.

Later, out on the dam, Gilbert lit a joint and offered me a hit.

"This is the life, huh, Danny?"

The sky stretched forever.

"Yup."

We carried our catch the five miles home in a bucket to give to Grandma to fry up for dinner.

Now I looked at my uncle, the guy who'd taught me how to piss like a man, brought me fishing, trained me to box, taught me everything I needed to know about drugs, guns, prison, and being a man. I'd always wanted Gilbert's attention. I wanted to spend time with Gilbert. I wanted to be Gilbert. The money and the drugs were sitting in front of me, along with the promise of joining up with the uncle I adored. But I knew what I had to do. I said no to him for the first time. "I can't, Gilbert."

"Just think about it."

He left, leaving the money and drugs on the counter. Frank found me out back sitting in a burnt-out truck.

"Danny, you know Gilbert's doing what he has to do, what he's going to do. That's not for you anymore."

"He left me a grand and two quarter ounces."

"Did you take it?"

"I took the money. I left the drugs." I flashed Frank the wad of bills.

"Good. Hell yeah, grab the cash." Frank laughed.

At R.I.F., a young woman named Debbie caught my eye. She was wearing a blue miniskirt and white boots with huge heels. She had long, beautiful hair—she was this gorgeous little thing, and she'd just turned eighteen.

Debbie was coming off an addiction to pills. She heard me share my story—it helped that the other kids looked up to me—and I could tell Debbie liked me.

At first, Frank was my ride to and from the meetings, but soon the kids were taking turns. It became cool to be the one who gave me a ride. So after the meeting I was talking about needing my own car, and Debbie said, "My parents are going to get me a new car. I can sell you mine." It was a beautiful '59 Impala. I didn't have a license at the time, but she let me drive it anyway.

We started going out after the meetings, to Du-par's for coffee with some of the other kids or out to dinner. She felt safe with me—because I scared her into it. I was in line at a burger place and she came to join me, cutting through the line. Some guy tried to rub up against her and I said, "Hey, asshole, what are you doing?"

He said, "What? What?"

I said, "Fuck you. You know what you did."

He went out to his car and reached in through the window like he was grabbing something.

I walked over and said, "You know, holmes, you better pull out a gun 'cause I have one."

He said, "Hey, man, what? What?"

I said, "You fucked up. You know what you did."

Then, finally, he apologized.

Afterward Debbie said, "Do you have a gun?"

"Not last I checked," I said. I told what is called a white lie. While I'd gotten rid of the guns buried in my parents' backyard, it wasn't like I didn't know where to get one.

She was impressed. She started calling me "Hard Guy."

I met Debbie's parents at the R.I.F. Family Night.

A girl spoke, a teenager. She said, "I've never heard my mom say I love you."

The mom was sitting right next to her. She said, "Well, you know I do; isn't that enough?"

"Why can't you say it?"

"Well, because you know it already."

I wanted to sock that lady. I was so angry. Shit from my childhood, pain I hadn't dealt with, boiled up through me. I felt like a whiny punk, but the emotion was so strong. My own parents had never once said they loved me. It felt like there was a whole world of parents who couldn't tell their children they loved them.

But Debbie's parents were cool. Her father was a bigwig at Hanna-Barbera Productions, the place that made the cartoons *Jonny Quest*, *Scooby-Doo*, and *Yogi Bear*. Debbie had a job there as an illustrator. Debbie's parents loved her, and, unlike my ex-wife Laura's parents, they loved me, too. I think they were probably motivated by the fear of what would happen to their daughter if she started using again. It can be incapacitating, that fear, that grief; to see your baby going through that shit, knowing you can't protect them always if they keep doing what they are doing. With me, she was staying clean, so it helped them feel safe. Debbie and I had only been dating a few months when her mom said, "When are you two going to get married?"

We thought it was a good idea—why not?—so we decided to do it. People can't understand why I seem so casual about marriage. But I didn't look at marriage like a lifelong commitment or a sacrament. I saw it as an opportunity for a good party, a way to make your old lady happy, and something to do until I didn't feel like doing it anymore.

Debbie was an angel—loving, happy, beautiful, full of life. Every day when she got home from work, she'd make a big show of giving me a picture she'd drawn for me—cute, funny caricatures of the two of us. Her parents bought her the new car she'd been promised—an MG Midget—so I inherited the Impala. My childhood friend Chubby's dad, Keeno, got the engine running right and Frank and I went to work on the body—we hammered out the dents, added Bondo, and sanded it to get it ready to paint. I wanted to make it primo.

One day, I was driving down Laurel Canyon by Fernangeles Park, a place where a lot of junkies hung out, and saw a guy hitchhiking. I had no idea who he was; I just wanted to show off my cool set of wheels.

I pulled over, and when the guy walked up to the passenger door, I heard him make a weird noise. It wasn't a sigh or a grunt—something between the two. What it really was, I was about to see, was the sound of all hope leaving a body. The hitchhiker was Dennis. My old crime partner. The one who'd gotten me locked up.

"Danny."

I gripped the steering wheel tight. "Get in, Dennis."

He got in the car and the first thing I noticed was the smell. It smelled like death. We sat there for a minute.

"Are you going to kill me?" He said it with resignation, like he was asking me if I was going to give him a ham sandwich for lunch and he was tired of ham sandwiches.

When I was sentenced, everyone knew the story of how I'd been busted and how Dennis had flipped on me. In our world, being a rat or a snitch was the ultimate sin, and one that carried the death penalty. In the joint, people would ask me, "You want us to kill Dennis?" I'd always respond that I was going to kill him myself. I had a friend named Charlie Fasanella who went to a hospital in Norco where they detoxed people in the criminal justice system. Dennis happened to be there at the same time. One day Dennis called "group" because he had something he wanted to share. It's something that happens at rehabs and psych hospitals. Everyone sat down in a ring of chairs, and Dennis opened with "I'm not doing good today."

My friend Charlie said, "You know who's not doing good today? Danny Trejo." Then he socked Dennis so hard it broke his cheekbone. I know this because Charlie was convicted of assault and filled me in when he caught up to me in Soledad.

There I was, sitting in the driver's seat next to the man whose testimony landed me in Quentin, Folsom, Soledad, the man who had put me away for potentially ten years, put me in the line of fire where I could've been killed, put me in a position where maybe I had to kill to stay alive. Here was the Judas. If Dennis hadn't caught me clean and sober, with a car and a fiancée, high on life, I would have killed him. I would have had to kill him just to save face in my community. But clean and sober, while I still hated him for what he did, I understood it better. I remembered the family photos I'd seen on the wall in his parents' house. Him in a graduation cap, fresh-faced, with a world of possibility ahead of him. That kid was long gone. I felt sorry for him.

Besides, I knew if I killed him, that would mean I'd have to give up my '59 Chevy, and I didn't want to give up that car for anybody.

"No, Dennis, I'm not going to kill you."

"It wouldn't matter, I'm dying anyway." He pulled up his sleeve. His right arm was the most disgusting thing I'd ever seen. He didn't just have abscesses from shooting up; he had a flesh-eating disease. His arm was black and green and looked like rotten meat. I almost threw up.

"Jesus Christ, Dennis."

Dennis told me that the Feds used him to bust people. From the moment he flipped on me they'd gotten him to set up more buys and let him keep half the drugs. When he was too strung out, they'd send him to Norco to get clean and then have him start all over again. I drove him a few blocks and dropped him off where Vineland and Lankershim merge.

"I'm really sorry, Danny."

A few weeks later, Dennis's body was found in Valhalla Park next to the cemetery in North Hollywood. I heard he'd OD'd and had been stabbed a number of times. Rumor had it that it was a hot shot—a deliberately fatal dose of heroin. At first the cops thought I might have had something to do with it. I didn't. Dennis had burned half the San Fernando Valley.

As an addict, Dennis's death was a matter of time.

Fifteen years later, a woman came up to me at a meeting. She said she wanted her daughter to get into CRI-Help, a program I was heavily involved in, to get clean. She told me Dennis was the girl's father.

"Will you kill her, Danny?" she asked. I was stunned. What kind of monster did she think I was? Had I really been such a dark and terrible person all those years earlier that she would even think it possible that I'd do something so reprehensible?

I said, "What is wrong with you? Of course not. I'll make a call and get her in today."

She collapsed into my arms and started bawling.

Debbie and I got married at a fancy hotel in Burbank and her parents paid for everything. My family was there, too. I think they were overjoyed at how my life had turned around, but, like the woman at the meeting, they couldn't say it. The night was fun, but I can't express how careless I was with the sacrament of marriage. It was a piece of paper to me. I figured if it made Debbie happy, then that was cool. This is horrible to say, but to me, being married meant little more than guaranteed sex.

We went to Palm Springs on our honeymoon, and Debbie's parents helped us buy our first house on Osborne Street in Arleta. We fixed it up nice and made a good home for ourselves. But some habits were too hard to shake. Infidelity was the culture I grew up in, and it went both ways. There's an expression: *"Una en la casa, una en la calle."* One in the house, one in the street. Growing up in Mexican culture, I was taught women are like the Virgin Mary. They have children and are therefore miracle makers, but since they're objectified, they can be dismissed. I am not proud of this, but, for lack of any other example, I had embraced this way of thinking. All the men I knew growing up had "one in the house and one in the street," and I would be no exception. There were women everywhere—at meetings, at work, in stores. And apparently, for some women, my being married made me an even bigger magnet. I had options, and I was open to all of them.

Debbie put up with my philandering. She wasn't blind to it. She joked about the women who called at all hours, but she was too young and sweet to call me out on it. I didn't pay attention to how she felt. I was stressing money and hustles.

Chapter 9

OLD RAGE

1972

I wasn't working at Carlisi's anymore. Frank Russo wanted me to hook up with somebody who lived near me who could help guide me in sobriety. Jhonnie lived too far down south and, as Frank Russo put it, "Danny, you went too deep in the system for me to be able to help you the way you need." It's kind of an ex-con way of thinking, but it holds true. We look up to people who did hard time for longer stretches in the fabled prisons like San Quentin and Folsom.

Sam Hardy was that guy, a huge country boy from Louisiana who did a straight fifteen for murder. He always spoke really slowly, with a pound of chew in his mouth. Once he described his crime to me saying, "Well, Danny. I got in a dispute with two gentlemen. I killed one of them and murdered the other."

Sam hired me to sell tools for a company he worked for. The first day I dressed up in a suit, drove around to garages and body shops, and asked if I could speak to the manager. I'd show them the tools, explain how good they were, say they were thirty dollars, and they'd blow me off. Sometimes I didn't even get that far. They'd see me walk in smelling of "salesman" vibes and would wave me off before I could even ask for a manager. After a few days of this I decided to try a different approach. I put on a white T-shirt, a long black leather coat, pressed Levi's with Folsom cuffs, and shiny black boots. This time, I pulled up around back in the alley. I'd let out a little whistle. A manager would see me and say, "You got something?"

I'd look over my shoulder, then open my trunk. "I got these tools, holmes."

"They look good."

"They're real good."

"How much?"

"Forty dollars."

"I'll take 'em."

You cannot fool an honest man. I knew all these assholes had a bit of dishonesty in them. They'd ask if I could give them receipts.

"C'mon, holmes. Does it look like I have receipts?" They'd laugh.

That first day I put eight hundred bucks on Sam's kitchen table. He couldn't believe it.

"What'd you do?"

"I sold them like they were stolen."

"Well, damn. We're going to have to make out receipts for all these sales, but you got a big commission coming."

Sam was great at talking me down from the rages I fell into easily those early years after I got out.

I'd learned as a kid to channel my shame into rage, and the only anger management lessons I'd gotten had come from Gilbert, which was kind of like having a giant teach you to tiptoe. One of Gilbert's tips came just after I'd gotten out of fire camp. We were in a bar called The Rag Doll with two older women. Gilbert went to get cigarettes and this drunk construction worker stumbled over to us. He wedged into our conversation with his back to my face and started talking to the girls. They shined him on.

I told the man to back off, and he said, "Punk, what are you going to do?"

I said, "Let's take this somewhere." I walked toward the bathroom and he followed me. The bathroom had a set of swinging doors, and the second he walked in I dropped him with a quick combination. Then I beat the shit out of him. He was lying on the floor, with no fight left in him, but I was still so angry that I pissed on him.

That's when Gilbert walked in. He shook his head and said, "Danny, you can beat someone's ass and get away with it, but you can't humiliate him. If you embarrass someone, they'll plot revenge until they die."

Later that night, we came out of the bar with the girls. I walked past a Cadillac and this guy popped out.

I heard a boom, and the whole night lit up.

I thought I felt something hit my chest. I fell down. The Cadillac peeled away.

Gilbert said, "Are you okay?"

When I dropped, I could have sworn I'd been shot, but it was just sheer shock that made me fall. I said, "Gilbert, let's go."

"What happened?" he asked.

"I pissed my pants," I told him.

Gilbert helped me to his car and when we got in, we both started laughing our asses off. Gilbert said, "That's karma, motherfucker!"

That was the first time I ever heard the word. "You got what was coming. Don't forget what I told you, holmes. Don't piss on someone after you beat the shit out of them. Never humiliate."

I wasn't pissing on people after bar fights anymore, but my rage was still right near the surface. There was a time I was on the 405 near Ventura and a guy in an El Camino pulled a U in front of me and flipped me off. A switch flicked. I chased him ten miles down the highway, on his tail the whole time, all but ramming into him. He exited at Wilshire and almost ran a red light at Wilshire and Sepulveda. I did run the light and stayed on him.

Then he hit a bunch of backed-up traffic and had to stop. I got out of my car and ran up to him yelling.

He was a big guy, sitting there with his hands up, screaming, "Wait, wait!" He was so scared, he wouldn't get out of his car. In a little kid voice he said, "I'm having a really bad day."

I said, "I'm going to make your day worse, motherfucker," but then I looked at all these businesspeople standing on the sidewalk, watching me with open mouths. They looked terrified. I had an image of me, a wild-eyed, tattooed Mexican standing there, yelling, and thought, *There's nothing but Republicans on this corner.* I imagined myself standing in front of a Caucasian judge with this Caucasian pool cleaner with his El Camino and fifteen Caucasian witnesses. I heard a Caucasian prosecutor say, "Your Honor, the crazy Mexican in question . . . ," and I knew it wouldn't go well for me.

Sam knew how to talk me down, and where Gilbert told me what to do *after* I beat the shit out of someone, Sam took it a step further. We were standing in his kitchen when he said, "The way I see it, if he ain't worth killing, he ain't worth fighting. And if he ain't worth fighting, then he ain't worth getting upset about. And since you're not upset, grab me a Dr Pepper from the icebox."

I knew I was doing better when someone cut me off and I could say, "That guy's sure in a hurry," instead of going after them.

After first admitting I had a problem with drugs and alcohol, something that was easy for me to do, the second step was believing there was something in the universe more powerful than me. It seems like that should have been easy, but to an egomaniac running on self-will, it was a barrier. I confused the God of my upbringing with a "power greater than myself."

To help redirect my perspective, Sam Hardy would stand on the beach with me and say, "Stop one of those waves, okay? The ocean's more powerful than you, buddy." He reminded me in not-so-subtle ways that the planet was more than capable of surviving without my contributions. He'd say, "The Chinese built the Great Wall, all four thousand miles of it, without your help. The ocean, the moon turning the tides, an avalanche on a mountain. There are a lot of forces at play in the world that lie beyond the reach of your control." Sam's point was that I was but a small thing in a big world. And knowing that helped me put my own struggles in perspective. Sam said, "Dan, don't take everything on your shoulders. The ocean, other people's behavior, they do what they are going to do. Since you can't control that, don't be distressed about it."

I learned to ask God to take my problems and defects of character from me. I was still going to be myself. I had to—everybody else was taken. But I asked God to make me more aware of those parts of my personality and better able to control them.

Because Sam had done hard time, he could get away with stuff that nobody else could try on me. Once, out of the blue, he said, "I love you, Dan." It caught me off guard.

I said, "What the fuck do you want?"

He said, "What the fuck you got?"

I said, "You ain't got nothing but a motherfucking dick, and I already got one of those."

He said, "What the fuck is wrong with you, Dan? Every time you hear the word 'love' you think someone's going to get fucked, whether it comes from a broad or a used-car salesman. You ain't got nothing but parole, and I already got that. I don't want your stinky ass."

"But you have to admit my ass is nice."

We laughed. By making a joke out of it I was avoiding sitting in the hard truth of what Sam was saying. Until then, I'd never once heard a man say "I love you" to another man. It was something that took me years to say.

The tool game was cool while it lasted, but I'd already hit every mechanic and body shop in the Valley. When things slowed, Sam suggested I find a job that kept me outdoors and involved manual labor, so I started a lawn-mowing company with Danny Levitoff, a friend from R.I.F. Levitoff was a good-looking white boy from the Valley who came from a rich family, but he was a stone-cold junkie. To get money for drugs, Levitoff held up a Jack in the Box on Ventura Boulevard. After the robbery, he ditched the gun but forgot to take off his ski mask. He was arrested five blocks from the Jack in the Box walking down Ventura Boulevard with a balaclava on. A wealthy white kid whose family had money and connections, Levitoff was lucky he was sent to R.I.F. for his punishment and not prison. It didn't hurt that Judge Hughes was the one who heard his case, either.

When Levitoff first told the story of his bust to all of us at R.I.F., he said he was so loaded he forgot to take the mask off. "Fucking stupid of me, huh?" he said.

We all fell out laughing. One thing people are most surprised by when it comes to recovery is the laughter. Laughter is a great healer. Some of my biggest laughs have come in meetings when people share their past fuckups in a place where they can laugh at them. Like it says in the twelve-step literature, "We are not a glum lot."

Before I met Debbie, Levitoff had said, "Come live with me and my roommates," so I went to live with him. One of the guys living there, a big guy, was loaded.

I said, "You're loaded, fucker."

"No I'm not. Fuck you," he said.

"I can't be around anyone who is loaded, so either you get clean or you leave," I said.

He left, and later Levitoff told me that was exactly why he'd invited me to move in with them—he wanted to get rid of that guy. Levitoff was worried about what the guy might do when he told him to leave, and he knew I'd take care of his dirty work.

Meanwhile, he did my clean work. Levitoff was the face of our lawn-mowing operation. I had him knock on the doors of prospective clients because I knew we'd have a better chance if they saw him than if they saw me. Early on in our business, we discovered that if some scary-looking tattooed Mexican knocked on the door, most likely no one would answer. One of our first jobs, however, was a freebie. There was a woman who lived in my parents' neighborhood who all the kids on the block called "The Witch." I knew her story and it was a sad one. One son had died in Vietnam, the other had been killed in gang violence, and her husband had committed suicide out of grief.

After her husband died, she never came out of her house. The lawn looked like a jungle. Levitoff and I did a job at another house in the neighborhood for people who lent us their lawn mower because we still hadn't bought one. Every time we did their house, we did hers. Without asking, we just started mowing her lawn, trimming the edges, and clipping the hedges to make them look nice. She never once came outside, but sometimes I'd catch her peeking at us from behind her curtains.

We'd been doing her yard for about two months. It was a hot summer day. Levitoff and I were cleaning up the clippings and I heard the front door open and close. I went around to the other side of the house and saw a huge crystal pitcher full of lemonade sitting next to two crystal glasses full of ice on the front porch.

I'd never told anybody this, but when I was in the pen, especially in Folsom Five Building, I had a fantasy about pulling a huge score, a massive drug deal or an armored-car heist. In my fantasy, I'd take suitcases full of money to Las Vegas, go to a fancy club where broads would be draped all over me, and drink whiskey out of a crystal glass. The most important part of the fantasy was the sound of the ice clinking on real crystal. I'd had drinks in plastic cups, tin cups, coffee mugs, and tumblers, but never crystal. It was one of my strongest and most vivid fantasies.

Drinking that lemonade on that sad lady's porch, I heard the sound of ice in a crystal glass for the first time. I can still hear the clinking. Levitoff had said something funny, and I was laughing. I was sweaty and tired—the good kind of tired, from work. That lemonade tasted a thousand times better than any whiskey after pulling a stupid crime would have, all because we helped a woman who'd suffered unimaginable loss. God knows how to work things out the right way, even fantasies. God has an awesome sense of humor.

A week later, we were finishing the job at the lady's house when a big white guy came walking up the sidewalk. He was about sixty years old, 6'4", and chomping on chew like a cow. He said, "Hey, Pancho, how much do you charge the old lady to do her lawn?" and spit out a stream of tobacco. As soon as he said "Pancho," I knew there was no way in hell I was talking to that asshole. I kept working.

"Hey, Pancho."

I thought, *If this fucker wants us to do his yard, he'll have to pay ten times the normal rate just because of how much of a dick he is.* I said, "Yeah?"

He said, "How much do you charge the lady to do her yard?"

"We don't charge the lady nothing." His face changed.

He said, "Come here, I want to show you something." He nodded toward Danny Levitoff. "And bring Paco."

At that point I thought the man would have to pay fifty times the rate if we were going to do his lawn.

Levitoff and I followed him down the street to his house. He opened his garage. It was loaded with beautiful tools and a huge workbench. He was the kind of guy who painted the walls of his garage blue and left white spots for each tool. There was a place for everything, and everything was in its place except for a hammer that was missing. There was a white outline of a hammer with no hammer in the spot. It bothered me.

He said, "I had a heart attack last year. The missus won't let me do strenuous work on account of that. If you do my lawn, I'll let you have all these tools." He pointed to a beautiful, brand-new mower, a trimmer, and a bunch of clippers and rakes. Levitoff and I looked at each other. We'd just been talking about how we needed to buy equipment to grow our business and how we couldn't just keep borrowing mowers from people whose lawns we mowed.

God struck again. Walking back to the old lady's house, Levitoff got philosophical. He said, "Danny, do you think God does these things on purpose?"

I said, "Of course He does, Paco."

We pissed ourselves laughing. After that, D&D Lawn Services really took off. I know the man gave us all that equipment because we didn't charge the lady anything. I ended up becoming really close with that old guy, and he never called me Pancho again.

Around that time, an old partner of mine from the streets, Jimmy Peña, reached out to me. We met in a coffee shop in the Valley. Jimmy was an ex-con who was heavily involved in getting people off drugs. He told me he was working for a new program downtown called the Narcotics Prevention Project. The N.P.P. was developed to treat heroin addicts using methadone. While methadone was being used in New York to treat heroin addicts, it hadn't taken hold in LA.

Jimmy knew I had a way of talking recovery to people. He'd heard I was chairman of the twelve-step recovery group in Soledad and had stayed active in recovery after I got out. He said he'd like to hire me to work with him and another addiction counselor, Norman Sprunck, at the N.P.P. Norm and a guy named Bill Wilson ran the hospital side of the N.P.P. while Jimmy ran the intake. It had always been a dream of mine to work in the field of treatment and recovery. I was already spending so much of my time doing what I could in meetings and reaching out to people, but to have a full-time job trying to get people clean was a gift from God. At the N.P.P., I'd be doing God's work and getting paid to do it.

I drove my Cadillac Eldorado down to the N.P.P. and discovered its location was a recovering addict's nightmare. There were dealers up and down the block and junkies nodding off everywhere. Jimmy met me at the front door. "Danny," he said, "Job One is to clean up the block."

Turns out Jimmy hadn't hired me because of my stellar counseling skills, just like Levitoff hadn't just wanted me as a roommate—what Jimmy needed was muscle to clear a safe environment for the clients. I whistled and got everyone's attention. "Everyone, get the fuck out!"

One dealer was resistant. I knew he'd done time, and I could tell he knew I had, too. I said, "Hey, holmes, you know you don't want to go back for this bullshit. Do what you got to do, just take it three blocks down the street. We can't have this shit around a place for recovery."

He sized me up. "Alright, man. Just for you."

It took me a day and a half, but I cleared all the dealers and users out of an area that was four square blocks. Norm was impressed. "Jimmy told me you were the right man for the job."

"Jimmy was right."

Most of my day work at N.P.P. involved assessing new patients in the morning and taking them to detox at the Metropolitan State Hospital in Norwalk. I was the only one with car insurance, so it was my job to chauffeur the patients. In those forty-minute drives I'd get more accomplished than your average social worker or psychiatrist. It was just like my psychiatrist at San Quentin, Dr. Berkman, used to tell me. He'd say, "Danny, there's no psychiatrist in the world who can help a man unless he deals with his drug problem first."

A magic happens when two addicts get together. We have a way of speaking to each other that cuts through the bullshit. They can't lie to you and you can't lie to them. Most of the clients had records, and they knew I represented a life of living clean on the outside of the fence. I was proof that you could get off the junk and get better. I never came on strong. No addict wants an unsolicited therapy session. I'd just say, "Let's go eat and relax." If they wanted to get into it, they'd open up, but getting them fed was key. Pancakes work miracles.

Another part of my job was taking clients to their court dates. One day I showed up to work wearing a suit.

Jimmy Peña asked me what I was doing.

"Hey, homie," I said, "don't you know that wearing a suit is the language of the court?" When people showed up to court dressed like *vatos*, or way too casual in shorts and huaraches, the court treated them as such. I've had judges cut guys loose to my custody just because I was wearing a suit.

To make it even more official, I had a laminated badge with my picture and *N.P.P.* written beneath it. I swear to God, when they saw my badge, a lot of officers of the court thought I was federal agent. One time I went to LA County to pick up a client and the guards let me in the back without going through security. I didn't know what was happening until one talked to me in copspeak like I was a Fed. It's amazing how far a suit and a laminated badge can get you. In 2001, an inmate at LA County Jail named Kevin Pullum was returning from trial on an attempted murder charge and simply walked out of Twin Towers wearing civilian clothes and a laminated ID with a picture of Eddie Murphy as Dr. Dolittle on it.

Another time I was picking up a client at LA County to bring him to Norwalk and a cop turned to me and said, "Trejo, you want me to cuff him?" I don't think he had a clue that, as a civilian employee, I didn't have keys to handcuffs.

I said, "Nah, I got him."

The guy was someone I'd done time with. He looked at me in amazement about what went down. He said, "What the fuck just happened?"

"He thinks I'm a Fed," I said. We laughed.

Around that time, Bill Wilson and Norm introduced me to a man named Dr. Dorr who ran a program called Western Pacific Med Corp. Dr. Dorr had opened his first methadone clinic in Glendale and wanted me to come work with him while I was still working for the N.P.P. I didn't have any counseling credentials, but they weren't as tough about that at the time. Back in the 70s and 80s, people were more concerned with results. We were getting junkies clean off heroin at the N.P.P. and Western Pacific and that was all we cared about.

I gave my share of the lawn-mowing company to Danny Levitoff and made my life full-blast recovery work. I'd hit the streets and talk to dealers I knew. A lot of them had customers who were flat broke and hassling them for more dope even though they couldn't afford it. The dealers knew which addicts would become colossal pains in the ass for them, so they'd kick them to me. One dealer sent me by a customer's house and I found two dudes, Little Joe and Tommy Andrews, on the front porch, nodding off with needles hanging from their arms. Turns out, I knew them both. I woke them up. "C'mon, let's go!" I said.

"Where we going?"

"Metropolitan State Hospital."

"Okay, Danny. Let me just fix one last time." Tommy searched the porch for a rig.

"You already got one hanging off your arm."

"Oh shit, thanks! You're right."

Chapter 10

UNA EN LA CASA

1975–76

Though I was helping a lot of people get clean, I was back for round two of being the world's shittiest husband. The excuse I made to myself was that I was doing so much good for so many people, I could be selfish in my personal life. Debbie was getting the short end of the stick. The rest of the stick I was saving for different women I had around town. Two who adored me were living together in an apartment in Van Nuys. They didn't mind sharing me and taking care of me. If we needed extra bread, they'd go to the clubs in Oxnard where women could dance fully nude and they'd bring home buckets of cash. I was living two lives. It was *"Una en la casa, una en la calle"* all over again, except in my case it was *"Tres o cuatro en la calle."*

When it came down to it, my bad behavior with women wasn't just about a male chauvinist culture. At its roots it was connected to something darker and more insidious, a family secret that I had carried with me from when I was seven years old.

One day after school, I was in the house with my dog, Hoppy, when my uncle David came by. My mom told me to take Hoppy and play outside. I took Hoppy out on the lawn while my mom closed all the windows and the venetian blinds. I didn't know what was going on, just that it was weird.

My mom and Uncle David were in there for what felt like forever. To tell you how innocent and naïve I was, I thought maybe they closed the blinds because they were going to surprise me with a present.

After what was probably forty-five minutes Uncle David came out of the house. He didn't look at me when he went to his car. My mother opened the blinds and stepped outside. Then she did something really odd. She went back inside, brought out a camera, and took a picture of me with Hoppy. My mother never took my picture. Then she went back inside and started making dinner for my dad. When I look at that picture today, I see a fake-happy, "I'm trying to be hopeful" expression on my face.

A couple of weeks later, my mom went to Mexico to visit family. While she was gone, my dad and I had the run of the house. My dad was always great with kids . . . except me. He could be funny and generous. He'd play tickle, find a quarter, all that stuff with neighborhood kids, while I just stood by and watched. I'd think, *Why the hell has he never found a quarter behind* my *ear?* One time, he even brought a little boy named Bernie home to live with us. Bernie's dad was a drunk who'd stumble around the streets all day. I hated Bernie. Luckily, he only stayed one night and wanted to go home the next day. I was jealous my dad couldn't be that way with me. But the weeks my mom was gone, it was different. We were buddies. We watched Westerns and went to grab tacos. One night, he said, "We should go by Lobby's and David's house on Saturday and cook up some *carne*."

I innocently mentioned that Uncle David had come by the house while he was at work one day.

"What?"

I said, "Him and Mom had something important to talk about so they put me out on the front lawn for a while."

My dad took it in, but it didn't seem like a big deal. Until my mom came home from her trip.

I woke up to screaming.

"Why was David here?"

"He's lying! I don't know why he's lying!"

My dad kicked in my door and dragged my mother into the room. He grabbed me by the throat and shoved his fist in my face.

"Tell me again what you said about David."

I'd never seen my father so angry. He was so furious, he was shaking. I froze. My mother was on her knees, crying. "Why'd you lie, Danny? Please! ¿Por qué mentiste?"

If I said the wrong thing, he might kill me. If I said the wrong thing, he might kill her. I knew whatever I decided to say, it was going to be real bad, so I decided to protect my mom.

"I lied."

My dad pulled his fist back like he was going to hit me. "If you ever lie to me again, I'll kill you."

When my dad left my room, I lay there thinking, *What the fuck? What the fuck did I do?*

After that, nothing was ever the same. Not with my mother. Not with my father. Not with me. I'd see her in the house and catch her looking at me. It was like she was wondering, *What do you know?* While I wondered, *What are you hiding?*

About a year after this went down my mom made me my favorite snack, fried okra, put it on the table, and asked, "Why did you lie about Uncle David coming by?"

She looked into my eyes and repeated the question.

I stared down at the okra on the plate. I couldn't look at her. I didn't want food; I didn't want to be there.

I said, "I don't know. I guess I'm just bad." I was taking the rap for something I knew I hadn't done and didn't understand. I didn't know what an affair was. I didn't know what my mother and my uncle were doing. But somehow both my parents blamed me for it.

She smiled. *"Come, come."* Eat, eat. She was mothering me and gaslighting me at the same time.

Ever since that day I've hated okra.

My whole life I've told people the same story about my mother. She was a saint. She took care of me as a child; she cleaned my clothes when they were dirty; she wrote me letters when I was in the joint. I always say that she was simple, that she loved her telenovelas and didn't really register what I did for a living until I was almost fifty and made a guest appearance with Luke and Laura on *General Hospital*. Later, when I did a run of episodes on *The Young and the Restless*, my mom's friends all called the house flipping out. Telling her friends I was an actor was one thing, but in terms of credibility, having them see me on a soap opera was something else.

"Oh, *mijo*," my mom gushed, "you're a star!" That was the story I told about my mother. But the truth is I never felt like she did any of those things out of love, it was more like it was her job. The whole reason my dad had married her was specifically for her to take care of me. I never felt truly cared for. My mother, for complicated reasons, brought a coldness to our house. And it was never part of the story that both of my parents had rerouted their anger at each other toward me.

They say we're as sick as our secrets.

My mother's affair with my uncle David continued for almost thirty years. A lot of people were broken by it. Two people died early because of it. My dad did for sure. And his sister—Uncle David's wife, my aunt Lobby. My whole family was broken because of the affair. The mark it left on me was indelible. My feelings about women became so twisted, I never trusted them after that.

I figured women were out to get you, so I had to get them before they got me. I wasn't violent, I was dismissive. If you were going to be my old lady, the other women were just something you had to get used to, and your feelings about them didn't rate. I was the only one allowed to have feelings in my house, just like my dad. If someone was going to lie, it was going to be me. If there was going to be cheating, I was going to be the one doing it. If someone was going to fuck someone over, I was going to do it first.

I think my mom's relationship with David threatened me so badly because it showed me that even if you locked a woman away in a house and denied her access to a car, as my father had done with my mother, she could still get you. For me to blame all women for that scenario, and even for me to blame my mother, who was living like an indentured servant under a tyrannical regime, didn't register at the time. It took me decades to figure this out, but at the time I was in protect-myself mode, and any woman in my path was paying the price.

The last straw with Debbie came when a friend of hers who was trying to stay clean was our houseguest on Osborne Street. The friend and I were up late watching TV one night, and I booked her. It was both a horrible thing to do and not that different from the crap I was pulling regularly. The difference was this time it happened under our roof.

The friend started feeling guilty about what had happened and made amends to Debbie. She was early in recovery, and I guess she missed the part that you make amends to people, "except when to do so would injure them or others."

Debbie was destroyed. She packed her stuff while I was out, moved back with her parents, and it was over. I got home that night to a half-empty house. I opened a drawer where we kept the cartoons she'd drawn of me and us together. That's when it really hit me how incredible she was and how much of an asshole I'd been. Never before or after has anyone loved me with unconditional adoration like Debbie. She never got angry with me. She had no fight in her. When Debbie saw me, she'd light up and melt. She'd get giggly. I took that innocent kind of love and trampled on it. And I realized that by being unfaithful to her under our roof, I'd done to Debbie what my mother had done to my father. I prayed every day that God would help Debbie find someone better who would love her the way she deserved.

I never heard from her again.

Chapter 11

THE TREJO NAME

1975

While I made a mess of my personal life, I was everyone else's cleanup guy, so I was the one my cousin called when Gilbert and some girl were naked in my mom's backyard.

If you're naked in a Beverly Hills backyard or on a beach in Saint-Tropez, you're sunbathing. But if you're naked in a Pacoima backyard, you're most likely fucking. I went over there and found them butt naked and loaded out of their minds. I started trying to reason with Gilbert. "Listen, Gilbert, I got to get you into detox at Reprieve House." Reprieve House was the first residential rehab in the San Fernando Valley started by Bill Beck, the same guy that started CRI-Help. I said to Gilbert, "You're violating your parole and if you don't get clean—"

The woman interrupted. She was sitting there, tits out, grinding her jaw, scratching her butt, and she said, "Do they take women?"

"*Shh, shh,*" I said, holding my fingers to my lips. "I'm talking to my uncle. Be quiet." Then I turned back to Gilbert. "If someone sees you, they're going to call the cops. You're going to get tested and—"

The woman interrupted again and I said, "Shut up! I'm talking to my uncle. I need to get him into rehab or his parole officer is going to violate him. Gilbert, go get some fucking clothes and get a towel for this woman. We gotta move."

He said, "I don't know. I want a Kool-Aid."

Fucking Kool-Aid.

Gilbert came back with a tumbler of Kool-Aid in one hand and his balls in the other. I said, "Gilbert, I've got a spot for you in Reprieve House but we have to act now. You ready to go?"

Gilbert said, "Nah, nah, fuck it. I don't want to go."

At that the chick sat up and announced, "I wanna go! Will you take me?" She was hammered, but dead serious. It caught me off guard.

Gilbert looked like he was reconsidering.

It wasn't the optimal situation, but to be diplomatic I said, "We'll all go."

Gilbert said, "Well, if she goes, I'll go."

I got them both clothes and brought them to Reprieve. The next day, Gilbert took off with a super gangster broad named Rachel Silvas. They ended up pulling a string of robberies that put Gilbert back in the joint. Rachel was on the lam for a while but is now doing life, on top of life, on top of life. The naked chick from the backyard, meanwhile, stayed, and for many, many years after that I'd see her around at meetings, sober, helping female newcomers get sober, and appearing to be having a great life.

As the cleanup guy, I didn't succeed with my uncle Gilbert. He ended up back in Folsom. At this point, he was one of the OGs of the California prison system. And that's when his son, also named Gilbert, started getting in real trouble. With his dad in prison, Little Gilbert's mother struggled to control him.

At six, he was busted the first time by the authorities for breaking into a dentist's office and stealing all his gold. I remember seeing dental equipment, fake teeth, and shit in his room and wondering where it came from. But, even as a former robber myself, I thought, *No way, this kid's too young.* Turns out, he wasn't. It was a cycle Little Gilbert would be caught in the next fifty years of his life. It was a cycle I knew well. His father was caught up in it. I was caught up in it. My other uncles and cousins were trapped in the same culture of destructive machismo. This was what it meant to be a Trejo man. What it was to live up to the Trejo name.

When I was four or five, my aunts and girl cousins adored me. They treated me like a Kewpie doll, dressing me up and putting makeup on my face and bows in my hair. It was innocent. We were innocent.

One day, my uncle Rudy came in the girls' bedroom, saw me in a dress, and went ballistic. "What the fuck are you doing?" He said it to my aunts, probably because he thought I was too young to know what was going on. I was.

He rubbed his face with his palms as if he were wrestling with something profoundly fucked up. For him, this was a Mexican *charro*'s worst nightmare come true. "*¡Ayúdame, Dios!*"

He turned to leave, stopped, then yelled over his shoulder, "Clean that shit off his face!"

We Trejos had to be masculine in every way, at every moment. One day at lunch at Elysian Heights Elementary the teachers brought the kids together to do a mass Hokey Pokey. I had already been so indoctrinated in the macho *Chicanismo* of my father and his brothers, I wouldn't do it and got sent home from school for refusing to participate. When my father came home from work, my mom told him I'd gotten in trouble at school. My dad demanded to know what I did wrong, and I told him I wouldn't do the Hokey Pokey. He had no idea what the hell I was talking about, so I showed him. When I got to the part where I said, "You put your right hip in, you put your right hip out . . . ," my father jumped up from the couch and turned off the ball game he was watching.

"What the fuck are they teaching you at that school?"

The next day my father took me to school and demanded to see the principal, Ms. Brooks. I sat outside the office in the waiting area and heard him yelling through the door, "I don't send my son to school for you to teach him to shake his ass! He's a man!" I never had to do the Hokey Pokey again.

If I ever did anything around my dad or uncles that wasn't considered manly, I was called a sissy. It was as humiliating as it was intended to be. I was taught to hate anything they considered feminine. It was a lesson I learned too well.

Little Gilbert, growing up with his father in and out of prison, didn't really have a chance. Like me, he took the same route that his father carved out for him. He was in and out of juvie, Youth Authority, boys' homes. When he was ten or so, he was placed in a boys' home out in Palm Springs. An old partner, Nolan Warner, and I rode Harleys out to the desert to check on him. When I got there, a counselor said, "We don't know where he's at, he just took off."

Riding back on Interstate 10 to Los Angeles, I saw a figure jump from the bushes by the side of the freeway. It could have been anyone, but it was Gilbert. This is the way God works in my life. I pulled off the road and called him over. He was tripped out to see me.

"Danny, I was just going to try and hitchhike. What are you doing here?"

"I'm here to pick you up."

I knew the boys' home wasn't the best place for Gilbert. Besides structure, he needed family love. He needed me. I could be a father figure to Gilbert, just like his father had been a father figure to me. Maybe set him on a different path. Nolan said, "What are you doing? You're not taking him back to Palm Springs?"

"Nope. He's coming home with me." I rode the 120 miles home with Gilbert on the back of my bike, clinging to me. No helmet, but cops were more chill back then. Letting Nolan take the lead on the freeway, I felt Gilbert's arms around my back and thought about how he was just about the same age I was when I started getting busted.

The first time I really got busted wasn't for violence or selling dope, it was because Tommy Provincio and I released all the cows at Roger Jessep's dairy on the corner of Branford and Laurel Canyon. We were walking around one night and heard the cows mooing. They sounded like they were suffering, so we climbed over a big fence, pushed the heavy sliding doors open, and set them all free. They couldn't wait to get the fuck out of there. They ran all over Pacoima. Those cows must have been in heaven for a few hours.

Because dairies are under the jurisdiction of the Food and Drug Administration, the Feds were all over the scene. Tommy and I got caught with cow shit all over our shoes and pants. It was hard to deny we did it.

If you put both those points on a line and kept going straight, you'd get to tenth grade, or when I was supposed to be in tenth grade. I'd already been kicked out of Poly, Sun Valley, Monroe, Van Nuys, and North Hollywood.

No school in the Valley knew what to do with me, and no school needed to figure it out after one Friday night when I went to James' drive-thru with a friend named Freddie T. and two girls. We were heading into the joint to order when two white boys jumped us. The four of us started throwing down in the parking lot. I was at a disadvantage. I was drunk off my ass. I don't care how good a fighter you are, if you fight when you're falling-down drunk and up against a guy with skills—and this white boy had skills—you're in for a tough time. He knocked me back to the car. One of the girls opened the door and I fell inside and reached for a wine bottle.

Gilbert had taught me that if someone grabs you, you should stick a thumb in their eye or bite them in the neck. That makes people think you're insane, and nobody wants to fight with crazy. Gilbert used to say, "I'm going to hand you your eye, holmes. You're going to take your eye home in your pocket."

I broke the wine bottle across the dude's head and stabbed him in the face with the neck.

He started screaming, so we hopped back in the car and took off.

I made it back to my parents' house, took off my clothes, dumped them in a pile, and went to bed. I was wearing pleated khakis and a yellow-and-white Sir Guy shirt with a matching yellow-and-white vest. This stuck in my mind because they were covered in blood and processed into evidence. About twenty minutes after I fell asleep, four cops busted into my room with their guns drawn.

"Get up, Trejo."

The room was spinning. I was still wasted.

"Put some clothes on."

I went for my closet, but a cop pointed to the pile next to my bed and said, "Put those on."

I was cuffed and taken to LA County covered in blood.

A few weeks later I was sitting with the public defender when the two white boys came into the courtroom wearing sailor uniforms. I looked at the judge, an old guy I was sure had been around during the Sleepy Lagoon case and the Zoot Suit Riots and most likely was not on the side of the Mexicans. The young man I'd fought had a big bandage covering his face. None of this was good for my case.

I was convicted of causing mayhem, scarring, and disfiguring and sentenced to fire camp.

Now, years later, I recognized the road Little Gilbert was on, and I wanted to keep him on my Harley, steering in a different direction. So I did. I steered us straight toward my house.

Chapter 12

THIRD TIME'S A CHARM

1975

When I brought Little Gilbert home with me, my girlfriend fell in love with him.

Joanne and I had been together for about seven months. I met her because, thanks to Dr. Dorr and my friend Bill Beck, I was involved in all the major treatment programs in the San Fernando Valley. I was at CRI-Impact just helping out when I overheard a counselor telling a young woman that all she needed to do was testify against her parole officer. I couldn't help but eavesdrop. Apparently, her corrupt PO had been using her parolees to deal heroin, and Joanne had been busted with thirty-two spoons and charged with intention to sell.

I had pulled Joanne aside and asked her what was going on.

"They want me to testify against my parole officer."

I said, "Okay, you have to do what you have to do, but you know, if you testify, you're going to be considered a snitch." She had no idea what I was talking about.

"But if I don't tell them she put me up to it, I'll have to go to prison."

"You might have to go to prison either way, but once you're inside and people know you snitched, it's not going to affect the PO, it's going to affect you."

I probably shouldn't have gotten involved, but my concern was for people to get clean, whatever that took. Joanne had been clean for a few months, her life was just getting back on track, and now she was confronting this. I couldn't tell her what to do or what not to do; I just wanted her to see the bigger picture.

Two weeks after that, Joanne showed up at my house crying. She said, "I ain't no rat!" She said she'd talked to her family and that a drug counselor named Jack Birch, who had been a street guy himself, had told her not to testify. She was scared. Me and some of the guys at R.I.F. found her a place to stay, and I told her to lay low, keep clean, and the rest would work itself out.

I knew a criminal defense lawyer in the Valley who was the main man when it came to drug offenses. He owed me a favor and kicked me to his associate, telling the guy, "Help Danny out." We started to prepare for Joanne's court date. The charges Joanne faced were serious. Possession of that much heroin with intent to sell could mean a decade in prison. It was disgusting that her PO was the one having her sell drugs. But I knew if she testified it would make her life inside hell. Better for her to face her punishment for what she did.

When the day came, I went to court with Joanne and her attorney. The case against her was presented and after opening statements were made, I slipped the lawyer a note. After reading it he said, "Your Honor, I'm here with Mr. Danny Trejo. He works with R.I.F. and is the counselor for my client. He'd like to say a few words."

The DA went ballistic. He said, "Your Honor, this witness was never provided! This is not—" Before he could finish, the judge held up his hand to shut him up. It was Judge Hughes of R.I.F. fame. I had expected him to be on the bench because he handled all the drug cases in Van Nuys.

Judge Hughes said, "I don't know if you know it, sir, but I happen to be one of the founders of R.I.F. It's a tremendous program!" Judge Hughes went on a long spiel about his work with R.I.F., and the DA knew he was fucked. "Continue, Mr. Trejo," said the judge.

"Thank you, Your Honor. This young woman has been attending meetings at R.I.F. and has been clean and sober for three months. She's working a strong recovery program and has made great strides in her life."

Judge Hughes turned to Joanne. "Are you going to meetings every day?"

"Yes, Your Honor. Except the days when I work a long shift."

"You have a job?"

"Yes, Your Honor."

The DA slammed a folder on his desk. Judge Hughes gave Joanne a thirty-day sentence but allowed her to serve it on weekends so she could continue to work. The DA wanted to kill me. Her lawyer turned to me and said, "I want you to work all my cases."

Before we left the courtroom, Judge Hughes pulled me aside and said, "Mr. Trejo, tell your client to return to court in two weeks and we'll evaluate from there." I knew exactly what he was saying.

I can't remember how much time Joanne did exactly, but it was over before she knew it. I'd drop her off every Friday afternoon at Sybil Brand Institute in Monterey Park. I still laugh thinking about that cute little thing standing in front of the prison's massive gate. Months passed and Joanne and I lost touch. Then I ran into her at a sober dance, and we went to coffee afterward at Du-par's. Joanne and I started seeing each other. She moved into my house on Osborne and we started a life together.

After I picked him up on the highway, I brought young Gilbert home to the house I was sharing with Joanne and told her that he was going to be living with us. She immediately made up the guest bedroom. Joanne was like that. When we first moved in together and she found strange men crashed on the couch in the morning, she didn't know what was up. But when I explained that this is what we do, we help others get off drugs and get their lives together, she fell right in with my program.

She was only twenty, but Joanne became a wonderful surrogate mom for this twelve-year-old boy. His case manager was okay with Gilbert living with us, because, as he said, "Danny, we don't know what to do or how to get through to this child. Maybe you can."

Before long, Joanne and I were talking about marriage. Like I said, to me, marriage was a good party. First was Laura, second was Debbie, third time's a charm, right?

Our wedding was at a church on La Brea. Joanne was already waiting in the church when I arrived in a limo. One of the guests, a friend of Joanne's, was standing on the sidewalk when I stepped out of the car. My first thought was *Wouldn't it be cool to hook up with her in the limo?* I made a joke to the woman about fucking in the limo, and if she had jumped in, who knows what would have happened? I was rehabilitated in many ways, but not as a groom.

Years later, my lawyer, Terry Roden, said to me, "Danny, I figured it out. You can't stand being married, but you love weddings."

For a couple years Gilbert did great. We had him in school and in sports. He was so hyperactive that the coach took him off the offense in Pop Warner football because he couldn't stay still and was always called for "illegal motion." When they moved him to defense and he was free to roam and hit people, he lit up the league. He was so good, the other teams tried to get him banned. Coaches kept demanding to see his birth certificate. And then his mother missed him. She wanted Gilbert back. I said, "Linda, this kid needs someone who can keep him in line. He's a great kid, but he needs to be checked. He needs to be pulled by the scruff of his neck, and you can't do that."

"He's my boy, and I miss him."

Gilbert went back to his mother and just kept getting locked up. He was an unstoppable freight train. At age seventeen, Gilbert committed the gang killing that put him away for the next thirty-eight years of his life.

Sadly, it wasn't a surprise for the family. My generation of Trejos, starting with Big Gilbert (since he was so young compared to his brothers he was practically my generation), were expected to be locked up. Toni, Coke, Salita, Mary Carmen and her husband, Ponchee, and I, we were all gangsters and dealers who ended up in jail or prison at some point. Little Gilbert actually served time in San Quentin with his dad, but everywhere Little Gilbert was locked up, Big Gilbert used his juice with the Mafia to make sure stone-cold *vatos* had eyes on his namesake. My uncle Gilbert may have been a gangster, but he would always do everything in his power to help those he loved.

Chapter 13

A SECRET UNRAVELS

1978

Joanne and I were married for three years, after which she left me for the same justifiable reason all my wives left me—it was like I was trying to send the message *You don't think I'm a dog? I'll prove it to you.*

Joanne moved on and out of the house on Osborne Street, and I decided it was time to make a switch myself. Someone in a meeting said they were leaving their apartment in Venice Beach, and I said I'd take it as long as there was no hassle and we could do it quickly. I checked out the place, we shook on it, and that afternoon a few friends helped me move my stuff in.

My first day living at the beach, I wandered onto the famous workout area in Venice called "Muscle Beach" and started lifting. Muscle Beach was open to the public, but if you weren't welcome, you'd find out real quick.

From then on, I was at Muscle Beach lifting every chance I could get. I think I loved it so much because the vibe in the place reminded me of the weight pile in San Quentin and Soledad, minus the stabbings.

My work in rehab had become all-consuming. I'd opened a new treatment center with Dr. Dorr called O.U.R. House (Ongoing Unity and Recovery) on Third and Western in Koreatown. We were also in the process of opening a new recovery house on Gardner, where we wanted to do more than take clients to receive methadone treatments. If they were really going to transition to a new life, we thought they should have a residence where they could get their lives together in a structured environment. It was a new idea at the time.

We had no shortage of clients. From lockup in Folsom, my uncle Gilbert would send me word and check up on me to see how I was doing. He sent me pictures of him on the Yard and joked about charging me three dollars for them. He also sent me clients. A lot of dudes in prison were worried about family on the outside who they knew were dealing with drug problems. Gilbert would say, "My nephew Danny is getting a lot of people in LA clean, holmes," and give them my number. I was getting tons of calls from family members of inmates who heard I could help.

Every day, starting at six a.m., I was tracking people down on the street and in drug dens, convincing them to go into treatment, taking them to job interviews, dealing with their parole officers, going to meetings, sponsoring dudes in the program. I was busy, and I loved it. In a way, the work tapped into something I'd felt when I fought fires back in juvie, and even what I felt when I defended underdogs in prison. Through drug counseling, I was helping people. I was making a difference.

I met Diana at North Hollywood Rehab, another residential treatment center I put together with Dr. Dorr. The first two things I noticed were that she was beautiful and that she had a broken toe. Since her room was up a small staircase, I made myself useful by carrying her to her room. I thought, *Damn, I like this lady*. But she was a client, and I didn't want to be unprofessional, so I didn't say a word and intentionally stayed away from her. I wasn't great at drawing lines in my marriages, but I respected that line in recovery.

Recovery is an intimate process. You see people at their worst, you hear their deepest secrets and biggest regrets. It's possible she noticed how close I was with other clients and wondered why I was all business with her. But the night I think her interest in me really sparked was at the circus.

When I saw the Ringling Bros. and Barnum & Bailey Circus was coming to the Forum, I called the office there and asked to speak to whoever dealt with group charities. A woman picked up and I described my organization and asked if I could get a discount for my clients. She apologized and said they had already handed out all the tickets they allotted for charities.

There was a guy who volunteered with us who owned a flower shop; he suggested to me that I send the woman flowers and a card. I wrote, *Thank you so much, please keep us in mind for next year.* She immediately called me back. She said she'd worked at the Forum for twenty years and had never been sent flowers. She ended up sending us thirty-six tickets.

We took two vans and a few of us drove our cars to bring thirty people to Inglewood. It turned out I had six extra tickets, each of which had a face value of $60. This was a shitload of money to any of us. My friend Jack Birch, the street guy who had counseled Joanne on snitching, suggested I scalp them before the show started and pocket the dough. The hustler in me liked that suggestion, so I stood out in front of the circus looking to make a sale. After a few minutes, a brother walked up to me. He was with six little kids. I'm sure I looked sketchy; I always did. The man said, "Got tickets?"

"Yeah."

"How much?" I checked the dude out. He was wearing gray khakis, a sweat-stained T-shirt that was completely covered in dust, and his boots had concrete on them. I could tell he'd just put in a hard day at work. The kids all looked like they were about the same age, so I knew they weren't all his. I figured he'd probably taken his kid and five of his kid's neighborhood friends for a once-in-a-lifetime experience.

"Free."

He looked at me sideways. "Free?" He got mad. "How the hell are they free?"

"Look, I was given these tickets and they're good, right down on the floor. I'm not looking to make money off them."

The guy studied the tickets, then studied me, and didn't trust any of it. I said, "Just see if they work. If they don't, I'm sure you can find someone who'll sell you tickets."

When I told Jack what I'd done, he was pissed. "Danny, you could have got three hundred and sixty bucks for those tickets."

"Don't worry," I said. "What I did is better."

The circus was awesome. All the clients were loving it. The elephants were running around, doing their shit, and I looked over and saw the man smiling and clapping. The kids he was chaperoning were in heaven. That man had given them a night they'd never forget. He caught my eye and thumped his chest and pointed me out to the kids. They all started waving and cheering. I caught Jack's eye and gestured toward the man and the kids. I may have missed out on some cash, but getting to see that guy be a hero in front of his kid, in front of his kid's friends, seeing the expression on his face, that was priceless.

Diana witnessed this and looked at me differently. I think she fell in love with me that night. I wasn't trying to impress her or anyone else. But as I've said many times: everything good that's ever happened in my life has come as the direct result of helping someone else and not expecting anything in return. We all felt good leaving the circus.

Diana finished her stint in rehab and found a job working in an office. We lost touch for a while, but after about six months she reached out to me.

I had just opened another new recovery house on Gardner Street in Hollywood with Dr. Dorr. It turned out she was living in an apartment just a few blocks away. Since we were overwhelmed with paperwork at the Gardner location, I offered Diana a part-time job helping us get on top of the workload. At that time, we were receiving state, federal, and city money to help with our programs, so I needed someone who could help cut through the red tape. Her work was so good that I said, "How much are you getting paid in your other job? Because I'll pay you more to come on board full-time." Diana started working at Gardner and soon after that, now that it was aboveboard, we started seeing each other, but we never moved in together. I didn't want to make that mistake again.

I was in my apartment in Venice the day all hell broke loose. My father called. He said, "She did it, she did it. She's gone." I told him to hang on, that I was coming to see him.

My mother had had a psychiatric break. In typical Mexican family fashion, no one had talked about it until the shit hit the fan. I was being told weeks after the fact. She'd done a few days under observation in the hospital before she was released and enrolled in an outpatient program where part of her treatment was to have talk therapy sessions. The counselor had recorded their sessions. For some reason I'll never understand, the man felt it was a good idea to play the tapes for my father. Tapes in which my mother admitted to having a thirty-year affair with Uncle David.

On the phone, my dad told me how he'd been brought into a family counseling session where the tapes were played. They destroyed him. The secret was out, and he snapped. He threw my mom's stuff out of their house. Alone, terrified, and humiliated, it took my father being brought to his knees in pain for him to reach out to me for emotional support.

Looking back, I think I might have some clue as to why the counselor violated my mother's confidentiality rights by sharing their sessions with my father. It turns out the counselor was the father of the guy Danny Levitoff wanted me to kick out of his apartment for using years earlier. It's just a hunch, but maybe the guy was still angry that I had pushed his junkie kid out on the streets all those years back and took it out on my dad. Whatever the reason, after my father threw my mother out of the house, he then went to his sister Lobby's and stuck a gun in David's mouth. The brothers used to have an expression in the joint about needing to be the first to act. If shit was even barely beginning to brew, they'd say, "Whoever gets down first, wins."

Lobby begged my father to spare Uncle David's life: "Don't kill him, Dan! Not in front of his children! I'll get rid of him. I'll get rid of him today!"

She did, and now the family was fractured.

I hung up the phone and drove straight to my parents' house in Arleta. I found my father on the couch, slumped over and broken. I'd never seen him like that. My mind was racing. Selfishly, I was angry he hadn't believed me all those years before. I thought, *I told you, motherfucker, and you called me a liar. You sided with her!* I was angry that he'd made me admit I was a liar when I wasn't. I was angry that my mother had made me snacks and gaslit me about why I'd "made up that story about Uncle David coming over." I thought about all the times my father was cool and friendly with other kids and not me. I remembered all the family picnics and barbecues when my dad would chum up to Uncle David, as if to emphasize what a liar he thought I was.

Between my father, my mother, and me, there was more than enough pain and tears and fear to go around. I couldn't handle my own emotions, much less his. For the first few weeks I just spent time with him, but he was inconsolable, so I went for the easy fix and asked him if he wanted me to fix him up with broads. It was the only thing I could think of. Something that would take his mind off reality. But he had no desire to see women.

I'd heard my mother had moved into an apartment in Lincoln Heights with her mom. I didn't know exactly. I didn't want to know. The whole family, myself included, was furious at her. But the split didn't last long. My dad, like me, was helpless around the house. Cooking meals, cleaning the house, doing laundry, writing checks—these were all things we had others do for us. Even in prison, I had fellow prisoners doing my laundry and cleaning my cell. My dad was the same, but the prisoner was my mother. She did everything for him. And she needed him, too. To feel like she had purpose. An identity. They were so fucked up together, but they were even more fucked up apart, so they got back together. In a way, I took it as another betrayal.

My dad called me and said he wanted me to come by and visit. I think he knew I was angry about everything that had gone down all those years ago and wanted to mend fences. I didn't really want to, but I came by and brought Diana so he could meet her.

When my mother was gone and I visited my father, the house had seemed neutral, like it was just a house. With my mother's return, the house felt cold again. She used the iciness to hide her secrets and control what people thought and felt, and even with the secret out, I still got the feeling she wanted to control how people reacted. I went to their house looking to make peace. My mother cooked dinner; we had moved past the hurt of the past. I knew my father wasn't going to change and my mother wouldn't change, either, and I accepted they were who they were. Diana and I spent the night. We didn't get it on in my parents' house but were joking around in the bedroom, and I guess we were laughing kind of loud. Having Diana there with me felt like armor protecting me against the anger and pain.

The next morning, we were awake and having coffee in the kitchen when my mother said she wanted to speak with me in private. I thought, *Maybe this is the moment. She's going to own up to all those years of deception. She's finally going to apologize.* She took me aside in the hallway and said, "I don't like the kind of stuff you are doing with that woman in my house. I won't stand for it in my home."

My decision to make peace with the situation dissolved in an instant. I'd fallen for her shit too many times. That day I waited outside the house, thinking she and my uncle were going to give me a present. The day she made me okra and gaslit me. And now, just when I thought she was going to apologize, she brought her moral bullshit on me just for fucking laughing.

The seed of my fucked-up treatment of women still wrapped itself like a vine around my ankles. I loved them, but how could I trust them?

It was always there, the Betty Crocker ready-to-mix instant rage. All my mom had to do was add the water. I saw red. I swear to God, I wanted to sock her right in her mouth. I wanted to stab her, not because I hated her or because her affairs were any of my business. I wanted to stab her just for saying that. I thought, *All these years you spent bent over, giving it to Uncle David, and you dare preach to me in my father's hallway about moral bullshit?* It brought me right back to the vicious animal I'd once been.

I didn't respond to my mother, but she knew she'd crossed a major line so hard she'd broken it. I grabbed Diana and said, "Let's go."

Chapter 14

LIFE AND DEATH

1981

For a while, Diana and I had fun. We went to meetings and traveled to recovery conventions together. We went to Palm Springs and Lake Tahoe. Life was good, or it should have been. But I was tough to deal with. She was a little, too. We started arguing, and it messed with our ability to do a good job at work. My reaction was to distance myself from her. Since we didn't live together, I could pick and choose how often I saw her. Our relationship was on-again, off-again, but Dr. Dorr had sold the recovery center on Gardner, so Diana and I were no longer working together when Diana found out she was pregnant.

I didn't know what to do, but it was her choice, and she told me she was going to have the baby. I said I'd always take care of her and our child. I knew that much, but I couldn't think beyond it. I was almost thirty-six years old, plenty old enough to have a child, but I'd lived a long time without that kind of responsibility, and I was selfish.

As the pregnancy progressed, I still saw Diana. We were in a weird limbo where we were together, but not. I wanted to make sure she was okay and felt supported. The future weighed on me. I was excited and scared and completely clueless.

One night, I went to Diana's and stayed with her in Hollywood. It was one of the days we were "on again," but the realness of it all was hitting me hard.

Her growing belly, and the new information that it was a boy, was a lot for me to handle. Maybe too much. I couldn't sleep that night. I lay there amped up until, in the middle of the night, the phone rang. It was my mother. She said my father had been in a bad car crash and was in a hospital in Marina del Rey. Diana and I took off. When we got there, he was in the ICU. Apparently, a kid working construction with my dad had a new Mustang. They might have been drinking, and he let my dad drive. They were racing another car, and my dad lost control, hit a telephone pole, and split the car in two.

Miraculously, the kid was alright. My father was not. For weeks while he was in the ICU they gave him medicine that messed with his glucose levels and his diabetes got out of control; the doctors were going to have to remove one of his arms and a leg to save him. At the hospital, I couldn't bear to look my mother in the eye. I felt like she was responsible.

In his bed in the ICU, my father looked small and frail. He'd loomed so large when I was a kid. And just like his younger brother, my uncle Gilbert, when he got angry he seemed to grow to seven feet tall. But ever since he'd heard the tapes of my mother in therapy, my father had wilted. He'd lost his will to live. He was a broken man. It wasn't like him to be reckless with another person in the car, and I knew he wouldn't deliberately hurt anyone, but the crash felt like the end of a slippery slope he'd been on since he'd learned of my mother's infidelity.

The night they told me they were going to amputate his limbs, I went into the parking lot and screamed at God. I said, "God, You motherfucker, either You work one of Your miracles and make my dad whole or You take him! Take him right now! Because my dad ain't going to want to live without an arm and a leg!" More than that, I knew he couldn't keep living with the knowledge of what happened between my mom and my uncle.

Just then, two LAPD officers in a cruiser shined a light on me. They said, "What are you doing?"

I screamed back, "What the fuck do you want?" Those were fighting words, but I believe God was looking out for me because they turned off the light and took off. They could have shot me. I was expecting a bullet. Most cops would have an ego when confronted like that, but I think they knew I was going through something heavy and had compassion for me.

The next morning, at six a.m., my mother called to say that my father had passed away. I knew God had listened.

*   *   *

My aunts and I handled the arrangements for his funeral, but there was still drama because no one from my family wanted to see my mother there. It was all fucked. I carried so much anger for this woman, but I knew I had to make sure I was there for her in her time of need because, despite her affair, she was shattered. I sat with her. I held her. I knew my aunts were going to freeze her out, so I made sure my friends were there for her and that they made her friends feel welcome.

Sometime after the funeral, my uncle Gilbert and I were over at my mom's house helping her with some gardening. He was just out of Folsom and clean for the first time in years. I had convinced him to take a job with us at Western Pacific Med Corp to keep him close to recovery. Gilbert seemed really hopeful for the first time since I'd known him. I was rooting for him. We didn't talk about it, but I knew Little Gilbert was gangbanging in the Valley and running wild.

I was trimming a tree in the backyard and my mother said, "Don't do nothing with this tree!" I moved to a new tree, but I noticed there was a big, dead branch on the tree she told me not to touch, so I went back to cut it off. I wasn't aware, but my mother had been staring at me out the window the whole time. She stormed out of the house. "I told you not to touch that tree! This is my house now! This is my house now!" She was screaming so hard, she almost couldn't get the words out.

I was trembling. I regressed to being a seven-year-old boy. I said, "The branch was dead, Mommy." In that moment, it was like there were two of me competing for space in the same body. The one holding out the branch in my left hand was a terrified little boy; the one holding the idling chain saw in my right was a vicious adult. After holding her during the funeral, making sure my friends were there to help buffer her from the death stares she was getting from my father's sisters, I flat out couldn't believe she was talking to me that way.

When she left, Gilbert said, "You were going to cut her with that chain saw. You know what, Danny? You have got to get out of here. You're trying to help her, but that lady doesn't want you here. You're going to kill her."

We left through the side gate and hopped in Gilbert's car. He twisted around to back into the street and said, "But if you do kill her, I'll help you bury the body."

Then we laughed. Laughter had always been our release when things got too insane.

After that day, I refused to see her again. The kicker was I heard she'd started seeing David again.

Diana and I weren't technically together, but we were still hanging out. A few weeks before she was due to give birth, I took her to a movie in Hollywood. I was parking the car when a man ran up to her window. I thought he was trying to jack us, so I jumped out and socked him in the mouth, cutting my hand on his teeth. It was the same hand I'd torn up once in Soledad when I'd punched an inmate. The man was known to be a snitch and had made a face at me from behind a thick pane of wire-meshed glass when I walked past the safety room he was in. I threw a left and nailed him in the face, and when I pulled my hand back through the jagged glass, I could see my bones through the gash.

When I punched this man in Hollywood, I aggravated that old hand injury and started bleeding like a stuck pig. I went to a hospital where they stitched the wound closed. I thought it strange they could fix it up so fast, but it was too good to be true. The next day I was in incredible pain and my left arm was swollen like a balloon up to my shoulder. I went back to the hospital. The human mouth is the second-nastiest thing you can cut yourself on after the mouth of a Komodo dragon. It was infected and it was bad. The night before, they'd simply stitched my wound closed over a bunch of bacteria from the dude's mouth.

When they saw how much my arm had swelled, they put me in the ICU and pumped me full of antibiotics. I wasn't improving, so they transferred me to Harbor-UCLA, a hospital that specialized in infectious diseases. I put it in God's hands. Time after time I was put under so they could scrape the bone with the hope of stopping the infection from growing. After about three weeks of that not working, a new surgeon came to look at me. When he saw my tattoos he said, "I hope you get to save that arm; it would be a shame to lose that tattoo."

"Do what you can, Doc," I said.

When I came out of surgery, I didn't want to look at my arm. I could feel something there, but I knew a lot of people who had lost limbs could still feel them. I didn't dare look.

Gilbert and his friend, a guy called Fury, came into the hospital room. Gilbert started joking with me about losing my left arm. He said, "Don't worry, when you go back to the pen, we'll make sure everyone serves to your right in handball so you can still play." He was fucking with me. He and Fury fell out laughing; they thought it was the funniest thing. That's when I knew I had my arm and I was going to be okay.

The doctor bandaged it up tight and I said I had to split. They didn't want me to leave, but I'd just received word Diana had given birth to a boy, a son we named Danny. I still have a picture of me with my bandaged arm holding Danny Boy in Cedars-Sinai. I was a father, and I couldn't have been happier. The second I held Danny Boy for the first time, I felt like a dad. I knew I had the responsibility of a lifetime in front of me. I had a reason to live, someone whose life truly depended on me. This is fucked up to admit, but since Diana and I weren't together, I felt like the moment would have been even more beautiful if Diana wasn't in the room with us. I know that sounds horrible, but I instinctively knew that child and I had our own journey ahead, just the two of us. I wasn't scared about the future. I focused on how amazing life was. And Danny Boy made being a father easy. God couldn't have made him more beautiful.

Chapter 15

THE FIGHT WITH GILBERT

1982

Gilbert's sobriety didn't last long. I got word he was using, and I knew my uncle. If he was using, that meant he was dealing. I could tell the person at Western Pacific who told me hated being the messenger because he knew how close we were, but we had a zero-tolerance policy. I'd warned Gilbert that he couldn't keep working at Western Pacific if he was using.

I found him in the office of our Reseda clinic.

"You gotta go, holmes."

"For what?"

"You're using."

Gilbert's mind was all over the place. "No I'm not! Why the fuck do you care?"

"We can't have this around the clients. You've got to go."

Gilbert got a crazy look on his face. As if from air, a knife materialized in his hand. It was that reflexive. I said, "You going to stab me, punk? You going to stab me?"

"Motherfucker, I've been shooting dope around you when we were lifting weights."

I said, "Fuck you. I'm going to come at you as soon as you're done stabbing me, and when you're done, you can go stab the grave of my grandmother, your mom, you fucking asshole, and then go stab the grave of my dad, your brother."

Gilbert looked down at his hand like it was doing something his head wasn't aware of. He held up the knife as if its existence surprised him. "I wasn't going to stab you, Danny! It was a reaction. It was a reaction!" I'd never seen Gilbert so hurt.

I grabbed him and pulled him close. "I love you, Gilbert. If you need help, we can get you help. Let me help you."

He couldn't even look me in the eye. "I got to go, Danny. I got to go."

"Gilbert, stay," I begged him. "We can help you."

Gilbert was and still is the only real hero I've ever had. With his magnetism, he could have done anything, been anything he wanted. I sometimes think that if Gilbert hadn't taken me under his wing when I was young, I might have crumbled into a ball of loneliness and depression and killed myself with drugs.

No matter what he was doing, Gilbert always had *time* for me, and the gift of his time and attention was something I needed as much as water. Gilbert made me feel like we could defeat anything in our path, as long as we had each other. When I was in trouble in Folsom and going in the hole, Gilbert said, "Danny, they can beat us with fists and clubs, but they can't eat us." What he said made so much sense. We could be down, but we were never out.

I loved Gilbert so much, I wanted him to have another shot at life, and I knew it was possible. I would have given anything to have been able to help Gilbert in that moment just like I had helped so many other addicts. The question was whether he could accept it. Turns out, he couldn't.

"I have to go."

Gilbert was so ashamed, he couldn't accept help. It's as if he believed in his heart that he was a lost cause, like when a doctor tells you you're terminal. When you feel like God Himself thinks you're a lost cause, you can't get help. Gilbert had made peace with the idea he was beyond help, even though he was wrong.

After he left, I went in the bathroom and took deep breaths. I didn't know if I was going to cry, scream, or shit my pants. I'd never felt that way in my life. I'd never been in a confrontation with Gilbert. Since I was a little boy, he'd been my North Star. Whether we were boxing or fishing or smoking weed, we were rarely apart when I was a kid. I was a boy who needed a male figure in my life, and Gilbert was that for me.

Now he was spinning. We'd backed each other's play for so long, but this time he was alone. The road we were on had split. I still loved him dearly, but I was powerless over his addiction. Within a week, Gilbert had committed the crime that put him back in Folsom.

Chapter 16

DANNY BOY

1983

Diana was an attentive mother and kept a good house. She was still living in the apartment on Gardner. She loved changing diapers and being a mom. She cleaned Danny Boy's clothes and sterilized his bottles. Danny Boy was a beautiful baby. He was a little doll. I thought he was the cutest kid in the world. Maybe God makes them so loving and affectionate, especially when they grow up in volatile environments, in order to help them survive. But the old me, the questioning me, the me who absolutely couldn't be "a man who stayed," kept my options open by living on my own in the Venice apartment. I came and went as I pleased. I always had my escape hatch—it wasn't heroin anymore, but I could lead a double life. I could be a family man and a bachelor who chased chicks at the same time. I thought, *As long as you give money, you are being a parent.*

After her maternity leave, Diana returned to work at a new job. I was busy opening new locations for Western Pacific Med Corp and running sober living houses in the Valley. While we worked during the day, Danny Boy stayed with an older white lady we called "Nanny" who lived in the apartment above Diana's. Nanny had lost her husband, and her kids were grown, so she welcomed the opportunity to look after Danny Boy.

During the next year I struggled constantly with self-doubt. Why was it that every time I lived with a woman, I felt trapped and preoccupied by thoughts like *What am I missing out on?* and *What's out there?*

There were times with Diana when I thought, *I can do this. I can make a life with this woman and have a little family.* But I liked my freedom too much. I was selfish. I had the best of both worlds—I had my little family . . . and I had my bachelor pad by the beach.

Life forced my hand. Diana had moved into an apartment in Los Feliz to be closer to work. I went over one night to visit Danny Boy and saw drugs on the coffee table and her connection sitting on the couch. I'd had a bad feeling for weeks. When I saw paraphernalia to fix—needles and a spoon—I lost my shit.

I grabbed the connection, pulled him onto the balcony by the throat, and held him over the railing. My sobriety is probably what bought me the extra two seconds of decision-making that saved me from making what would have been a terrible mistake. I said, "If I ever see you around here again, I'll kill you."

I went in the apartment and grabbed Danny Boy. Diana was crying. I said, "If you ever go near this child again, I'll kill you." In that moment, I meant it, but it didn't dawn on me that that was the exact same thing my father had said to my birth mother when he took me away from her. Then I carried Danny Boy out the door. He slept through the whole thing. I put him in the back seat of my 1976 Oldsmobile Cutlass Supreme and drove around Hollywood. It was late, and I didn't know what to do. My big concern was that it was a weeknight, and I knew I had to work early the next morning. I'd had Danny Boy at my apartment with me before, but that was on the weekends, and even then I'd had broads there who would help take care of him.

I was young, I was immature. I was, in a strange way, entitled. I viewed child-rearing from the perspective of a convict—take it as it comes, survive another day—not a fully formed, caring adult.

I was trying to think of a "late-night" meeting where I could find women I knew who'd be willing to look after him. I cruised down Santa Monica, but the groups of people who usually lingered on the sidewalk after the midnight Hollywood meeting had already left. I headed west by Ohio Street, but the parking lot of the church was empty. I started looking for hookers. I knew most of the people on the streets and there were a few prostitutes I knew through recovery who I trusted and could pay to take care of Danny

Boy, but I didn't recognize the faces of any of the women at the IHOP on Sunset Boulevard. I headed east and pulled over to the curb on Formosa by the Seventh Veil strip joint, but the lights were off. I was getting desperate. I needed the village of my friends in recovery to help me, but none could be found. I looked at this little boy swaddled in a blanket in the back seat of my car and almost lost it. I felt so overwhelmed. Then I remembered Nanny.

She answered the door in her muumuu. As soon as Nanny saw Danny Boy, she said, "My baby! My baby!" I told Nanny that Diana was using drugs. She said, "I know. I saw some things that scared me."

"Listen, I just need to get settled. I'm not sure how long it's going to take for me to figure something out, but I didn't know where else to turn. I have to work tomorrow and I don't know what to do."

She was so excited. "You just leave him with me. I'll take care of him for as long as it takes. I love my baby."

Danny Boy woke up. He saw Nanny and said, "Me want mac a cheese, mac a cheese, Nanny."

"Bring him inside." Nanny immediately went into the kitchen and started making Danny Boy macaroni and cheese from scratch. Nanny never did any of that from-the-box stuff. She was a saint. I told her I'd be back in the morning.

"We'll figure it out. I have him. He's my baby."

I drove back to Venice thanking God for putting Nanny in my life the whole way.

Diana ended up in prison for drug offenses, but Nanny and I worked it out. Like many divorced couples of the time, I became a weekend dad, working all week and bringing Danny Boy back to Venice on the weekends to hang out with my friend George Perry and me. George was an old pimp from San Francisco I'd connected with at a meeting at CRI-Help. George would become one of the most important friends in my life. He had been in San Quentin in 1935, the first of his six stints there. We didn't need small talk. We were on the same wavelength. He got me. I needed a friend like George during those years. On the weekends Danny Boy, George, and I were our own family unit.

Danny Boy was my beach partner. He was hilarious. We'd see women on the beach and he'd say, "It's just me and my dad. My mommy left," and they'd immediately melt like butter on a hot pan.

George was in awe.

"Did you teach him to pick up girls, Danny?"

"Nope."

"It's genius."

God had worked things out. I was able to keep Nanny afloat financially, and she kept me afloat with my son. She was a great influence on Danny Boy. One time, he'd just come from her place and when he got to my apartment he said, "Daddy, I need a chore. I need a chore to do." I made him pick up some papers, just something to do, and gave him a ten-dollar bill. When George and I took him back to Nanny's the next evening, Danny Boy slipped the ten-dollar bill in the pocket of her muumuu. When George saw that, he almost cried. George was a stone-cold ex-con, and that gesture of kindness and generosity melted his heart.

All in all, my life was in balance. My work in rehab centers was steady and going well; I became a fixture at Muscle Beach; and I was offered a job as supervisor of my apartment complex, so I had free rent. (The owners were having issues with people not paying their rent on time and they knew if it was me knocking on doors that wouldn't be a problem.) On weekends, George and I took Danny Boy to the beach. He had a three-wheeled, battery-operated motorcycle-thing. We'd walk with him between us, and there was a game he liked to play. He'd stop, and with an exaggerated, exhausted sigh, he'd say, "Flat tire." Then we'd mime helping him change the tire. A block later it was the same thing. Near sunset one Sunday night, the sky a blood-orange band on the horizon, Danny Boy stopped for the millionth time and sighed like an old man.

"Another flat?" George said, and stooped down next to him. I watched them pretend to change the tire. Those days could have gone on forever.

Part Three

INMATE #1

Chapter 17

RUNAWAY TRAIN

1985

There was a good-looking tattooed kid in a meeting who mentioned he'd been doing extra work in film and television. I was intrigued. He said there was an agent named Sid Levin who specialized in "hard-looking" types like us and set people up with jobs. He got paid fifty dollars a day just to be in the background of film shoots. The idea appealed to me. I was at the methadone clinic and mentioned what I was thinking to Dr. Dorr. He lit up. "That's great, Danny. I bet if you got your face out there it would be a great advertisement for the work we're doing."

I took a few gigs as a background performer, an extra, and I got paid fifty bucks a day. Fifty dollars doesn't sound like a lot, but at the time the extra bread really helped keep Nanny and me afloat. Even better, I found that film sets were good places to find clients for our clinics. Back then, cocaine was everywhere—in the production offices and on the prop trucks. I was seeing a lot of people in a lot of trouble. I knew my message of sobriety could be useful.

In one of my first background gigs I was cast as a convict (surprise) on a TV show. The other background people and I were in a holding tent waiting to be called to set. Some of the guys were bitching about the quality of the steak at lunch. We were literally sitting next to a table called "craft service"—food that productions provide for the cast and crew that is available the whole time they are filming. The table was loaded with every kind of food imaginable.

I couldn't believe it. I'd just been sitting there thinking about how awesome it was to be on a job, getting paid just to hang out, where the bosses fed us for free, and this guy was complaining about his filet. I said, "In what other job do you get fed three times a day and have a table full of food whenever you're hungry? You're playing a convict, bitch. Eat a baloney sandwich."

About a month later, I was home and my phone rang. It was late, close to midnight, and I considered not answering, but I remembered Jhonnie Harris telling me what I had to do whenever someone's hand reaches out for help. "You have to be there, not for them," Jhonnie told me. "For you. It helps you."

I picked up, and it was a kid who'd heard me talk at a meeting about getting clean. I couldn't even put a face to his name—I'd given out my phone number to so many people. I could tell he was young, maybe nineteen or so. He said he was at work, that there was a ton of cocaine around him, and he was afraid of using. I took down the address. I figured it was just some warehouse where this kid and I would sit in my truck, drink coffee, smoke cigarettes, and shoot the shit. I agreed to come help him get another twenty-four hours under his belt.

When I got to the address, there were trucks and lights and people everywhere. It was a film shoot. I'd wandered onto what turned out to be the set for the movie *Runaway Train*.

I was looking around for the kid when an assistant director came up and asked me what I was doing. From my experience being an extra, I knew he was probably ready to jump on my case for not being where I was supposed to be. But when I said, "I'm just looking for a friend," he gave me a once-over.

"You have a good look," he said. "Do you want to be an extra?"

I knew what he was talking about, but I played like I didn't. "An extra what?"

He told me they were doing a prison scene and could use background people who looked like convicts. "Can you play a convict?" I thought of Soledad, Folsom, San Quentin.

"Yeah, I'll give it a shot." The man said the gig would pay eighty dollars cash. Eighty dollars was thirty more than I'd gotten for doing background work. The guy grabbed a wardrobe lady handing out prison blues and told me to change. I started taking off my shirt when I heard a man yell, "Jimmy Peña," from across the set. He'd mistaken me for my homeboy who'd gotten me the job at the N.P.P. I looked up and saw an older white guy running in my direction. Halfway across the set the man realized he had the wrong guy. He said, "Danny Trejo!"

It had been almost two decades since I'd seen him, but I recognized Eddie Bunker immediately. Years later, when my son Gilbert's friends met Eddie for the first time, he was just sitting there quietly but his resting face was mean enough to scare the shit out of all of them.

Here, he was all smiles. "Danny, I saw you win the lightweight title in San Quentin."

"Eddie Bunker? Damn! What are you doing here?"

Eddie was a career criminal and famous in Los Angeles. I'd actually met him decades before. Back in the Valley in 1962, he sold my uncle Gilbert and me the plans to do a heist of a big-dollar poker game, a scene later portrayed in the Dustin Hoffman flick *Straight Time*—a film based on Eddie's book *No Beast So Fierce*. In those days, before he realized he could make more money fictionalizing his ideas for crimes, Eddie sold detailed plans for robberies.

Eddie was a troubled kid who grew up in state homes and juvenile detention centers, but he was always known for having a brilliant intellect. His nickname in prison was "The Brain." In San Quentin, Eddie was the youngest inmate when he arrived, but he scored so high on an aptitude test that he was offered the job of captain's clerk, the most powerful position in the prison. While the warden dealt with the big political issues, the captain dealt with the day-to-day of running a prison, and his clerk was the one who put all the requests in front of him to sign. There were so many requests a clerk had to get the captain to sign off on—prisoners being moved to different cells and guards being assigned different shifts. If you didn't like a guard, Eddie could move him. If someone wanted a particular person in their cell, Eddie could do that, too. Sometimes it was done to be close to a friend, sometimes it was done to be close to a foe, sometimes it was done to gain a lover.

But the thing that made Eddie most famous in the joint was his ability to write writs. There was a big drug dealer from LA in Folsom named Denis

Kanos who'd gotten busted. His case was affirmed, meaning there were no appeals left. Eddie, who happened to be doing a jolt in Folsom at the time, looked over his case file and said, "Denis, I think you've got at least three writs here."

The thing about writs is that they had to be written perfectly in legalese with no grammatical or spelling mistakes. Eddie had that gift. He got Denis's case overturned, and after that everybody paid Eddie to write writs for their appeals. Eddie wasn't racially political when it came to writs. If you had the bread, he'd work on your case. That's how Eddie came to be so tight with the shot-callers in the Black Guerrilla Family, the Aryan Brotherhood, and the Mexican Mafia.

When Eddie got to San Quentin, he was so young that they housed him in the more secure North Block, where they could keep a closer eye on him. It was next to Death Row, and he shared a vent with Caryl Chessman, a murderer who was a celebrity among the literary set. Foreign journalists and famous writers visited him all the time. Caryl and Eddie struck up a friendship through the vent, and Caryl told Eddie he should be a writer. A silent film star named Louise Fazenda, who was married to the producer Hal Wallis, met Eddie when she volunteered in one of the boys' homes Eddie lived in and took a shine to him. She encouraged him to pursue an education and even bought him the typewriter he used to write his first books.

Now Eddie told me, "I wrote this movie. I mean, I adapted the screenplay. What are you doing here?"

"I came to help a kid, but I can't find him."

"Are you still boxing?"

"I'm training, not fighting pro. But I'm in shape."

"I'm asking if you still box because there's a fight scene in the movie where Eric Roberts fights another inmate. The director, Andrei Konchalovsky, needs someone to train Eric. He could use the help. You'd get paid three hundred and twenty bucks a day."

I loved the sound of that. I said, "Eddie, how bad do you need this guy beat up?"

"I don't need him beat up, Danny. We need you to train him."

Eddie had me hit a heavy bag to show Andrei what I could do. When you're sharp on a heavy bag, it sounds like cannons going off. I made sure I made that thing shake. I could tell it got Andrei thinking.

Dad visiting me at the Burbank house, right before I went to live with him, 1949. I was reluctant to leave my aunts and my girl cousins to move in with my dad and stepmom.

Me and our dog Hoppy on the front lawn, 1951. My mom took this picture right after my uncle David left after he visited her one afternoon. I was trying to plaster on a fake smile because I knew there was something strange about that visit. (*Courtesy of Alice Trejo*)

Temple Street in Lincoln Heights with my second gang of girl cousins, 1947. Thankfully I was surrounded by so much great female energy when I was a young boy.

Me and Joey Meyer, right after a robbery, early 60s. We'd just gotten high as kites with the proceeds of the crime. I didn't know if I was pulling robberies to support my drug habit or shooting dope to support my robbery habit.

FROM LEFT TO RIGHT: Me, Toni, Gilbert, Coke, Eddie, and Mary Carmen. Family party, dancing in the kitchen, early 50s. Back in the days when it wasn't unusual to live fifteen to twenty to a house.

My First Holy Communion, stoned on weed, staring at the crucifix, early 50s. I felt deeply unworthy to receive the Eucharist, but I wasn't going to piss off my grandparents and parents by not going through with it.

My birth mother, Dolores Rivera King. I never knew until I was an adult why she hadn't been in my life since I was three.

Portrait of my dad from before I was born, early 40s. Movie-star handsome was Dionisio.

Dad in Burbank when I was five, 1949. My father spent so little time with me when I was a child, but I was always excited when he'd visit.

Dad and Alice in a Mexican American version of *American Gothic*, late 40s to early 50s.

It was through boxing in San Quentin, Soledad, and other prisons where I first tasted what it felt like to be a celebrity, 1966. I would have gone pro when I got out if California didn't deny boxing licenses for convicted felons for two years after release.

Dogs have been my constant and best friends my whole life. Here I am with Hoppy at my grandmother's, early 50s.

My father and Alice at Pop's Willow Lake, where they used to have beauty pageants and all kinds of things, early 50s. I truly loved life in America in the 50s.

My dad after he'd wrecked his car, 1949. Besides construction, my father worked in auto body shops, so this would have been easy for him to repair.

The biggest day in a young Mexican Catholic's life—the sacrament of First Holy Communion, 1951. Here I am with Betty (*left*) and Emma (*right*) on their big day. I had to get stoned to deal with my First Holy Communion the following year.

My father and Alice in the early days of their courtship, early 40s. He was a single father looking for a woman who would help him take care of me.

LEFT TO RIGHT: Me, my dad, Edwina, Betty, Emma, and the neighborhood girls, 1954. My dad always seemed to come alive around other kids, just not me.

Dad, me, and Alice at Alice's mom's house, mid-50s. Witness my dad's version of "smiling." He was a gangster!

Me holding the piñata for Alice at her sister Mary's house, mid-50s. Alice came alive around her sisters and her mother. It would take years for me to understand her.

Hunting with my dad, early 50s. We Trejos were all good with guns from an early age.

BACK ROW, FROM LEFT TO RIGHT: Uncle Art, Dad, and Uncle Fred. FRONT ROW, FROM LEFT TO RIGHT: Uncle Rudy and Uncle Gilbert. The Trejo men, late 40s. A lot of machismo all wrapped up in one shot.

Dad in his zoot suit days, 1948. My father was in the 38th Street gang, the gang at the heart of the infamous Sleepy Lagoon murder case that was the basis of an Edward James Olmos film called *Zoot Suit*.

Hoppy on a hunting trip, early 50s. I loved dressing up my dog!

My father fishing off the Redondo Beach Pier, early 50s. His dream was to own a pickup truck with a camper and to fish up and down the West Coast.

My uncle Gilbert at eighteen, fresh out of boot camp and ready to start training as a paratrooper, 1956. Most of my father's brothers served in the military. I would have, but I already had too much of a record for the Marines to accept me. *(Courtesy of Gilbert Trejo)*

The pond in the backyard at my parents' Arleta home, next to a spot where I dug a stash hole to hide cash and guns, 1960s. When my mother told me my father wanted to put in a new sprinkler system near the pond, I begged her from prison to tell him no.

Visiting Gilbert in Folsom with Grandma, early 70s. As an ex-con, I wasn't supposed to be allowed to visit, but the captain liked me and let me in.

Gilbert was very in touch with his Mexican and Yaqui heritage, 1975. My grandmother, his mother, always reminded us we were descended from indigenous warriors.

Before prison officials removed weights from the California prisons, 1980s. Here's Big Gilbert getting his daily workout in.

Big Gilbert in Folsom in the mid-70s. While he was there, he handled negotiations between the Mexican inmates and production, allowing Michael Mann to finish filming *The Jericho Mile*, something Mann was eternally grateful for.

Gilbert's son, Gilbert, when he was living with me and Joanne on Osborne, mid-70s.

My cousin Little Gilbert in Youth Authority, shortly after his Pop Warner days and not too long before committing the crime that would put him behind bars for the next thirty-eight years of his life, mid-70s.

My first wife, Laura. She served me divorce papers when I was serving time in Youth Training School. I used them to keep score in dominoes.

My mother, Alice, and my second wife, Debbie, at our wedding, 1971. My lawyer later joked, "Danny, you don't like being married much, but you must love weddings!" Debbie was such a kind soul.

Debbie at our apartment in the Valley, 1970. I was out of the pen, but I was still up to shenanigans.

Not unlike with my first two wives, I fell in love with Joanne, my third wife, at first sight, 1976. Easy to see why!

Diana and me in Palm Springs, late 70s. We were working in the field of recovery together and traveling all over California. This picture was taken just before Diana found out she was pregnant with Danny Boy, our son.

This is me with my son Gilbert, 1988. This is the photo Gilbert would show me when he was directing me in *From a Son* to get me in the emotional state I needed to be able to work on the film.

My son Danny Boy, 1981. He was absolutely the most beautiful thing I had ever seen.

Ringing in the New Year with Maeve when she was pregnant with our daughter, Danielle, 1989.

With Gilbert when he was fresh from the hospital, March 20, 1988. And no, they do not come with instruction manuals!

With Danielle when I took the kids with Maeve to go visit their grandmother in Arleta, 1990.

On a family bike ride off the boardwalk in Venice, 1990. FROM LEFT TO RIGHT: Gilbert, me, Maeve and Danielle, and Danny Boy.

Me and my little men, Danny Boy (*left*) and Gilbert (*right*), in 1989, before Danielle was born.

The infamous family photo, 1990. Tears were spilled before, during, and after. Maeve was always trying her best to have us do "normal" family things. *(Jimmy Forrest)*

Coaching my kids' T-ball teams has been one of the highlights of my life. That is what real men (and women) do! Here I am with Danny Boy, early 90s. *(Ronnie Brown)*

To be able to work with my best friend, Eddie Bunker, and legends Robert De Niro, Val Kilmer, Jon Voight, and Tom Sizemore on *Heat* is probably my fondest film memory, 1994. I will always be grateful to Michael Mann for including me. But I'm sure he felt, *Who better to play the armed robber?*

Eddie Bunker was my best friend and confidant and a man who knew me all the way back to our days in San Quentin together. I know he watches over me. Val Kilmer is one of the actors I became closest with in my career and we still keep in touch. 1994.

God made it so Eddie and I both happened to be in Paris at the same time, 1996. Walking around the City of Light at night, I had to pee, so I went under a bridge off the Seine. I said, "Hey, Eddie, doesn't this wall remind you of Folsom Prison?" He said, "Mexican, you're in Paris. Can you forget about Folsom for just a minute?"

My son, Gilbert, directing me in his feature film debut, *From a Son*, 2018. The work I did on this film is the proudest I've been of any work I've done as an actor. And as a father, I couldn't have been prouder. *From a Son* felt like the completion of a long circle and a passing of an artistic torch from father to son. *(Frank Ockenfels III)*

Donal and me at the opening of his restaurant, La Vida, in Hollywood in 2010. A cool spot that unfortunately didn't last! *(Angela Weiss)*

He held up his fingers, the way directors do with their hands to mimic a film frame, and stared at me. I joked to Eddie, "That's the most ridiculous gang sign I've ever seen." But Andrei's wheels were turning.

"Contrast," he said. "Contrast!"

I was unaware of it at the time, but Andrei had already hired an actor to play the convict who fights Eric in the jailhouse boxing scene. The guy was tall, thin, and pretty, just like Eric. Andrei realized that pairing wasn't going to work.

Andrei took my face in his hands and gave me a kiss on both cheeks. He said, "I want you in movie. I want you to box Eric Roberts in scene. Contrast! You look like this and Eric looks like that. Contrast makes movies! You be my friend! You be in movie."

At that, he walked off. Eddie said, "Congratulations! You've just caught lightning in a bottle. You got the gig."

I joked to Eddie, "Hey, Eddie, 'friend' don't mean what it does in the joint, does it?"

He laughed.

"Listen, for three hundred and twenty bucks Eric can beat me with a stick. But if that old guy's going to kiss me, I'm going to have to get paid a lot more money."

Eddie said Andrei was a Russian aristocrat and that's how people did things in Europe. We went to grab a cup of coffee, and I noticed Eddie's demeanor change, like he was struggling with something.

I said, "Eddie, what the fuck's up?"

"Nothing."

"What the fuck are you talking about? How long do you think I've been around?"

Eddie lowered his voice like we were back on the Main Yard.

"Danny," he said, "I was only supposed to be out here for the week. I'm scheduled to head back to New York tomorrow, but they extended my trip for another two weeks." He paused, then admitted, "I'm on methadone, holmes, and I only had enough take-homes to get me through today."

I said, "Eddie, do you know who you are talking to? I run a string of methadone clinics. I can help you."

I don't know if Eddie thought I was joking or what. He got upset with me.

"Don't be fucking with me, Danny. This is serious shit." He was panicking.

I said, "I'm not fucking with you. I have a string of clinics out here with a cat named Dr. Dorr. Tell me where you're staying, and tomorrow morning I'll pick you up at five thirty and take you to Western Pacific Med Corp in Glendale. We'll get you a temporary transfer."

He said, "Really? You better not be fucking with me, Mexican!"

The next morning, I found Eddie standing on the sidewalk in front of his hotel in Hollywood. At my request, a doctor had shown up early to Western Pacific. He called the clinic in New York, verified Eddie was on the program, and transferred his prescription.

God was doing His work. If I hadn't shown up to the set that night, Eddie would have gone back to shooting dope. And if Production had sent Eddie back to New York like they were supposed to and I hadn't answered that kid's call, I wouldn't have my career.

The whole time I worked on *Runaway Train*, I never saw that kid I was trying to help. My guess is that he gave in to temptation and started using again.

After we got to set, I told Eddie to bring Eric to the back of the stage, where I would be hitting a heavy bag. I wanted Eric to be on board with me training him, and I knew if he watched me work a bag over it would accomplish a hell of a lot more than a conversation. As soon as Eric saw me pummeling that bag, he turned to Eddie and said, "I want to learn how to do that."

When the time came for us to film the boxing scene, the stunt coordinator asked me to walk through some of the action. "Show me a jab," he said. I threw a couple of jabs.

"Those are beautiful, Danny. Straight, sharp. I'd hate to get hit with one of those," he said, "but the camera will never see it." He explained to me he'd had trouble in the past working with professional boxers. In movies, you have to throw wide, looping shots so the camera can read them. I did what he told me.

We set up to film the scene and it immediately took me back to the fights I had in prison. Just like in San Quentin and Soledad when I fought for the title, the place was packed, everyone was screaming, and I was ready. When Andrei yelled "Action!" it was like the whole world slowed. Even though the scene was two men fighting with a huge crowd watching, it felt like it was all about me. I knew what I had to do. As long as I was controlling the action, I could get Eric to do exactly what Andrei wanted. If Eric had to throw a left and open up for the camera, I knew precisely how to move to get his body in the correct position. I loved everything about the experience.

Between takes of the fight scene, the assistant director, the guy who'd first asked if I could play a convict, came up to me carrying my headshot and waving it around. "Danny!" he said. "Today your agency submitted you to be an extra!"

I laughed. "Guess I got lucky getting in on the game early."

"You sure did. I would have stuck you in the crowd. Now you're pulling SAG money." He seemed as surprised by the course of events as I was. "We can always put you back on eighty dollars a day if you want?"

"Nah, I'm good."

He laughed and patted me on the back.

Movies had saved me once and now I was really in one. Back in Folsom, in 1966, I was put in solitary confinement. Every time you hit a new joint, you hit the hole first, or madhouses like San Quentin's B Section. When I rolled into Folsom, I never even hit the Yard. I was chained and taken straight to the pit of Building Five while I waited for classification. There was no time limit set on when they had to classify me. I'd been deemed an "Institutional Convenience" in San Quentin, which meant I was such a pain in the ass, involved in so much contraband business and bullshit, that any prison in California could do what they wanted with me and take their time doing it. Folsom looks just like Dracula's castle. That's why it's called Castle de Dracula. Its walls were cut from massive slabs of granite. In the summer, it gets to over 110 degrees. In the winter, you could die of hypothermia. If Folsom is known as the dungeon, I was in the dungeon of the dungeon. I still have nightmares about Building Five.

I was stuck in a six-by-ten cell with an iron door. A six-inch slit in the door was the only opening to the world. I didn't have contact with anyone but the guards. They passed food through the door twice a day. It was not slop. One thing about Folsom, the food is good. To keep from going insane, I did push-ups, sit-ups, as many as I could every day, and played out movies in my mind. The two I kept returning to were *The Hunchback of Notre Dame* with Charles Laughton and *The Wizard of Oz*. Every day I'd remember a little bit more of each one. I searched my mind to connect the stuff I knew and vaguely knew and totally forgot. It was incredible how much came back. I'd get excited. If you've seen or heard it, your brain's made some imprint of it and filed it away. Those memories set me free. Anytime the guards would yell, "Shut the fuck up, Trejo!" I'd come back with, "Water, she gave me water!" from *Hunchback*.

I'd replay the scene where Dorothy and the Tin Man, the Scarecrow, and the Cowardly Lion cross the poppy field. The first time I saw *The Wizard of Oz*, that field seemed like it stretched for miles and miles. Until I worked in movies, I didn't realize that was a painting. Then I'd recount them seeing Emerald City for the first time. Acting it out, I could see its beautiful, emerald-green spires shining in the distance. As Dorothy, I'd say, "There's Emerald City. It's beautiful, isn't it? He really must be a wonderful wizard to live in a city like that."

Acting wasn't new to me. I'd acted to survive my childhood. I'd acted like I wasn't scared when I was terrified. I'd acted when I robbed joints. In Folsom, I acted to keep my sanity. I had to move; I had to speak out loud; I had to hear my own voice.

"You perfect rat, look what you've done! I'm melting, melting!"

What I was up to wasn't lost on the other prisoners. Word got back to Joey Abausto, a man I'd done time with in Sierra Jamestown, a man who'd trained me as a boxer (he was a great boxer but an even better trainer), that I was screaming like a madman in solitary. Joey circulated a petition among the general population in Folsom to have me released from the hole because he was afraid for my mental health.

Now that I was doing it for fun, not just to make it through solitary, I loved acting, I loved the feeling. Like a new drug, I was hooked.

The first paycheck I got from *Runaway Train* was so big, I was sure they'd made a mistake. I told Eddie I was going to hit the bank before they realized their fuckup. He explained that we got paid for overtime and for meal penalties if we hadn't been fed in six hours. It was insane. It was the most I'd ever been paid in my life. I wanted to cry. I still didn't get the concept of meal penalties. How could there be a meal penalty when the craft service table was a free-for-all? I was at the craft service table making three sandwiches I wanted to take home for Danny Boy and myself when a production assistant found me and told me I was in meal penalty. I thought she was busting me for making sandwiches.

"I can put them back."

She laughed. "No, Danny. Make as many as you want. I'm just telling you that we're going into meal penalty and you're going to get a pay bump."

The world of movies was just getting better and better.

Between takes one night, I was standing in the alley next to the warehouse where we were shooting, smoking a cigarette, when I saw a kid roll up in a beat-up Datsun. He pulled a suitcase out of the trunk and went inside. I followed him and watched as he unzipped the suitcase and started handing out bundles of cash to the actors, the stuntmen, and the crew. Back in the 80s, per diem varied wildly depending on what job you had. Stars like Jon Voight and Eric Roberts got big slabs of cash. The criminal in me was fascinated.

The next week, I made sure I was in the same spot on the same night. Right on the button, the kid showed up. Eddie joined me and lit a smoke.

"What are you doing?"

"Just having a cigarette, like you."

"That all?" he asked.

I said, "Eddie, you know how much cash that kid is carrying in that suitcase? He's all by himself in a dark parking lot. Man, I could snatch that no problem."

"It's tempting," he said, "but, Danny, with your look and who you are, that's chump change. You're going to make so much money in this business. Even if that kid had sixty grand, that's a pittance compared to what you're going to make if you don't fuck this up."

I couldn't believe Eddie had so much faith in me. He was hugely successful. What he said helped me believe I could make it in the film industry, and in doing so, I could spread the message of sobriety in a world that deeply needed to hear it. Eddie stubbed out his cigarette and turned to go inside. He stopped. "But if you're planning on moving on that suitcase, I want in."

Then he laughed his deep, slow laugh.

Eddie Bunker. Man, he was a legend.

*   *   *

After *Runaway Train*, I wanted to keep working in film. I liked those over-time checks. Bring on the meal penalties! The stunt coordinator was so pleased with how I handled the fight scene, he hired me for his next job. I'd be a background artist but would get bumps for doing stunt work.

On my third movie, *Penitentiary III*, I finally got to play a character who had a name. I was See Veer, a baddie. The producer/director, Jamaa Fanaka, told me I could work as an extra until my speaking scenes started.

George Perry was visiting from San Jose when I started work on *Penitentiary III*. He'd gotten into a fight with his teenaged daughter, Lisa, and needed to leave town to get perspective. He was going to stay in Venice with me. The day he called to tell me he was coming, I saw Jamaa Fanaka at the production office and told him I had a friend who'd done a lot of time who could play a perfect OG convict. I wanted George to have a gig when he got to LA.

When I went to work the first day, I brought George because I knew they'd think he was cool. George wasn't a pimp or a drug dealer when I met him—he'd gotten married and left all that behind. But he still had pimp style. Like a real pimp, his fingernails were immaculate. His whole demeanor was that of a well-dressed woman. You could never rush George to get dressed. He'd lay out his outfit and his shoes and make sure everything worked together at a level that was beyond me.

We were walking from the parking lot to the set when a huge blue Rolls-Royce pulled up. George saw it and said, loudly, "Who's the pimp?"

It was Jamaa. I said, "Jamaa, this is the cat I was telling you about!" Jamaa took one look at George in all his finery, smiled, and said, "Congrats, you're in the movie!"

George didn't hear him. "What'd he say?"

"He said you're in the movie, holmes."

George was so excited. We both were. It's easy to become jaded, but this was big stuff for me and George. It was so far from the world we came from.

George and I would often get coffee and have a smoke outside the warehouse where the set was. One day, a big black limo pulled up and a youngster got out. He was Italian and wearing a slick suit. He said, "Why do I think you guys don't belong here?"

We said, "We don't." He laughed. It turned out he was Anthony Gambino, the son of the crime boss. He was there to see Leon Isaac Kennedy, the star of the movie. Apparently, Anthony had invested in the project. We told him we'd walk him in. We were entering through a side door when Leon stepped out. He greeted Anthony but tried to stop me and George from coming in. Anthony snapped at him, "Hey! They work for me!" I don't know if he was joking or just trying to be cool, but after that Leon and everyone else was scared shitless of me and George.

We were paid in cash at the end of every day. We were making $120 a day, but we always went into overtime, so we were stacked with cash. We usually finished shooting at two or three in the morning, and then I'd drive us back to Venice. After a particularly long day, George was squirming around in the passenger seat, messing with his shoes. He seemed perplexed.

"You alright, George?" I asked.

He looked at me with wild eyes and waved a wad of cash in my face. "Danny, I'm going to need bigger socks."

George still kept his money in his socks. Street habits die hard.

I met Maeve while we were shooting *Penitentiary III*. I first saw her at a meeting, and she knocked me out. I actually went with a guy who was interested in her. The second I saw her I thought, *Fuck that, I want her for myself.* I went up to her and said, "Call your mom and tell her you're going to be taken care of for the rest of your life." She looked at me like I was crazy.

A friend who'd given her a ride had bailed on her, so I took her home on the back of my motorcycle. When she was settling in behind me, she said, "Nothing's going to happen, just so you know."

She was new to sobriety. I respected that, so I gave her space. Truth was, I had made the first move and went back to playing like I didn't care. Maeve found me after a meeting one night and asked me why I'd pulled back. She felt ready to be in a relationship. We took it slow. We went on proper dates. We fell in love. Well, a warlike love.

Call your mom and tell her you're going to be taken care of for the rest of your life? My thinking was fucked. I couldn't see it at the time, but I was offering to make her my prisoner. That's the way the men in my life did it. My friend

DJ Bennett said, "My old man was a Green Beret and my mom was whatever the fuck *he* said she was."

It always busts me up when I hear that, but the laughter comes from a dark place. It's such a true statement about the world we grew up in.

At the time, Maeve was living with a roommate, and I liked it like that. We were becoming serious, but not serious enough for me to give up my bachelor pad. Maybe two weeks after Maeve and I got together, she started picking up Danny Boy from Nanny whenever she came over to my place. She didn't have a driver's license, but she could still drive better than most truck drivers. Maeve knew Diana was in prison and thought Nanny was babying and spoiling Danny Boy. Those were details I missed, but Maeve dialed in on them immediately.

One time, Maeve said to Danny Boy, "Now we're going to pick up your toys before we head back to Nanny's."

Danny Boy turned to her and said, "Connie never makes me pick up my toys." (Connie was the girlfriend I had before Maeve.)

Maeve said, "That's why you're not going to see Connie anymore."

I liked how Maeve was mothering Danny Boy. I didn't think too much about what kind of father I wanted to be, but I sure knew what kind of father I didn't want to be. I knew I didn't want to condemn my son with my fucked-up values—specifically, the chauvinistic maxim of "one in the house and three on the street." Most of all, I didn't care if my son was the leader of the Mexican Mafia or a state senator—I wanted him to know I'd love him no matter what.

My style of parenting must have been rubbing off on George. Shortly after finishing *Penitentiary III*, I was walking down the boardwalk in Venice with Danny Boy. George was following behind, and when I turned to let him catch up, I saw he was emotional. "What's up, George?" I asked. He said he'd seen little Danny Boy put his fingers in my belt loop and it got him choked up.

"I need to get back to San Jose and make things right with Lisa."

"I'm glad my counseling helped you figure that one out," I said.

We laughed.

Chapter 18

GOODBYE TO ANOTHER LIFE

1986

When I started working on movies, I didn't know it, but I was stepping into another life. But my uncle Gilbert was still in my old life, playing out that alternate timeline. He got out of prison, hit the street, and jumped back into what he knew best. He was collecting money for the biggest drug dealer in the Valley. If Gilbert showed up at the door, most people paid up immediately because they knew he was a serious dude. If you couldn't pay, he'd take your boat or your cars until you could.

In worst-case scenarios, he'd get dark. Gilbert never raised his voice. If you have to scream, you've already lost. Instead, Gilbert would call someone who was late on their debt and say, "Tomorrow, I want you to call your wife and tell her that so-and-so, your oldest son, died. We can work out how it goes down, but it's going down. Decide what kind of accident it will be, because you don't want to have to tell your wife her child died because you didn't pay your bill."

He'd do it so calmly and matter-of-factly that whoever was on the other end of the phone would move heaven and earth to make their debts right.

But Gilbert himself was in a free fall. I knew it. He was living in Sylmar but would ride his Harley all the way down to Venice every night to see me and George after we got off work. He'd be waiting for us in my apartment with takeout from the pizza joint down the street.

Gilbert always carried a knife, a sword, and two pistols. One night he told me that even though he had thirteen grand in cash on him, he'd robbed a liquor store for eighty bucks on his way to my place. He was as addicted to the adrenaline spike he got from robberies as he was to drugs. It was a line crossing I knew well. At the end of my running days, I didn't know if I was pulling robberies to support my drug habit, or doing drugs to support my robbery habit.

Gilbert was in full-on fuck-it mode, the way I was when I was on the run with Dennis, the way my dad was when he was racing in that Mustang. You're doing everything you can to push it till you get stopped by a tree, by the cops, by a bullet.

We had a conversation about him selling cocaine. He said it was no big deal.

"No big deal? Remember Chuey's?"

Chuey on Temple Street had been our connection for heroin back when I was fourteen. A few years later, Chuey had something new for us.

Gilbert picked me up early to head down to Temple Street. When we pulled onto his block, we saw Chuey's whole family out on the front porch. His old lady was in her housecoat with curlers in her hair. The kids were crying. Gilbert parked.

"Where's Chuey?" he asked.

She pointed inside. "Oh, Gilbert, he's on that shit."

"What shit?"

"That shit!"

Gilbert gave me a look and we walked into the house. The place was torn up. There were pans on the kitchen floor and broken dishes. We heard weird noises coming from the back room.

The curtains were drawn, but even though there was only a small stream of light coming through the window, we saw shit strewn everywhere. Chuey was a junkie and a dealer, but he was a family man. His house had always been tidy. Chuey's neighbors knew what he did, but they understood that was his way of providing for his family. Chuey's family weren't into drama; they weren't loud and crazy. None of what we were witnessing was like the Chuey we knew. We heard him mumbling and cackling from behind a sheet hanging over a closet door.

"Chuey, you in there?"

"Gilbert?"

"Yeah, it's me, *carnal.*"

An old man's hand pulled back the sheet. Chuey was shirtless, hunched over, and holding a machete. He started waving it around. He looked like he'd aged twenty years since we saw him last.

"What the fuck is going on?" asked Gilbert.

"The shit. I'm on that shit!" Chuey pointed at a dresser with the machete.

"What shit?"

"That shit!"

Gilbert told me to open the drapes a pinch.

"No, Gilbert. No! They're out there."

"No one's out there, Chuey. Just a little light, holmes, so we can talk to you."

I pulled back the curtain. I've seen a lot of shit in my day, but the transformation of Chuey was shocking.

"Is this the shit he's talking about?" I pointed to a big mound on top of the dresser that looked like a beautiful chunk of mother-of-pearl.

"Yeah, that's the shit," said Gilbert.

"We've got to help you, Chuey. Maybe start with some water to drink."

Chuey let Gilbert take the machete from him and help him to his feet. Meanwhile, I wrapped the hunk of alabaster in a T-shirt and stuck it in my coat pocket. Chuey's wife was beside herself. "He's not the same. I don't know what to do, Gilbert."

"We'll be back. We'll try and figure something out."

We got our heroin from his wife and headed back to the Valley. When we got to Gilbert's apartment, I put the alabaster block on his coffee table. Gilbert looked surprised.

"What the hell's that? You took that?"

"He said it was the shit."

"Good job."

"What are we supposed to do with it?"

"Fix it."

I spooned a big scoop off the chunk. It was a beautiful, crystal white. I said, "Is this enough?"

"Yeah."

Turns out, it was way too much. The purest cocaine I've ever done in my life just so happened to be the first I ever tried. I didn't even know what it was called until that day in 1962. I shot the whole spoonful and immediately had what I thought was a heart attack.

"Fuck!" I took off running out Gilbert's door and down Vineland. I didn't know where I was going, I just knew I had to move or I'd die. Gilbert chased me down in his car. "Get in, get in."

"Gilbert, I'm dying. What is that shit?"

"Cocaine."

Now Gilbert was selling the shit. In my apartment in Venice, Gilbert laughed and said, "Danny, coke is not a drug like heroin. It's a commodity, that's all. A commodity that lets me stay up late and sell more heroin."

The last night Gilbert came to see us he dumped his motorcycle on my neighbor's lawn. The guy started to say something but shut up quick when he saw Gilbert's face. Gilbert was so warm and caring, but he could chill a person to the bone with just a look. Like my dad, when Gilbert flashed anger it seemed like he grew to eight feet tall.

Gilbert came in with a pizza and fried zucchini sticks. They were covered in grass. He apologized and ate it anyway. Gilbert was emotional. He told me how proud he was of me and how sorry he was for starting me on drugs and crime.

I said, "Fuck that, Gilbert; if you hadn't, I'd be at home somewhere watching the news. You made me who I am. My experiences made me who I am. There's nothing I would change."

He nodded silently and said, "I'd better be getting home." He was wasted. I knew he had a thirty-mile ride ahead of him.

"Why don't you just stay here?"

"Nah, it's alright. I love you, Danny."

"I love you, too, holmes."

I'd come a long way from the days when I couldn't say "I love you" to another man. With Gilbert it was understood and unconditional.

He gave me a hug and walked out into the night. He always looked like a movie star, even when he was wasted.

After he left George said, "Danny, I think Gilbert was making amends to you." But Gilbert had nothing he needed to apologize to me for.

My cousin Sal found him a few days later in his apartment. He'd OD'd. Gilbert had seventeen grand in cash and eight ounces of cocaine and heroin on his person. There were guns everywhere. I told Sal to get rid of that shit before he called the paramedics. In my mind, none of that stuff defined Gilbert in life, and I didn't want it around him in death. We buried him a couple of days later at Valhalla Memorial in North Hollywood. When I got home from the funeral, I wept like a baby. I felt truly lost. Half of me was gone. Whether Gilbert was in prison or not, we were never out of touch. He was the defining relationship of my life, and now I was alone, left to carry on without him.

Chapter 19

FIRST CLASS

1987

In one of the first interviews I did, the journalist said, "You always play the Mexican with tattoos. Aren't you afraid of being typecast?"

I said, "I *am* a Mexican with tattoos." But there was truth to what she was saying, so it meant a lot to me that I was cast as an Italian gangster in *Death Wish 4* with Charles Bronson. Bronson was everything I hoped he would be. His face, his look, his gestures—he was one of the only men I'd ever met who reminded me of Gilbert. They both could turn people to stone with a look.

In the film I played an Italian mobster named Art Sanella. We were in a restaurant doing a scene, and the director told us to figure out some conversation to have in the background. There was an old OG character actor in the scene named Perry Lopez who kept telling us what the conversation should be. Perry was a Puerto Rican from New York who'd been a contract actor in the old studio system. He was a legend among Latino actors. A young guy at the table with us kept telling everyone within a five-mile radius he went to Hooliard. I asked Perry, "What's Hooliard?" He laughed. He said, "Juilliard, Danny, Juilliard."

Perry went back to informing us what the conversation should be, and the young guy said, "Who the fuck made you the director?"

Perry looked like he'd been punched. I snapped. I said, "I did, motherfucker. Do what he says or I'll beat you to death."

Everyone got quiet, and I could feel someone hovering behind me. It was Charles Bronson. He'd seen the whole thing. I thought, *Damn, I'm just starting my career, and I probably ended it right here.* Bronson gave me a once-over and said, "I heard you're some kind of drug counselor."

"I am."

He smiled. "I like the way you counsel." I was in with Bronson.

After that film, my acting career heated up. I got a gig that filmed in Philadelphia called *Shannon's Deal.* Boarding the plane to Philadelphia was such a fucking thrill. I thought, *I'm really an actor!*

The only other time I'd been on a plane before that was a couple years earlier, when Danny Boy was about four. I was asked to speak at a narcotics convention in San Francisco and we flew out of Burbank. It was awesome to fly for the first time, but most of all, I felt like I was really being a dad, taking my son on exotic adventures. We hit turbulence on the flight. Since it was my first flight I half expected it would be a scary roller-coaster ride, but people who knew better started to panic. Danny Boy yelled out to the other passengers, "Don't be scared! Don't be scared! Hold up your hands and say, 'By the power of Grayskull!'" Grayskull was a magical castle in his favorite cartoon, *He-Man and the Masters of the Universe.* Everybody on the plane followed his instructions, and I saw smiles on all their faces.

"They're not scared now, Dad!" Danny Boy beamed.

At the convention, I was speaking at the podium, and to the roomful of self-diagnosed, recovering drug addicts I said, "We don't drink, either!" because total abstinence is what we were about.

At that, Danny Boy came running across the stage dancing and chanting, "Don't drink! Don't drink!" almost like we had staged it. The place fell out. He was my little sidekick.

I was starting to see parts of the world I'd only dreamed of. For *Shannon's Deal,* I couldn't believe they flew us first-class and put us up in an incredible hotel. And, of course, there was a per diem. I was a convicted felon. I'd spent most of my young adult life locked up. I'd heard of Philadelphia and had seen it in films and heard about it in history books, but I couldn't believe I was actually there. Walking around Philadelphia gave me a "wow" feeling.

It was my first film on location and my first time going against production company wishes. Another actor named Tommy Rosales and I were told explicitly not to go to a neighborhood that was considered bad news. As soon as we got done with work that day we hopped in a cab and told the cabdriver to take us directly there.

It wasn't shit. We found a bar and danced late into the night.

When I wasn't working, I hit meetings and the streets to find people who needed to get clean. Dr. Dorr's hope of my higher profile bringing clients to Western Pacific Med Corp was being proved right. More and more people recognized me from the screen, and there was this look of amazement on their faces. I'm not saying being in a film or on TV should give you some kind of special validation, but as a drug counselor it was working in my favor. Even in my best months I wasn't bringing in a ton with the acting jobs I was doing. By Maeve's and my standards it was great; sometimes I'd bring in an extra $700 a month with acting jobs, but if someone had seen me in a couple of TV shows, they figured I should be able to buy a mansion and a helicopter just for walking across a screen. To think I was that successful and to see me still working in recovery made them think I must really care, and I did. I still do.

At Western Pacific I spent all day bringing people in off the streets, but I wasn't as receptive to the idea of bringing a new baby into our home. Maeve was pregnant. I wish I could tell you I cheered and bought her flowers when she told me, but I didn't. I reacted badly. I asked Maeve what she wanted to do, and she said she was going to have the kid. I didn't want her to. I didn't feel ready to have a second child. She didn't care. She said, "Fuck you. I'm having the baby. If I have to, I'll live in a shelter."

We were at a standstill—or, rather, she knew what she was doing and I didn't—when I had to go to Hawaii for a job on *Guns*, a film with Erik Estrada.

Erik was distant in the preliminary meetings, a bit aloof. He'd act weird and competitive when people recognized me. He didn't understand it. It had been too many years since he was Ponch on *CHiPS*, and no one gave a shit anymore. It was a good reminder to me to always have a higher purpose than Hollywood.

I'd been cast late in the process. For our flight to Hawaii, Production explained they were tight on cash and we all had to fly coach. I was cool with that. When we boarded the plane in LA, Erik and his girlfriend were in the back with me. But right before we took off, a stewardess came back and whispered something to Erik. Erik and his girlfriend stood up and followed her into first class. She pulled the curtain shut behind them.

I stared at that curtain, fuming. I thought of my first-class flight to Philadelphia with the big seats and the special service. *Why the hell did Production take away my right to fly first-class when it was in our contract?* I started imagining the whole thing was a setup from the get-go, like some arrangement had been made between Erik and the producers on the down low where they told him to pretend he was going to fly coach, and they'd switch it up before we took off. I'd been out of prison and sober for almost twenty years at that point, but the slightest hint of what I thought was disrespect still sent my brain spinning. I stewed about how I'd been played, lied to, and, most importantly, made a fool of. Yes, I had agreed to what the producers asked when everyone was in it together, but as soon as my costar and his girlfriend left me back behind the curtain, I got pissed. I wanted to get up and make a stink.

Instead, I channeled Sam Hardy, sat back, and looked out the window. It was a beautiful day. I had a row of four seats all to myself. My mind was going back and forth. I was telling myself I was being disrespected while another part of my brain was pinching me to remind me that I was in a plane with an empty row and going to Hawaii for the first time. I'd never been, but I'd seen the pictures and it looked like paradise.

A man and woman who looked to be in their seventies were sitting in front of me. The woman took the man's hand and said, "Can you believe your promise to me that we'd go to Hawaii on our golden anniversary is finally coming true?"

I was eavesdropping, staring at their hands through the gap in the seats. The man's hand was as big as a shovel and rough like leather. Maybe he poured concrete or welded. Whatever he did, you could tell by his hands that he was a manual laborer. A manual laborer taking his wife on a trip he promised her fifty years ago and had probably been saving for throughout their whole marriage. I was slapped back to reality. Who the hell was I to feel like I was getting the short end of the stick? I felt like the biggest asshole in the world.

God always has a way of sending me messages to check my ego and will.

I marveled at the old couple's love for each other. It made me think of my relationship with Maeve. Maybe we could get a nicer house in Venice, with a big kitchen. Maybe this baby would bring us closer. Maybe we could take trips together when we got older. Maybe she would be all I needed; maybe I'd be all she needed. I couldn't say any of that. I never trusted the future. I was scared that Maeve might leave me, but I wanted to be free. Why did I have such a problem thinking about being with the same woman for life?

"Excuse me," I said. "I have this row to myself and if you want some extra space, I can trade with you."

"That's so kind of you," said the woman.

We made the switch, and when I got up, one of the producers on the film who was also flying coach smiled at me and gave me a thumbs-up. Everything was exactly as it was supposed to be.

A few hours into the flight, I twisted around to check on the old couple. They were making out like teenagers. I thought, *Oh gosh, Lord, I didn't have to see that.*

The movie was goofy but fun. People ask me if I mind doing B movies and the answer is, every time I do a movie and my involvement helps it get made, that means people are getting paychecks that assist their families in putting food on the table. Plus, movies are what they are: the people you meet, the conversations you have, the life that goes down while you're making them—*that* is the gold.

I think the main reason I keep getting jobs with the same people is that they know I carry myself like a worker among workers; I take it one gig at a time; I give them 100 percent focus, my best effort; and I don't rock the boat. A lot of people get wrapped up in their own importance. You can try and steer them to the right way of thinking—I've spent more than half my life working that beat—but usually you can't save people from themselves if they're hell-bent on fucking their lives up through egomaniacal behavior. Some people never appreciate what they have and are always focused on what they don't.

The episode with the seating arrangement was an opportunity to check my ego. Eddie Bunker said it best. He said, "Danny, the whole world can think you're a movie star, but you can't."

Chapter 20

PARTY OF FIVE

1988

When I got back from Hawaii, I told Maeve to grab her stuff and move in, but she insisted that she wouldn't move unless Danny Boy was there with us full-time. It didn't seem right to her to bring my second son home to a place where my first son only lived part-time. But taking him away from Nanny was going to break her heart. I didn't know how to cut the cord. Then Nanny fell and broke her hip and never came out of the hospital. The universe forced the decision. Danny Boy was already with me that weekend, and I told Maeve, "Get your stuff. Danny Boy's with us now."

At Nanny's funeral, Danny Boy held me tight. The attention he received and the complexity of loss overwhelmed him. It was a lesson in mortality he was too young to learn. He stuck close to me and Maeve and wanted to get out of there as soon as we could. On the drive home he said to me, "Daddy, I'm glad you were there. I don't ever want to go to another one of those things."

The night Maeve's water broke, I didn't know it had. I had a terrible migraine and was in the bathroom throwing up. When I came out, Maeve was gone. She had a friend take her to the hospital. I wish I could rewind the clock, but I can't, and I've since forgiven myself for not being in the room when our baby was born. When I got to Cedars with Danny Boy, Maeve was holding him swaddled in a blanket. Just like Danny Boy, he was the cutest thing I'd ever seen. The child I hadn't wanted melted my heart immediately. We named him Gilbert, after my uncle. It was Maeve's idea. She knew how much I looked up to him.

We started making a home in our tiny apartment. I'd built a crib for Gilbert, and he shared a room with his older brother, who just adored him.

It all worked out so well that we just kept going. For the first time in my life, I really dedicated myself to being a proper stay-at-home dad and a good partner. Maeve was juggling the kids and her studies at Santa Monica College. She was supportive of my acting career but privately worried one of us had to have a "real" job, especially with all these mouths to feed. And another was on the way. Twenty-seven months after Gilbert arrived, Maeve was ready to go to the hospital to deliver our daughter, Danielle. Just like when she gave birth to Gilbert, when it was time to go to the hospital I came down with a migraine. The headaches were real but psychologically convenient. This time she didn't let me chicken out from taking her. She said, "I don't care if you are dying, you're driving me to the hospital." When we got to the entrance to Cedars-Sinai, she said, "You can just drop me off right here."

I said, "Don't be silly," parked, and took her inside. I was debating privately whether I should go in the delivery room or not when Maeve's contractions got so intense, they brought lights into the room we were in and she delivered the baby right there.

At one point, the pain got so bad, Maeve started screaming, "Oh God! Oh God!"

I said, "Scream, 'Oh, Danny!' I'm the one who did this."

She shot me a look that said, *You fucker*.

I remember the moment Danielle's head crested. I looked at the clock. I wanted to remember that moment for the rest of my life. Holding that little baby girl was a fresh start for me. Being with her from her first breath meant my relationship with her was a blank slate and could be written however we wanted to write it. I will forever be grateful I got to experience that. The doctor gently handed me Danielle, and the first thing I said to her was, "No one will ever hurt you." When the doctor offered to let me cut the umbilical cord, I couldn't do it. I had *just* promised her nobody would hurt her.

"Don't worry, Mr. Trejo, she won't feel it."

"But *I* will." It wasn't a joke. It was the first time I'd been in the room for the birth of one of my kids, and I'd bonded with Danielle so hard that I would never want to cut the cord, literally or figuratively.

Maeve stepped in, took control, and had the doctor make the cut. Danielle threw her hands in the air and cried.

"I told you not to hurt her, holmes."

The doctor smiled. I don't think he'd ever been called "holmes" before.

Chapter 21

AMERICAN ME

1991

In 1991, two Chicano scripts rolled through Hollywood that both centered on the formation and growth of La Eme, the biggest Mexican gang in the California prison system. Since I was a high-profile Chicano who'd done time, both movies reached out to me. They knew my involvement would give them credibility. One was called *American Me*, directed by and starring Edward James Olmos. The other was *Blood In, Blood Out.*

When I sat down to read *American Me*, I was excited. Olmos was just coming off an Oscar-nominated performance in *Stand and Deliver*, and now he was making a movie about a world I knew intimately. But my initial excitement quickly changed to dismay. Ten pages in, I knew there were going to be problems. In the opening scene, the mother of Montoyo Santana, the character Edward James Olmos plays in the film, is raped by sailors the night of the Zoot Suit Riots, leaving her unsure of who Montoya's real father is. That was straight-up untrue. I knew it was untrue because Olmos's character was based on a real guy in the Mexican Mafia named Rodolfo Cadena (aka Cheyenne).

That wasn't the only problem. About twenty pages later came a shocking scene in which something violent happens to Santana in juvenile hall. Because of what happened later, I won't mention what it was. The whole thing was a fire started in falsehoods I don't want to add fuel to. The truth is

Cheyenne had never been abused in that way and the fact that (in the script) he immediately got revenge on his attacker didn't matter. I know this sounds harsh, but no person who'd ever been violated in that way could ever rise to the top of a prison gang. They could be killers and bad motherfuckers, but they'd never run a gang. It wouldn't happen. More importantly, it didn't happen.

Another big concern I had was that any movie about the Mexican Mafia would have to be okayed by the OGs in prison. Before I signed on to either project, I was definitely going to have to find out what the shot-callers thought about it.

And, finally, somewhere before page thirty in the *American Me* script, I saw that the writers called the gang La Eme. This is the actual name of the Mexican Mafia, and I had a feeling using it would be a big no-no for Joe Morgan, Robot, Donald Garcia, and Sailor Boy, some of the La Eme bigwigs I'd known since my days in juvie, YTS, the Deuel Vocational Institution, and San Quentin.

I knew just how serious and deadly La Eme was. I'd come up with the guys, but my uncle Gilbert was the one who really knew the older shot-callers. I was lucky; because Gilbert was so respected in the pen, I got that level of respect passed on to me. When I got to prison, Gilbert cautioned me about joining the Mafia. He said that was a contract for life and we shouldn't have any part of it, so I stayed away, but that didn't mean I wasn't friends with the guys. Sailor Boy and I starched our clothes together in YTS. Robert "Robot" Salas was a good friend. Donald Garcia and I had gone back since junior high. Gilbert was good friends with all of them, especially Joe "Peg Leg" Morgan, the current head of the Mexican Mafia.

Even though we weren't members of a gang, Gilbert and I were classified as "sympathizers," a designation that wasn't casual. Ramon "Mundo" Mendoza, a hit man for the Mexican Mafia, later commented on my friendships within the organization. Mundo said, "Danny Trejo is blessed. He was friends with people on both sides of the line, but always got respect."

I'd done time with these men. They were serious *vatos*. Their world and their lives were being represented—or, I suspected, misrepresented—in the film, and I couldn't imagine they'd be happy about it.

*   *   *

Edward James Olmos had arranged a meeting to discuss the script. We were to meet in Jerry's Famous Deli in Encino. Edward was bringing his agent, and I took Eddie Bunker. I knew if anyone could suss out truth from bullshit, it would be Bunker. We were sitting in a booth, waiting for them to arrive, when Eddie glanced up and said, "They're here."

I turned around and saw Edward in full cholo wear. He was in a County blue shirt buttoned up at the top and flying open on the bottom. He wore County blue pants. The only thing he was missing was a hair net. This was a business meeting. Eddie and I were dressed like casual businessmen.

Edward greeted me with an *"Órale, ese, ¿qué onda?"* I was confused, obviously not by the greeting but by his appearance. Edward was an actor, a great actor. He'd never been part of a gang, and he'd certainly never done time in prison, but here he was, playing like he was an OG from the streets. I figured he was most likely employing some kind of Method approach to the role he'd be playing in the film.

I love actors and I love movies. Replaying movies in my head helped me survive the times I was in the hole in Folsom and Soledad, but I knew the difference between real life and make-believe. Actors are incredible at making people believe they are a divorced dad, or a woman with a secret, or a soldier-killing Nazi, or a boxer two fights past when they should've hung their gloves up, but they are not those things. I don't think there's ever been a mobster who can play a mobster better than Ray Liotta or Robert De Niro or Al Pacino—that's an actor's job. But those roles extend only as far as make-believe allows. Robert De Niro's never actually beaten a man to death, and even though Edward James Olmos played a zoot suiter, he wasn't one; my father was—he was a *verdadero* zoot suit gangster from 38th Street, the gang at the center of the controversial Sleepy Lagoon murder case, the focus of the movie Edward starred in called *Zoot Suit.* My mom was from Ford Maravilla, the same gang that Joe Morgan came up in in the late 30s. I had too many personal connections to the liberties Edward was taking with the story for any of it to sit well with me.

But honestly, my biggest problem probably had as much to do with my insecurities as with what Edward James Olmos was doing. Him dressing up as a cholo made me question whether Edward, an incredible actor, a lifelong devotee to the craft, wanted to bond with me not as a fellow artist but as a gangster of some sort. Did he look at me and see the person I'd been in my past life—a life I'd worked so hard to put in my rearview mirror?

It wasn't the first time I'd experienced this dynamic. It was something I was overly sensitive about, but I felt like certain Latinos in Hollywood viewed me as a gangster, not a peer. To them, I was a circus curio from the hood, a world they'd certainly recognized, but never inhabited.

The meeting was off to a confusing start.

We ordered sandwiches and matzo ball soup and started talking about the film. Edward got straight to the point and asked if I was interested in working on the project. Eddie Bunker immediately raised one of our chief concerns.

He said, "Edward, did you talk to Joe about this film?" He was referring to Joe Morgan.

Olmos said, "I met with Joe. He gave the okay."

Immediate red flag. As soon as Eddie asked Edward the question, I could sense his demeanor shift. If prison had taught me anything, it taught me when someone was backing up. There seemed to be a hint of deflection and deception in Olmos's answer. I glanced at Eddie Bunker and saw that he shared my doubt.

I got down to business. "Look, Edward, the problem is there are things in this script that aren't true." I told him some of my concerns.

Edward said, "I know, but it makes more theatrical sense for the piece."

I was hoping he'd say, *I know and we're going to address that*, or, *We're going to figure out a way to tell our story without twisting the truths of real people*, but he didn't. He was married to the idea that the fictional arc of the script was more important than letting truth get in the way of a good story. This might be true in the offices of Hollywood producers, but it wasn't in the world I knew. I couldn't believe how casual he was about details that were so critical.

I offered yet another point of contention. "Eddie, Cheyenne was killed by Nuestra Familia, he wasn't killed by his own gang." That was huge. The day Cheyenne died in 1972, he knew there was a hit on him. So did the guards. They offered him the option of staying in his cell in Palm Hall at the Chino Reception Center. Instead, Cheyenne walked out on the tier and was stabbed over fifty times by Nuestra Familia gang members. He is remembered by La Eme as being a martyr, not someone who would be killed by his brothers.

Edward said that detail was theatrical, too.

Jesus. I couldn't believe what I was hearing. Still, I tried to be diplomatic. I liked Edward James Olmos and had deep respect for what he meant as an actor in the Hispanic community. I made a statement couched in a joke. "Edward, the people you're talking about are not theatrical people." Eddie Bunker and I shared a dark laugh at that one.

From their reaction, I got the sense that Edward James Olmos and his agent didn't like the way the meeting was going. I don't know what they were hoping for. I can't imagine they didn't know there were going to be issues. Maybe they were praying I wouldn't question the script and I would just be happy to be considered for an acting job like a regular Joe Schmo actor at a meeting campaigning for a part.

I was full of unanswered questions. The biggest was what the La Eme bigwigs really thought about all of this. All the talk of theatricality and "interesting character arcs" set my mind racing. Hollywood has always told stories of gangsters, some loosely based on their lives, others taken straight from court transcripts, but I had never found myself so squarely in the intersection of fiction and reality.

Looking back, I honestly believe Edward James Olmos's utter brilliance and mastery in the world of acting and film blinded him to some degree to the deadly seriousness of prison politics and how much sway it carried on the streets—even if (in a deeply ironic way) it was the central theme of the script he was directing. There's no poetic license when you're pissing off the wrong people.

A lot of it was just common sense. I would rather have a rabid dog as a friend than an enemy.

Eddie Bunker leaned in. From his position as captain's clerk in San Quentin, there was no one in the world who knew the ramifications of prison politics as well as Eddie Bunker. He said to Olmos, "Edward, are you sure about all this?"

Eddie Bunker was trying to make Olmos see where this whole thing could go sideways. But Olmos was clearly determined to make this version of the film.

We finished our meal, and I agreed to meet Olmos at his office the next day to continue discussing the project. I was hoping he would sleep on some of the issues we'd raised and rethink some things, but my gut told me he was set on the story he wanted to tell.

The next day I got my answer.

When I stepped in Edward's office, I found him decked out in cholo wear again. Edward wasn't the only one who'd slept on the issues we'd covered the day before. After leaving Jerry's Deli, I struggled to identify what really bothered me so much about his costume. I knew my conflict was deeply rooted in all the time I had spent as part of gangs or in prison. While I appreciated his dedication to portraying a life he didn't live or even know—that's what actors do—what bothered me lay in the heart of my own feelings of what being a cholo meant. When you take the dress and the code of a cholo, or a Crip, or a Blood, or a Mexican Mafia member—or an Aryan Brother, for that matter—you become something that is no longer Mexican, or Black, or white. When it comes to gang wear, how you are dressed is not merely a costume, it's a declaration that you are committed to a life of crime, for which you're willing to sacrifice the well-being of those around you—moms, dads, wives, sisters, brothers, children.

To me, real Mexicans, whites, and Blacks were the kind of men who worked hard and took their kids to Little League practice when they got home. Perhaps I was overreacting. After all, I was already interested in taking the part of Geronimo in *Blood In, Blood Out*, another prison gang movie where we'd all be decked out as cholos. But these were the feelings I was feeling, for better or worse. I guess you could also argue that I myself was playing by gang rules in arguing against the liberties Olmos took with the script. But the untruths made me deeply uncomfortable. I'd watched plenty of movies about organized crime, but I never knew the players personally before. And I knew too much to keep my mouth shut. I didn't want to play the middleman, but I smelled danger.

Edward said that he wanted me to think about the part of Pedro Santana, Montoya Santana's father, who disapproved of his lifestyle. I looked at the part and immediately wasn't interested. I told him I would think about it.

I didn't tell Edward I wasn't interested in the part of Pedro Santana because it reminded me too much of my own father. I didn't bring up the controversial aspects of the script again. I didn't have to dig any further into those complicated corners, because Edward made the decision easy. What totally killed *American Me* for me was when Edward told me that any actor considering working on *Blood In, Blood Out* would not be a part of *Ameri-*

can Me. That was the final blow. There were so few parts in Hollywood for Chicano actors as it was. I thought it was unfair that when two projects that would employ a ton of my Chicano brothers finally came along, one of the movies would deny entrance to the other. Especially coming from someone who was involved so deeply in *Chicanismo.*

We left it with me telling Edward I would have to run it by my agent. But one thing I didn't mention was that right before I went to the meeting, my cousin Sal had called me from LA County. When I picked up the phone, Sal said, "Danny, Joe Morgan wants to call you." They were both in High Power, a section of LA County for high-profile or especially dangerous prisoners. Sal sounded concerned. "Are you alright?"

We both knew a phone call from Joe could be ominous.

"I'm good, Sal. How are you?"

"You know how it is. Just facing this case."

"Just call me if you need anything, okay?"

"Yeah, Joe is going to call you at five p.m. at Bunker's house."

"Tomorrow?"

"Today."

I knew what he wanted to talk to me about had to be serious business. By calling me at Eddie's, it was clear Joe Morgan didn't want to put a red light on me by calling my house.

"Tell him I'll be there. Be good."

"You know it, holmes."

He hung up. Of course Big Joe knew about the movie and of course he already knew I'd met Edward James Olmos the day before. From his cell in San Quentin, Chino, or LA County, very little went down in the world that Big Joe didn't know. And this upcoming phone call confirmed my suspicions. Joe wasn't happy about the film.

Joe Morgan was the son of an Irish American father and a Croatian mother, but he grew up in Mexican neighborhoods. He was as hard as they came. He'd joined the Maravilla gang when he was a kid and quickly rose through the ranks. Joe had lost his leg from a gun blast and got the nickname "Peg Leg." The loss of his leg didn't stop him. Joe was still one of the best handball players I'd ever seen. He spoke Spanish perfectly and had an incredible presence. When you got near his cell, the molecules in the air got heavy. Joe only talked to people if they were his best friends or if he wanted them dead. I knew Joe didn't want me dead, but he wanted something from me.

That afternoon, I headed over to Bunker's. He'd already put on a pot of coffee. Eddie Bunker made the best coffee in the world. At five p.m. on the button the phone rang. Eddie answered.

"What's up, Big Joe? You good? Yeah." He listened for a bit. "Yeah, he's right here," and handed me the phone.

I hopped on the line.

"Danny? *¿Que pasó?*"

"I'm good, holmes."

He said, "I hear you're up for that movie, *American Me*."

"I'm up for both of them, *Blood In, Blood Out*, too."

He got straight to the point. "Which one are you going to do?"

I said, "C'mon, Joe. I'm going to do *Blood In, Blood Out*, holmes."

He was happy. He said, "Good, that's the cute one!" We both laughed. Then he said, "La Onda," stretching out the word. La Onda was the name of the fictional Mexican gang in *Blood In, Blood Out*. I always laugh thinking about Joe Morgan calling *Blood In, Blood Out*, a movie about a gang of stone-cold killers, "the cute one."

"*Vacay un chingón de pedo*—there's going to be a lot of problems with that other movie," Joe added.

"I figured."

He talked about Olmos directly. "That *baboso* is running around saying he met with me in Chino and got my approval. It's all bullshit. I refused to see him. There's a lot of bullshit in that script."

"That's what I tried to tell Eddie."

He said, "You know, Danny, you could do that other movie . . ." He was saying he wouldn't hold it against me if I did *American Me*.

I said, "No, Joe. I've got too much respect."

"Gracias, holmes. *Vatos* got enough respect for you that you could get away with it."

"Thanks, Joe." Then I asked him, "Hey, Joe, what about the crew and the other actors?"

He laid any concerns I had to rest. "The crew and the actors are just workers, holmes. They're just getting a paycheck."

"*Órale.*"

That was a load off my mind. I knew many of the actors involved in *American Me* and didn't want them to have any trouble. Joe said, "Be good, Danny. Good checking in with you," and hung up.

The crazy thing is that *Blood In, Blood Out* was a movie that covered many of the same themes as *American Me*—racial politics in prison, murder, betrayal. The difference was that *Blood In, Blood Out* was a piece of fiction. It never tried to present itself as the real story of the Mexican Mafia.

Months later, when we were up in San Quentin shooting *Blood In, Blood Out*, I heard that *American Me* was running into problems in Folsom with the Sureños there. In fact, someone from Production reached out to me to offer me a job if I would go to Folsom to serve as a "consultant" on *American Me* for two days. My suspicion was they needed diplomatic clout to help them. But I didn't want any part of it. Later, after the movie was about to be released and rumor of trouble was brewing, William Forsythe, who played J.D., the Joe Morgan character, reached out to me and asked if everything was going to be alright. I told him, "Of course, William. The actors will have no problems. You're just a worker getting a paycheck." I told him I thought he'd done a great job in the film, because he had. William Forsythe plays a hell of a gangster.

I had no idea just how bad things were going to get. The word on the street was at least eight people died because of their involvement in *American Me*, maybe ten. Four outside and four to six inside. One of the guys murdered was a Mexican Mafia member named Charlie Manriquez who had fallen into disrepute because of his drug use. He was given a pair of Levi's, some tennis shoes, and money to buy weed to be an extra in a scene and act as an unofficial "technical advisor" before being gunned down in Ramona Gardens.

Another guy was shot seven times just for being in the deep background of a scene where he sits in a car. A community gang liaison named Ana Lizarraga, the top consultant on *American Me*, was executed outside her home in front of her son. Besides being warned about not getting involved in the project, like Olmos, Lizarraga falsely claimed that she, too, had met with Joe Morgan and gotten his approval. Olmos was like a kid playing with a grenade, thinking the whole time it was a sparkler. The violent aftershocks rumbled for years. Southern *vatos* I knew, who were in prison in the years that followed, hated the fact hits were out on Sureños who'd been involved in the production. A lot of these men were simply drug addicts who needed money for a fix when they agreed to be extras or do bit parts in the film.

It's a horrible chapter made worse because it was all so avoidable. The average viewer or film critic wouldn't even know the difference between *American Me* and *Blood In, Blood Out*. I do not condone the violence. But even if it's wrong, it's irresponsible to pretend there might not be repercussions.

The *American Me* saga brought my past life as a convict front and center. However far I'd come from the fire didn't mean it wasn't still hot. Edward James Olmos had just come off an Oscar nomination; his star was in the ascendant. I think that might have blinded him to what otherwise might have been more obvious. Those of us who had done serious time on the streets and in prisons knew threats from prominent gangs could and should never be dismissed, but not everyone has that background. Producers and Hollywood don't always necessarily understand the nature of the people they are representing. I will never discount the contribution Edward James Olmos has made to Hollywood and his constant advocacy for Latinos, but the whole episode was, in my view, unnecessarily reckless. If Edward James Olmos had studied Cheyenne a little more, maybe he could have told a deeper story while still not glorifying violence and crime.

That might be my biggest problem with *American Me*. While the producers said they wanted the film to encourage kids not to follow that path, it illuminated it in big Hollywood lights. *American Me* made a California prison gang known only to prison insiders into an entity with worldwide fame. Ramon "Mundo" Mendoza later spoke about the recruiting power the film *American Me* had on Chicano youth. He said *American Me* "elevated the public awareness of an organization that was becoming more than just a prison gang." And he added that this was something that was "not lost on the impressionable, aspiring gang members who now viewed joining the Eme in the same light that a kid from the other side of the tracks would aspire to join our country's armed forces."

Even now, whenever Crips or Bloods start shit with the Mafia, they say, "You know what happened in juvie to that Cheyenne guy?" *American Me* gave them a critical jumping-off point from which they felt emboldened to disrespect the Mafia—causing confrontations that led to even more deaths. Other gangs felt if a Mexican American made the movie, it must be true.

This story isn't new. It's well documented that there was no shortage of voices cautioning Olmos, finding contradictions in things he'd said, or expressing dismay at the final product, including police officers hired on the film and an associate warden hired as a consultant. But he couldn't hear it from anyone. Production on *American Me* was slated to start at Folsom State Penitentiary. The train had left the station, and I'd said all I could say.

Chapter 22

CELL C550

1992

The first few weeks on *Blood In, Blood Out* were spent in Los Angeles re-hearsing and doing wardrobe fittings. While I was comfortable with the script, I found myself still walking the line between my two worlds—my past as a convicted felon and my new vocation as an actor. Maybe because of my conversations with Olmos, I was feeling sensitive to the differences between my background and the way I became involved in the film indus-try. I know this was more my issue than theirs, but it seemed to me that the other actors in *Blood In, Blood Out* spent a lot of time in rehearsal talking about where they had studied, what school of acting they came from—Stanislavski, the Method, the Actors Studio, whatever. They talked a lot about Shakespeare. I think they were doing it with each other to establish who had more cred in that world and to remind me that, in their world, I had no cred.

I talked about it with George. I'd gotten him a job doing extra work on the film so he was in heaven. He joked that I was the greatest agent in the world. I said the actors were talking about Shakespeare all the time in re-hearsal because they knew that wasn't my scene. He told me to not take it personally, that it was simply the language of their court, and who better to play a prisoner in San Quentin than me, a man who'd been through it?

Besides, it wasn't as if I had never studied acting.

It was true. I thought about when I was twelve. Gilbert, Bobby Ortega, and Charlie Diaz were getting high. I was eavesdropping on them talking about a robbery they'd just pulled. Gilbert saw me peeking through the door and said, "Come in, Danny Boy. I'm going to teach you something." Gilbert handed me his Army-issued .45. He told me to point it at the mirror and say, "Give me all your money."

I was so skinny and the gun was so big, I couldn't hold it steady with one hand. Charlie and Bobby laughed.

There I was, gun drooping, thin-voiced. "Give me your money!"

That just made them laugh harder.

"That won't scare anyone, *ese*. Say it meaner, with feeling!"

I tried again. "Give me your money!"

"Use both hands."

I did, but the words still sounded weak coming out of my mouth.

Bobby had the idea to hand me a sawed-off shotgun. That felt different. It felt good to hold. Easy to cradle. It made me feel like I was in charge and could hold off an army if I had to.

"*¡Escúchame, putos!* Give me all your fucking money!"

That was it. The guys clapped and hit me on the back. "You got it, holmes! You're a scary *hombrecito*."

Looking back, they were probably just high and having a laugh about how ridiculous it was to coach a little kid on how to pull a robbery. But to me, it was no joke. From infancy on we develop the masks we wear to get by, pretending we're not scared or hurt, that things are alright. This was my first real "acting" lesson. I had to make someone understand I was not fucking around and would take their life if I had to. Long after my uncle and his friends left the room, I kept staring at myself in the mirror with the shotgun in my hand, making my voice deeper and more menacing.

"Give me the fucking money!"

That was the one. I looked at my reflection. I liked what I saw.

When it was finally time to start rolling film on *Blood In, Blood Out*, the whole production moved to San Francisco. Taking the van to San Quentin brought me emotionally back to where I was in 1965, more than twenty-five years earlier. We parked outside the prison's walls and George turned to me and said, "Danny, one of the actors is packing a knife."

It was true. I said, "Give me that knife."

The man said, "I'm not going to let one of those motherfuckers disrespect me!"

He was like a fish who protested too much when told to strip and spread 'em. I said, "Listen, we're actors, they're killers. Give me the fucking knife."

I handed George the knife and he stashed it under a seat in the van.

When we stepped onto the Yard, everything was quiet at first until a massive noise erupted. If you've never heard it before, it's the most intimidating sound in the world. It's the sound of three thousand prisoners screaming and banging. I call it "The Motor." Inmates were yelling my name and things like, "Hey, Trejo, we told you you'd be back! Danny, move into my cell! You look better now!"

The effect on my fellow actors was obvious. They fell into step behind me as if by staying close, they'd be safe. George whispered in my ear, "Ask them where's Shakespeare now, motherfuckers!"

Even with their trepidation, the actors didn't fully understand the dangers in prison. Right off the bat, we were all handed safety vests to wear when we weren't filming. Some actors refused to wear them—they said it disrupted their ability to stay in character.

Taylor Hackford, the director, asked me to explain why the vests were necessary.

I said, "If anything happens, the guards will know who not to shoot."

Everyone put on their vests.

Being back at San Quentin was heavy enough, but it didn't fully hit me until filming moved to the South Block. We were climbing the stairs to the set and with every step, my heart pounded harder. When we reached the flight between the fourth and fifth tier, I stopped. I was standing on the same steps where Tyrone stabbed the man who tried to kill me. At the top of the steps we hung a right, and the assistant director led us to the block of cells where we were going to rehearse. The production had the cells C545 to C550 blocked off for filming. C550. My former cell. I glanced at George. He looked like he was going to cry. He pointed to the heavens.

After rehearsing the scene, when the actors broke off for wardrobe and hair and makeup, George suggested we pray. We went into my old cell and got down on our knees and thanked God for our freedom from drugs and alcohol, our freedom from prisons, and we thanked Him for our kids and our lives. I'd come full circle.

During the weeks we were filming, I found we had more freedom to roam than I thought we would. At the risk of bragging, I knew I had the respect of the inmates and was safe. Early on in filming, about eight Northerners came up to me and asked me where I was from. I don't know if they thought I might throw down my San Fernando Valley credentials, but I just said, "C'mon. I'm from Hollywood, *putos!*" They laughed.

Against Production's wishes, I went out to the pile where the weight lifting equipment was. There was a huge *vato* pushing almost four hundred pounds on the bench and curling hundred-pound dumbbells. This was before officials pulled weights out of the prison system because cops were complaining they were seeing ex-cons hit the street with twenty-two-inch biceps. The dude pushing iron was the kind of *vato* you picture when you think of Mexicans to be scared shitless of. He was wearing blue shorts. I finished a set of pull-ups and walked over to him.

"What you doing?" I asked him.

"Time," he said. He wasn't much into small talk.

"No," I said. "What you doing wearing blue on the Yard?" The man explained he'd made shorts out of pants he'd taken from LA County Jail before he'd been shipped up to San Quentin. His name was Mario Castillo and he was from Baldwin Park. I was impressed he was wearing Sureño colors in a Yard full of Norteños.

In the old days, all Mexicans in the California prison system were unified, but in the late 60s things began to change. The inciting incident was a murder over a pair of shoes.

The dividing line in the California prison between Northern and Southern California Mexican gangs is in Delano, a small farming community just north of Bakersfield and south of Fresno. Even the town of Delano itself is divided by a single street. It's as crazy as it sounds, but that's the way it is. Before Centinela and Calipatria and other new huge super prisons were built in the southern part of the state, most Sureños were sent to prison in Northern California, right into the heart of our supposed enemies.

When we shot *Blood In, Blood Out*, San Quentin had become a Northern

Reception Center, making the balance between Norteños and Sureños even more weighted toward Northerners than it was in my time there in the 60s. Mario gave absolutely zero fucks. I immediately liked him. He didn't just have the balls to wear blue on the Yard, he was funny, too. Serious, but funny. I said I could probably get him some work on the movie.

Mario wasn't interested. He said, "Word's come down that no Sureños work on the movie. All the guys you got are Northsiders."

The prison politics between the Sureños and the Norteños wasn't just playing out on the weight pile, it was bleeding into the production. Because of the *American Me* fiasco, Joe Morgan had decreed that no Southside Mexicans in Folsom or San Quentin were allowed to work on either production. Early in filming, Taylor Hackford asked why it was so hard to get Mexicans involved. A few Mexicans were coming out, but they were Border Brothers, Mexican nationals who were in prison in the United States and would be deported as soon as their sentences were over. I said, "Taylor, we are doing a movie about Southern Mexicans in a Northern Reception Center."

Taylor said, "What are they worried about?"

I said, "More than likely, colors." I explained the significance of blue and red. I said, "Red is the color worn by Norteños, and blue is for Sureños."

He said, "Oh, okay. We'll make it work, whatever's right."

One thing about Taylor Hackford: he was willing to listen to the men who knew. He said, "Danny, do you think we can organize a meeting with the Northerners?"

I talked to George who (being from San Jose) knew some of the shot-callers from Nuestra Familia. We organized a sit-down. The first thing they said was "We don't want you disrespecting Northerners."

I said, "This movie is not about north and south. This movie is about Mexicans; it's about Chicanos; it's about before we separated and things went bad." That's when they got specific.

They asked, "What about the colors?"

I said, "We're not flying colors—nobody is wearing blue or red." So for the entire course of production, we all wore brown, a neutral color that stood for all Chicanos. It was agreed that Native American inmates could wear red in the film because that has historically been their color.

Filming wasn't without its hitches. A couple of days before we finished filming, the actor who I'd taken the knife from was "playing the dozens" (engaging in joke talk) with one of the San Francisco heavies. Things turned more serious when this actor said, "¡Soy mafioso!"

A line had been crossed. Immediately the tier went silent. It felt like the temperature had dropped fifty degrees. The feeling in the air was an old feeling I knew well—it was the feeling like shit was about to jump off. Immediately I moved the actor back and George interceded with the Northerners. A crisis had been averted, but if there were any more slips, violence would be inevitable. I was glad we were almost done.

The thing I'm most proud of is that when we finished shooting *Blood In, Blood Out*, my fellow actors regarded me as a peer and not as a convict. We were the actors and not the killers we played. I'd gotten over my earlier insecurities and, in turn, gained a deep level of respect for the artists who had put so much time and care into crafting their characters.

Before the film was released, Buena Vista Pictures, a subsidiary of Disney, changed the name to *Bound by Honor*. I guess some executives felt the original title was too violent for the brand.

I made some great friends on that movie. Besides Taylor and the cast, I actually got close to some Nuestra Familia members and talked to them about getting clean. Two of them have stayed off drugs since then, and that was over thirty years ago. Another inmate, Briley "Chato" Perez from Hayward, is still one of my good friends. He says that I showed him another life was possible and he has been out of prison and clean for over fifteen years.

But Mario was the person who made the biggest impact on me at Quentin. After our brief encounter, I never forgot about him. Fifteen years later, I was speaking at a recovery convention in Burbank. I entered the event center and from across the room I saw a big *vato* with his back to me. I knew immediately it was Mario. It turned out that after a few more stints in prison, Mario was clean and sober and determined to never go back. At the time, I had no clue the role Mario was going to play in my life.

Chapter 23

MI VIDA LOCA

1991

We finished filming *Blood In, Blood Out* and Production was planning a big wrap party in San Francisco. A lot of the locals who'd worked on the film were going to come and the cast begged me to stay, but I just couldn't. I had to get home and give Maeve a hug. Being around so many men who were locked up and missing their families made me miss mine more than ever. Back in the 60s when I was in prison, I was lucky. I had nothing on the streets and no one at home missing and waiting for me. I wanted it that way. But now I had three children and a great woman and I didn't need to wait for a parole board to tell me I could see them. All I needed was a plane ticket.

On the flight home, I prayed to God to let me be present, attentive, and loving. To have received the amount of respect and acceptance I got from the inmates in San Quentin made me emotional. To get that kind of respect back when I was an inmate meant you had to be feared, but to get it for having made something of my life after I got out was a hundred times more fulfilling. It was an incredible gift from God to go back to a prison I hadn't been sure I was going to make it out of alive and to make art there.

The time from when I landed at LAX until the car service took me back to Venice might have been only twenty minutes, but it felt like a year. The first thing I did with the kids was go down to the beach and play in the sand while Maeve made us dinner. Lying in bed later that night, I looked over at Maeve, Gilbert, and Danielle snuggled together asleep and thought, *You have this family. You have this beautiful thing. Why don't you want to keep it like this, Danny? Fuck whatever's out there. Whatever you feel like you're missing out on. This is everything you need.* I was in bed with everything I held dear in the world and it wasn't enough. I thought, *What the fuck is wrong with me?*

If I was more self-aware, I could have seen that Maeve and I were both emotional, immature, volatile people who wanted control and didn't want to be controlled by the other. Especially me. Among my dad, my uncles, and their friends, you'd be thought of as weak if you didn't have control of your woman. One of the men, without looking up, would say to his wife, "Get me a beer," and all the other wives would get up, ask all their husbands if they wanted a beer, and go with her to get them. If one of the wives took a job, they'd clown her husband at barbecues and get-togethers, saying, "Anna, is it okay if Art drinks a beer?" There was only one way to be a man in that world.

I knew I was never going to commit to a monogamous relationship. Every day I was flirting, I was furtive; my life belonged to the world outside our apartment. I never checked to see how Maeve felt about me doing my own thing. If I wanted to go out, I went out. I didn't ask permission; I didn't say when I would be home. Suckers did that. Suckers had to run it by their old lady anytime they wanted to do something.

"Where you been?" *None of your business.* "Where you going?" I didn't necessarily know.

Whenever Maeve moved out or kicked me out, I'd be good for a bit, but we'd miss each other. And this cycle continued happening long after we had children. All of it was too much for me to understand. I just never saw myself as that stay-at-home, one-woman guy.

The next day, I was in the pool holding Gilbert and Danielle. They were so small cradled in the crooks of my arms. I caught Maeve looking at me like she knew. She knew how much I loved her and I loved my children, but I wanted to be a person I just couldn't be. It was like she knew that that feeling of us being a family unit who shared the same roof might only last another two days, two months, or five years, but she was determined not to let the specter of any potential future breakup cast a pall on the present. She called to me from the barbecue grill, "Danny, kids, out of the pool! The hot dogs are ready!"

I told Maeve that when George and I were in San Quentin, I had a terrible time with my emotions. That was big for me. I'm not really one to reveal my soul troubles. Maeve suggested I talk to her mom, who was a therapist. She said, "Danny, I think you're suffering from PTSD. You've been traumatized by the knives and the guns and the violence, by being in prison so long. All the stories of men you've hit, on the streets, in boxing rings, through steel grating—average people haven't been through that. Average people haven't robbed a liquor store at gunpoint. Your experiences aren't normal. You've been through a lot."

What she said was true. But I could only think of the people on the other side of those scenarios. "I've put people through a lot."

"Yes, you have. But guilt without self-awareness makes it worse."

The first time I robbed a store, I was fourteen, almost fifteen. My friend Mike Serna and I were back at my house after school one day, fucking around, when we went into my uncle Art's room and started pulling stuff out from underneath his bed. I knew he had a gun there and I found it. It was a .22 pistol with a broken barrel. Art had told me he was going to take it to get fixed, but it would still fire if you held your hands over the cylinder. Mike and I took it in the backyard and test-fired it. Art was right. It worked, but it burned the shit out of our hands.

Right then and there, we decided to do our first job. It wasn't planned, but we'd been talking about robberies we wanted to pull for so long. That was the day. We took my uncle Rudy's pink-and-white '57 Ford Fairlane 500 convertible. Talk about brass-balled idiots. Not only was I years away from having a driver's license, our first robbery getaway car was a pink-and-white convertible. We headed down Penrose to San Fernando and hung a right. Our target was the Far East Market on Lankershim in Sun Valley.

On the way we kept saying to each other, "Let's do this!" and pumping ourselves up. We parked off San Fernando by a wrecking yard and approached the store from the south. I was ready. Adrenaline made everything move in slow motion. My senses were on overdrive. We came through the door and found an older Asian lady behind the counter. I pulled out the revolver that was tucked in my pants with both hands. Just like I'd so carefully rehearsed in the mirror two years before, I said, "Give me your fucking money."

Mike was screaming, "You heard him!" The lady opened the register and handed me eight one-dollar bills. Mike yelled, "The cigar box. The big bills are in the cigar box!"

I looked behind the front counter and saw the box. I pointed to it with one hand and the barrel of the gun drooped. Right then, an Asian guy came running out of the back of the market screaming and waving a cleaver. Mike and I hauled ass in the opposite direction from the car and made our way over fences and through a back alley to get to the Fairlane. When we hopped back in the car, we started laughing hysterically. It was such a rush. We'd made eight dollars. All of that for only eight dollars. We didn't care. What we cared about was the high we got from the experience. Mike suggested we call ourselves "The Laughing Bandits."

We laughed then, but now I thought about the lady we'd robbed and how scared she was and how funny it was to Mike and me when we ran out of the store. It's something I'll always be ashamed of—bringing fear to people like that woman. When you bring a gun to a robbery, anything can happen. When someone gets killed during the commission of a crime and the criminal says, "I never meant for anyone to get hurt," they're full of shit. It's murder, plain and simple. The second you pull a gun in a robbery, all consequences are on you.

Part of the problem was we didn't think what we were doing was necessarily wrong. When we robbed people, we didn't think of them as people. We thought of them as money and a way to get something we needed. We weren't taking from them so much as giving to us. We figured if they had money, that meant they could get more. When I got sober, I stopped doing that to people, but there were many other parts of my life where I was still selfish.

The world of sobriety requires inward circumspection. I'd been in that world for so long, and I felt ashamed of who I'd been and what I'd done, but I'd never really given much thought to the insane masculinity I'd grown up in and how that had shaped me. I just figured if I stayed sober and helped other people get sober, I was doing everything I needed to. I didn't look at the little boy who was me and what happened to him and how all of that informed who I became as a man.

I thought I was just another dude with really bad nightmares.

Maeve was deeply in love with me and I with her, I just couldn't express it or show it in a conventional way.

I have so much respect for her for how she carried herself during those years. Maeve will tell you that even before my acting career hit, I had a kind of aura around me, whether it was at meetings or walking down the Venice boardwalk. It wasn't always easy to stand in my shadow, for her or our kids. If you asked me, I'd swear I had no ego around any of that stuff, but even that is a bullshit, egocentric thought. But when *Blood In, Blood Out* came out, my life really changed. However infamous I was in LA circles, I now had legitimate, worldwide fame. I was on a new ride, and I didn't know if we were going to survive it as a unit.

Right on the heels of *Blood In, Blood Out*, I was offered a gig on an Allison Anders movie called *Mi Vida Loca*. It was about young girls growing up in gang life and how the ruthlessness of the world tears them apart. *Mi Vida Loca* was an important film for me to do after the whirl I had been caught up in—walking away from *American Me* and being elevated by *Blood In, Blood Out*. Both films wanted to show the other side of gang life, but it's something *Mi Vida Loca* truly accomplished.

Mi Vida Loca focused on the real loneliness and despair that are the by-products of gang life—the suffering of the families. No one was going to make a two-hour movie about brokenhearted parents and children, but *Mi Vida Loca* spent real time showing the dark and still moments—scenes of pregnant girls standing in line at the Department of Social Services trying to get food stamps, a mom crying in her kitchen because her daughter was killed in a drive-by shooting, parents picking up their son's bullet-riddled car from impound.

Allison Anders is an artist. She just got it. She understood that young people think they're invincible, that bad shit might happen to other people but not to them. They think they're the smartest dealers and the baddest motherfuckers who've ever walked the earth. Allison knew how enticing gang life is to kids in the *barrio* and got the fact that it's hard to teach anyone anything when they think they know everything already.

It had been years since I'd been in a gang, but it was the one lesson Gilbert had failed to teach me. We were not invincible. So many of my old homies were dead, casualties of the life. The battles we thought we'd won had consequences we thought would never matter to us. I was in constant contact with widows, widowers, fathers, and motherless children. Coming up, we didn't value our own lives, or those of the people around us. And I'd spent years trying to make up for it.

Chapter 24

THE RIGHT THING

1991

While Danny Boy's mother, Diana, was in the pen, I had established contact with Diana's parents, Danny Boy's grandparents, who were living in Long Beach. I'd take Danny Boy down and drop him off so he would see his grandparents. When he was five, I got into trouble because when he arrived at their house in Long Beach and they asked him what he wanted to do, he said, "Let's go to the beach and check out babes!"

Diana's mom called me and said, "Danny, what are you teaching this child?"

Shortly after that they moved to Lompoc, a small town a few hours north on the central coast. After Diana got out, she went to Lompoc to live with her folks, and I let Danny Boy stay there for longer and longer stretches, especially in the summer. One time, I went to pick Danny Boy up and Diana's mom called out to him in the street. I stood and watched him play with a group of about ten friends. He was in heaven. In Lompoc, Danny Boy had big yards to play in and a bunch of friends. It was like Mayberry. I half expected Opie to come strolling up the street with his fishing pole. On the other hand Venice, where we were living, was all gangs east of the beach: Venice Trece, Crips, Bloods. Kids Danny Boy's age were joining up. The only gang of kids Danny Boy was going to fall in with in Venice was an actual gang, and then it was just a matter of time before the shit started. I was working with drug addicts, and Venice was a great place for me to be since there were so many of them around and I could help them get into treatment. But my kids' mothers and I had our own histories of drug problems, and we all knew our kids had it in their genes. In Venice it was just a matter of time before trouble came for them. Maybe it wasn't the best place for them to grow up.

Out on the street in Lompoc, Danny Boy heard his grandma call him, and even though he was excited to see me, I could tell he was having a hard time leaving his friends.

"Okay, Dad, I'll be there in a minute," he said. I watched them say good-bye to each other and it broke me a little inside. Danny Boy was happy in Lompoc.

When we got back to Venice, I told Maeve what I'd seen and asked her what she thought. Maeve had treated Danny Boy like her first child. He was ten now and Gilbert, who was three, had grown up with his big brother. The two of them shared a bunk bed in the same room where Danielle had her crib. They loved their older brother with all their hearts. It would be extremely hard to part with him, but Maeve tried to see the big picture. Diana and her parents were all good, responsible, loving people with decent jobs and nice houses.

Maeve said, "It might be better for Danny Boy in Lompoc. It's time to consider letting him live with his mom."

"I don't want to be away from my kid," I said.

"He's only a year or two away from the streets here, and you know it," Maeve said. "He'll be safer there."

"Well, what about Gilbert and Danielle? They need to be safe, too."

"They're babies. We have time to figure out our lives and get out of here," Maeve said. And the truth was that it would be hard for Maeve and me to move. Maeve had grown up in Venice, and because she was managing the apartment where we were living, collecting rents and overseeing repairs, we lived rent-free. It was the hood, but it worked for us. But Danny Boy had a ticket out and maybe he should use it.

With Maeve's approval, I went to Danny Boy and asked him if he liked being in Lompoc with his mom and grandparents. He did. "What would you think about living there?" He looked like he was struggling with something.

"I'd never want to do anything that hurt your feelings, Dad. You're my dad."

"You could never do anything that hurt me, Danny Boy. You're my son, you will always be my son. I love you more than anything. So tell me: Do you like it up there?"

He nodded. He'd been relieved of the responsibility of my feelings. "I love it up at Mom's."

"You have a lot of friends?"

"Way more than down here. And, Dad?"

"Yeah?"

"I get sad sometimes that Mom doesn't have a kid with her. She's all alone."

I went back into the kitchen and called Diana. "How are the schools in Lompoc?"

She started yelling. "How can you do this? Why are you doing this to me?"

Her mother got on the phone. "Danny, what's going on?"

"I just asked Diana how the schools in Lompoc are in case Danny Boy wanted to go to move there. She must have thought I was messing with her." His grandmother got so excited, she started hyperventilating.

"Oh, you have to understand, Danny, they have the best schools here. The schools are incredible, the teachers are incredible." The idea of Danny Boy living in Lompoc was clearly something they'd fantasized about for a long time.

"Alright, I'll talk to him about it, but I think he'd love that."

Danny Boy moved to be with his mother and grandparents in Lompoc. Maeve or I drove up every weekend to pick him up and bring him to LA to see Gilbert and Danielle. A lot of times we drove the kids up there to see Danny Boy. Gilbert and Danielle missed him something fierce. We all did. It was hard, but it was the right thing.

Chapter 25

THE FIXER

1995

An actor named Raymond Cruz, who I'd met in Venice, took me to meet his agency. He thought I needed better representation. I don't think Raymond's agent saw much in me, but to keep Raymond happy, they kicked me off to a junior agent named Gloria Hinojosa who'd just started at the company. Gloria was funny, she was cool, and, most importantly, she was a hustler. As soon as I signed with Gloria, my career took off.

The first gig Gloria got me was *Baywatch*, in which (surprise) I played a Harley-riding ex-con who was too much of a dick to let his kid take part in a program for kids from the *barrio*. It was fun, everyone was cool, and I got paid to hang out at the beach a few blocks from my apartment.

Work was fast but not diverse. I got offered a part in a prison flick called *Last Light* with Kiefer Sutherland and Forest Whitaker. It was Kiefer's directorial debut. I was cast again as (surprise) an inmate. My official character name was "2nd Inmate." Privately, I thought, *Second inmate? Damn, I'm heading backward.*

Early in production, Kiefer had brought a friend onto the project who ended up being out of control. Kiefer may have thought the guy's wildness would make him a convincing inmate, but on a movie set, unpredictability just causes big fucking headaches. Whenever the AD would say, "Rolling," for filming to begin, the guy would start belting out, "Rolling on the river," loudly and aggressively.

By the time I arrived, that guy was gone. When Kiefer figured out he was too volatile, he had to have security escort him off the set. That's when things took a funkier turn. I could tell something was eating at Kiefer; he was struggling. I said, "What's wrong, Kiefer?"

He said, "Nothing."

But a week later, it was clear it wasn't just "nothing." Kiefer called me from New York and told me he was worried about this guy, that after he fired him from the movie the guy threatened him and his kids.

I was an actor, but I was also seen as a bit of a fixer. I had a reputation for knowing how things operated on the streets. If people had problems that they didn't think had a legal solution, they hit me up for advice and help. I told Kiefer not to worry about it.

I found out who the guy was, and George and I spoke to him. The man was upset because Kiefer had promised him after so many days of work he could get a Screen Actors Guild card, and that's why he was hounding him. I tried to be diplomatic. I said, "Maybe the card didn't work out on this one. But if you don't cut it out, someone might put an M-80 in your ass and light it." That seemed to do the trick. The next day he sent flowers and an apology to Kiefer's wife.

What I learned about Hollywood is that if I helped someone with a problem, they either became my best friend or they grew distant from me. Kiefer was legitimately grateful. As for the others, maybe they felt that by asking for help they'd revealed a weakness. This was a pattern that went down a few times in my film career. I understood why people came to me—I was considered a legit hard man, not just a dude who played one—but the dynamic wasn't always comfortable. It was the same shit I faced on *American Me* all over again. I'd think, *Did you want to hire me because I'm an actor, or because I'm an ex-convict?*

Whatever my private concerns about how I was perceived, it was clear Hollywood casting agents saw me as a baddie. The following year I was hired to play Johnny 23 in *Con Air*, a serial rapist who is part of a group of convicts planning an escape by stealing a prison transport plane. *Con Air* was a macho fest from the start, both the film and the production. Nothing was said or done that didn't become a dick-measuring contest. Benny "The Jet" Urquidez, a world karate and kickboxing legend, was hanging around the set because he was training John Cusack at the time. Guys were always pulling pranks during production. One time it was raining and someone pulled on the tarp we were sitting under. Water got on me. I jumped up in a flash and said, "What the fuck?" Benny saw how pissed I was and pulled me away.

"These dudes don't get what our kind of anger is, Danny."

I got into some conversations with dudes on that job that always funneled to the same conclusion: "How do you think I would do in prison?" It's a strange, almost universal fascination of men. They don't get how messed up a question it is. First of all, anyone who would ever ask it is probably not going to do well in prison because you already know what they're scared of. Being molested. How would they do? Maybe if, like a lot of kids who were in juvie with me, they hit someone in the head with a bat or a chunk of concrete or stabbed them, they'd start to build a rep that might shield them from some of the violence. But you had to commit violence to avoid violence.

I knew what the actors were getting at, but it was foolish. People have this fantasy about "holding your mud," that if you stood up the first time anyone challenged you, you'd get to do unmolested time. It's bullshit. I knew a white kid that went in, got shit from some Mexicans, and fucked two of them up in his cell. The dude was bad. Two nights later they found him in his cell with his beanie on and his throat slit ear to ear. A pool of his blood on the tier was what alerted the guards. He did what he was supposed to do, what people on the outside think you have to do for people to leave you alone, and two Mexicans went in his cell and took his life. If you go in you have to go with your race, put in the work, and only then will you have some protection. Even then, you still have to fear your own guys. Prisons are breeding grounds for paranoia and insanity. All it takes is for one dude in your clique to say something—be it because of jealousy or suspicion. Once a rumor is whispered, true or not, you're already on the defensive, and a lot of times the penalty is death.

You've got to be really careful if you get involved with stupid shit like drugs and gambling, anything that could cause you to be in debt, because if you cause problems, you get regulated by your own crew. Or you pay protection and walk around the Yard like a bitch. For people who are recognizable and known when they go in, their only option is to pay for protection. I've seen pictures of famous guys in the joint with their "posses," but they are paying them one way or another.

Before my dad married, when I was living at my grandparents' house, I did everything with my aunts and cousins. The house had four bedrooms. Grandma and Grandpa slept in one; my dad and uncles Art, Rudy, Fred, and Gilbert shared a room; my aunt Carmen and her husband, Manuel, shared another; and the other eight of us—my aunts Margaret, Reyna, Lobby, Carmen's four daughters, Mary Carmen, Coke and Toni (the twins), and Salita, and I slept in a room with four beds at the end of a long hallway.

I was the youngest, and if you see pictures of me when I'm little, I'm always with girls—four here, five there, nine there. We did everything separately from the men, even meals. That's why I didn't know I could pee standing up until my uncle Gilbert told me. We played make-believe and dress-up and played with dolls and our dog, Blackie. We screamed, we laughed. What I remembered most, and missed in the male-dominated environments I was in later, was that there was no competition. If one of the girls could throw a rock harder, it was cool. No one questioned it. No one contested it.

Con Air, on the other hand, was like the streets and prisons where guys competed over who could hit harder, pee longer, do more push-ups, pull more chicks, even spit farther—men were playing the same dangerous game in the safety of a movie set. Nic Cage was cool as hell, though. As testosterone-driven as that set was, I made more friends on *Con Air* than almost any movie I'd ever been in—John Malkovich, Steve Buscemi, Ving Rhames, Jesse Borrego, Dave Chappelle, and my homie Emilio Rivera. Emilio really impressed me. He reminded me a lot of me, the way he came up, how he handled himself on set. And for the record, John Cusack is a legit kickboxing badass. *Con Air* ended up being a good flick, but sometimes playing sick dudes like Johnny 23 gets to me. I've seen too many of them in real life.

As far as working with big Hollywood stars, my next film took everything to the next level. *Heat* put me in with the big boys. I'd met the director, Michael Mann, a few years earlier when I was cast in *Drug Wars: The Camarena Story*, a miniseries about Enrique "Kiki" Camarena, an undercover DEA agent who was tortured and killed by the cartel in Guadalajara. I got to talking to Michael after doing a scene he complimented me on. I'll never forget; he had a reputation for being tough as nails, but he came up to my trailer after a scene where I verbally attack Treat Williams. Michael had told me to go after Treat hard on one take, and I did, and I think it took everyone by surprise. Michael knocked on my door and I could have sworn I was getting fired. Instead, he said, "Danny, that was an Emmy-worthy performance." I thought, *If scaring people is Emmy-worthy, I should have won a ton of them.*

I wasn't even hired on *Heat* to be an actor. Eddie Bunker and I were brought on as armed-robbery consultants. When production started, the first time Michael Mann saw me, he called me Gilbert.

Mann had shot *The Jericho Mile* ten years earlier in Folsom, but I never put it together that he was there at the same time my uncle Gilbert was.

I told Michael that I was Danny, Gilbert Trejo's nephew.

At first he looked confused, like he thought I was mistaken or he was seeing a ghost. Then a look of recognition washed over his face. He said, "Oh yeah, Danny. We did the Camarena miniseries together."

Michael said Gilbert had made it possible to complete filming on *The Jericho Mile*. To film in any working prison, Production needs the cooperation of the inmates. The Blacks and whites were on board, but the Mexicans weren't. Gilbert and some other Mexican shot-callers handled the negotiations and got the Mexicans to okay the flick. Gilbert even snagged himself SAG union days. I told Michael that Gilbert had passed. He was genuinely moved.

After we'd worked all that out, Michael said, "Danny, there's a part in this movie I think you'd be right for." At the time, the character's name was Vince or something similar; I don't think he was even Mexican. The script went through two revisions while I read for the part, but on my third try, Michael just handed me the script and said, "Danny, you have the part. I'm sorry, but I can't call this character anything but Gilbert Trejo." He said it almost apologetically, but to me it was the greatest honor.

Heat is a heist movie, one of the greatest, most thrilling heist movies of all time. It starred Val Kilmer, Robert De Niro, Al Pacino, Jon Voight, Tom Sizemore, Amy Brenneman, and Ashley Judd. On top of my part being named after Gilbert, Jon Voight's character was based on Eddie Bunker. The first day Jon went to set he brought a picture of Eddie into the makeup trailer and said, "Make me look like this." The end result was so good, every time I watch the movie, I think of Eddie.

Heat was the first time I felt in complete awe of the people I was working with. It was like I'd been painting houses for a long time and suddenly found myself in a Van Gogh. De Niro is a living legend, but he was so patient with me and taught me so much during our scenes. He's the kind of actor who puts the script down and works out the moments. It isn't the words with Robert De Niro, it's the space around them. When we were blocking out my death scene he said, "Danny, how do you think we should play this?"

I said, "Bob, what do you think?"

He said, "I think you are already dead and just holding on long enough to ask me to kill you." That angle made it so powerful.

In the scene I ask him, "Where's my Anna?" and he says, "Dead." I moan in a combination of pain and hope leaving my character's body. When Mann yelled "Cut" on the scene Bobby said, "Great job, Danny," and helped me off the floor.

When we were working, I watched Robert on set. He was always kind but conserved his energy for when it mattered. A shooting day can sometimes be seventeen hours. It's a lot and you have to give full energy to every take. Watching De Niro, Kilmer, and Voight, I learned a lot about how they saved it for when it mattered.

There's an unreality to movie sets that exists nowhere else in the world. There was a time (it's changing) when certain people, usually actors and directors, were allowed to get away with terrible behavior. I've seen actors say awful things to crew members, and you knew that if it happened anywhere else that grip or electrician would have fucked them up, but because it was on a set they didn't want the production to grind to a halt or to risk getting a bad reputation. I saw an actor once get in the face of a young wardrobe intern and make her cry. I said, "Lighten up."

He stood as if to challenge me, and I said, "You better think about what you're doing." He knew I meant business. I called Eddie and told him what happened. He said, "I get it, but before you kill him you should reach into your wallet and tear up your SAG card, because you'll be killing the star of the movie."

I told Eddie to pick me up, and while I was waiting, someone from Production came up to me. This never happens, but they offered to double my pay if I would stay and keep this actor in line. Looking back, it was a small price to pay to protect their investment.

Hollywood needs muscle, too.

*   *   *

When *Heat* wrapped, I gave Michael Mann a photo of Gilbert in the pen that was never supposed to be taken. It was definitely not one for the Feds—it was all the shot-callers. As far as I know, Michael has that picture of Gilbert hanging in his office to this day.

After *Heat* came out on VHS, I watched it with Maeve, Gilbert, and Danielle. The kids were still little, and even though I was right there with them, it was still hard for them to watch. It was the first time they'd seen me die on-screen. Gilbert was the only one who managed to stay on the couch. Danielle and Maeve had to leave the room. I went in Danielle's room to give her a hug. She held on to me like she wanted proof I was really there. My death scene in *Heat* felt real to her because she was so little, but it felt real to me, too. I was acting under my uncle's name, my son's name, dying with nothing left to live for. It was where my life had been headed and how it might have gone.

Chapter 26

MRS. FINLEY'S AMAZON

1996

Maeve and I weren't getting along, and by *not getting along* I mean we were explosively combative around the clock. We could be laughing, fighting, making love, and fighting again in the space of an hour. It was too much. It was never one thing, it was everything. I was on the outs with Maeve, and privately I felt like she had really pushed it past the point of no return with me. That's why I was particularly excited about jobs that required me to travel. In 1996 I filmed two movies in Manaus, Brazil. The first was a French flick called *Le Jaguar*. The second was *Anaconda* with Jon Voight, Jennifer Lopez, Ice Cube, and Eric Stoltz.

On *Le Jaguar* we were bouncing between Brazil, Venezuela, and Paris. The rain forest blew my mind. At breakfast the first morning in Venezuela, two huge, beautiful macaws were hanging around a huge open-air restaurant that was attached to the hotel we were staying in. They were smart as shit. One would fuck with you while the other stole your breakfast. I got another breakfast and the other bird fucked with me so the first one could steal my second breakfast. I tried to make friends with one by holding my hand out, and he gave me a side-eye look that said, *Where the fuck are you from? Do you see my beak? I will take your finger.* From then on, I'd get three bowls of oatmeal from the caterers—one for me and two for my new buddies.

We moved production to Brazil, and when the plane started accelerating for takeoff, a beautiful macaw kept pace with the plane as long as it could. I wondered if it was one of my pals from breakfast looking for one last bowl of oatmeal.

We filmed in a village about twenty miles from Manaus, the capital of Amazonia. Nestled in the heart of the rain forest, Manaus is the main city in the "lungs of the world." During the day we'd walk out to this jungle area where they'd built the set. Production gave me a rental car, and after work all the background people and I would go into Manaus and dance all night. I spent every day and night with the background people on that movie, all natives from Brazil. Their energy was so positive, warm, and disarming, but they were proud. The indigenous people of Manaus always said they were the only people who never made a treaty with the Portuguese and the Spanish, because while they'd conquered the coasts, they never made it that far up the Amazon.

Heading back to Canaima, Venezuela, to shoot additional village and jungle scenes, from the air I saw huge chunks of the rain forest missing because of logging. It looked like the earth had huge scars in it. The forestry person in me from my camp days was sad. Approaching Canaima, we flew over Angel Falls, the highest waterfall in the world. I'm not the biggest green crusader in the world, but God's marvels are breathtaking, and I said to somebody, "This must be where God comes to vacation."

In Venezuela, there had just been a coup. My guide and I were walking downtown and I happened to be wearing paratrooper boots. These five fifteen-year-old kids holding AKs started screaming at me, asking where I got my boots.

I wanted to play dumb, so I let the guide talk and I just kept saying, "Americano."

My guide told them, "He's an actor from America. He got them in America." They demanded a receipt. They wanted my boots so bad—they thought I'd gotten them on the black market.

I think Production was worried about how much socializing I was doing. When we had a week off filming and another client of Gloria's, Gil Birmingham, and Richard Duran (a fellow actor in the film) were taking advantage of it to travel, Production wouldn't let me go anywhere.

I said, "But Richard and Gil are going to Peru."

They said, "Because they'll stay with the tour or near the hotel. We've watched you. You go into the absolute worst neighborhoods in Manaus to party—even though it's sober partying. We'll pay you extra just to stay in your hotel. In fact, if you stay in your room, we'll pay you even more."

During the filming of *Le Jaguar*, I went to Paris for a wardrobe fitting—all the way to Paris to be outfitted as a tribesman in a loincloth. Movie budgets! So I flew to Paris, and as soon as I got there I found a meeting. I introduced myself as Danny from Los Angeles. Everyone was speaking French, so I didn't know what they were saying, but it was cool, because even if I don't speak the language, the language of recovery is something I recognize anywhere.

Afterward, a guy came up and said he was from LA. He asked me to coffee. Over Marlboros, he told me he had married a Frenchwoman. He said he took her back to the United States on their honeymoon, and when it was time to go home, she said, "Thanks for the citizenship, I'm staying." He preferred Paris, so he split. The last thing he said to her was, "Thanks for the citizenship!"

Because he spoke French and English, he was kind enough to show me around, so the next day he met me at my hotel and we walked around past the Louvre and other sights, and it was amazing, and then we were walking along the Seine when I saw this huge cathedral. I knew exactly what it was, but I was shocked because I hadn't put it together that Notre Dame was in Paris. For some reason I always thought it was in Rome.

The square was completely empty and there was a mist in the air. It reminded me of the first night I stepped into the Yard in San Quentin. But instead of imposing, the cathedral was beautiful, holy, calming, the opposite of the Right Now. It was the Forever. I almost fell to my knees. I came so close to crying, my friend asked me what was up. I didn't want to get into all those months spent in the hole, reliving *The Hunchback of Notre Dame*. I just said it meant a lot to me. He could see how much I was moved, so he was moved. Before we left, I said, "Sanctuary!" channeling Quasimodo, and we laughed.

I got back to my hotel and called Eddie Bunker. His wife told me Eddie was in Paris shooting a flick called *Chameleon* with Seymour Cassel. We were walking under a bridge near the Seine at night when I had to piss. I was pissing up against a granite wall and I said, "Hey, Eddie, doesn't this wall remind you of Folsom?"

He said, "Mexican, you're in Paris. Can you forget about Folsom for just a minute?"

School and I hadn't always gotten along too well, but later that year, when I was shooting *Anaconda*, I couldn't help remembering my fourth-grade teacher at Elysian Heights Elementary, Mrs. Finley. Mrs. Finley wore colorful dresses and big wooden bracelets that clanked together. She was fine as hell and liked me a lot.

Mrs. Finley was obsessed with the Amazon River. She taught us that the Rio Negro pulls sediment from the tributaries, and that giant water lilies called *Victoria amazonica* grow long stalks when the river is high, and the lilies stay high above the water when the river recedes. She said her bracelets were from the Yanomami tribe, who live in the rain forest.

We'd yell, *Ya no, Mami*, because it sounded like Spanish slang for "Stop it, Mommy!" She'd laugh and we'd laugh with her, but then Mrs. Finley would raise her arms and say, "Children, the stars in the night sky above the Amazon are overwhelming! Overwhelming, I tell you!" Then she'd shake her arms so her bracelets knocked together.

We asked if she'd ever been to the Amazon, and she said no.

I couldn't believe she talked about it so intimately, like she had lived there. "If you've never been there, how can you talk about it like you do?"

She said, "I just know."

Of all the teachers I ever had, the only one I paid attention to was Mrs. Finley. She taught me that if you imagined with intense focus, you could truly believe you were somewhere else. It's a skill that had proven valuable in prison.

Early into filming *Anaconda*, we were chugging in a huge old wooden ship up the Rio Negro when we saw water lilies the size of Volkswagen Beetles sticking out of the river on giant stalks. They looked like something from Dr. Seuss.

Ice Cube tripped out. He said, "What are those?"

I said they were called *Victoria* something and grew with the rise and fall of the river, and when the river receded, they stuck out of the water, waiting for the river to rise again.

A few minutes later, someone said something about the color of the water and I said, "That's why it's called the Rio Negro, 'Black River.' The water from the tributaries in the mountains is black with sediment. It mixes with the water coming from the ocean."

Everyone was looking at me like *How the fuck do you know that?*

Ice Cube said, "Damn, Danny, I thought you were supposed to be a gangster."

I said, "When I was doing time, I did a lot of reading, holmes, to make up for my lack of education."

I was lying. I couldn't tell him about Mrs. Finley.

A few weeks later, I had to shoot a scene in which I get eaten by the giant anaconda. While the rest of the cast was back at the hotel, I was alone with the director and the crew.

Chugging home down the Rio Negro, I stood at the ship's bow. The crew was in the stern trying to sleep. I looked up, and I'd never seen so many stars in my life. There were layers upon layers of thousands upon thousands of stars. I started laughing. I laughed so hard I woke everyone up. The director said, "Danny, what's so funny?"

I threw my hands in the air just like Mrs. Finley and yelled, "The stars in the night sky above the Amazon are overwhelming!" I laughed even harder. "Wherever you are, Mrs. Finley, you were right!"

Two nights later, Jennifer Lopez showed up to work wearing wooden bracelets she said were given to her as a present.

I said, "They're from the Yanomami tribe."

She looked shocked. "How did you know?"

"Mrs. Finley."

Ice Cube laughed. "You're a trip, Trejo."

When I got back to the hotel that night, I called Maeve and the kids and told them I wished they were there and that I wanted them to see the stars in the night sky above the Amazon. I was learning so much through travel, even though I hadn't had the chance until now. I wanted my kids to know the beauty of the world and different cultures.

Chapter 27

DOMESTIC LIFE

1996

When I came back from trips, I always brought the kids presents. In Brazil, I picked up a blow dart for Danny Boy that the indigenous people used to kill frogs. Maeve said, "Are you crazy?" She held up a dart. "Can't you picture one of these sticking out of Gilbert's eyes?"

Maeve finally got tired of me fucking around, tired of us fighting, tired of me threatening to move out, tired of me telling her to move out. I think she figured every time I moved out, there was the option of me coming back. So she left.

It was harder than I thought. I was a single dad again. And on top of everything, I lost my pad in Venice. I got into beef with the owner of the building, a tough old Irish American broad from Chicago or Boston or one of those places. We butted heads and I was asked to leave.

At least Maeve was kind enough to find me an apartment in Santa Monica near where our kids were going to school. I missed Maeve. I'd cook the kids' breakfast, shaking cans, making noise, throwing flour around, pretending I was a master chef, then come out of the kitchen with a perfect stack of straight-from-the-box pancakes.

I knew I didn't want to be like my dad, and I'd been out of prison long enough to see some good families and to watch how they worked. Families that were shaped around love, not rage. Dads who weren't afraid to say "I love you" to their kids.

I didn't have specific goals or ambitions for my kids, except that, more than anything, I wanted them to feel loved. My dad got along great with my cousins and the other kids in the neighborhood, but not me. He acted like there was something wrong with me, and he couldn't give me attention or show me affection. He never told me he loved me. So I never paid much attention to other kids when mine were around. I told them I loved them in private and in front of people. Danielle would kiss me. I'd kiss the boys. The boys hated it, but I'd do it anyway.

Gilbert was doing T-ball, and the kid was no Babe Ruth. The whole team, in fact, was made up of the leftovers of the T-ball draft. We were like the real-life Bad News Bears. I was helping to coach, and every week I saw dads yelling at their kids. But I told the kids on my team, "Don't worry, I don't care if you hit it or not. Get an out. Just try." That team didn't win a single game all season, but they tried. We'd do a call-and-response where I'd ask them, "What's the only failure in life?" and they'd all answer, "Not trying, Mr. Trejo!"

When Danny Boy was down visiting from his mom's in Lompoc, I'd take the kids to the Cheesecake Factory in Marina del Rey. I'd pile Danny Boy, Gilbert, and Danielle in the car, and Danielle would look at me and say, "Daddy," then she'd make an old-person face and hold her hands out. "My purse!" She'd never go anywhere without a purse. If you see any pictures of Danielle starting from age four, she always has a purse. I'd shut off the car, go upstairs, grab a purse, run back down, and she'd look at it and say, "Does this purse match my shoes?" She said it so matter-of-factly, I almost wanted to laugh, but the purse-shoe color coordination was no joking matter to Danielle. I'd take her back up to the apartment with me and have her pick out a purse that matched her shoes. Danielle taught me a lot of things, but most of all, she taught me patience.

When Danny Boy and Gilbert would roughhouse, Danielle and I would be sitting on the couch, eating snacks, and she'd say, "Boys stink!"

I'd say, "You're right, boys do stink."

One time she said, "It's stupid to hurt somebody else for no reason." Out of the mouths of babes. The way I grew up there was a certain toughness I had to have to survive—I was tough at the drop of a hat. In the joint—even in juvie—I lost my ability to argue or get angry. I would go straight to rage. The best defense you can have at your disposal is that rage, because with it you can kill someone if necessary. When I got out of prison and was taking clients to court, I was amazed to see attorneys arguing. I kept waiting for one of them to hit the other. Where I'd come from, the bottom line to every argument was a murder. I wanted my kids to be able to defend themselves— even Danielle learned to box—but I wanted them to see fighting as a last resort.

The boys' roughhousing was a kind of play I understood. Both my sons could fight. They had it in them the way all Trejo men did. But Gilbert had an additional weapon. I'd stopped arguing with Gilbert when he was five years old because he was winning every argument we had. He was such a master manipulator of language that part of me hoped that instead of being a defendant someday in the future, he'd be a high-priced lawyer. Sitting with Danielle on the couch, throwing popcorn at Danny Boy and Gilbert tussling on the floor, I wished all three kids could stay like that forever—in a world where the falls were cushioned by thick carpet and taunts were brushed aside over a bowl of popcorn.

Even though we were farther away from the beach than we were in Venice, we'd still walk down to the beach and eat at the Sidewalk Café. There was a playground there, built on sand, where Gilbert lost every Ninja Turtle toy known to man. That park was a black hole for toys. Sometimes I'd work out at Muscle Beach while the kids hung on to the fence and watched.

Venice was a community where people could fly their freak flags. There were fire-eaters; a guy who juggled chain saws. Harry Perry, a roller-skating guitarist. They were all my friends and would keep an eye on the kids for me if needed.

It was my friends from the Venice boardwalk community I turned to when I needed help. When Danny Boy was little, I'd leave him with break-dancer kids. Danny Boy would get on a piece of linoleum and spin, making money from the crowd. Another only-in-Venice-Beach babysitter was Louis Offer, a guy with crazy tats and red hair styled in devil's horns who was always down on the boardwalk with his iguana. We all loved Louis. He would have taken a bullet for my kids.

When Gilbert was six or seven, my friend Eric Feigin was in a motorcycle accident and didn't have a place to stay, so I moved him in to help with my kids. He'd take my kids to the witch store, where there were spell candles they could smell and crystals and stuff like that. The folks I had babysit my kids were never of the generic variety.

We often walked down to the beach with Dennis Hopper and his son. They only lived a couple blocks away from us; his son Henry and Danielle were about the same age, and Henry loved Gilbert.

I'd been close friends with Dennis for a few years by then. We met when my old girlfriend Connie—the same Connie that Danny Boy told Maeve never made him pick up his toys—brought Dennis to a meeting to hear me speak. He was newly sober and Connie and her friend Monica thought he'd get something out of hearing my story.

We hit it off right off the bat.

Dennis said, "Danny, if you can stay clean, anybody can do it!"

I laughed and said, "That seems to be the general consensus around here."

From that day on, we were inseparable. Dennis lived in Venice in two Quonset huts joined by a cross bridge. We did everything together—hit meetings, went to art openings, and watched his beloved LA Clippers' games. Dennis always drove, which worked for me, because he had a bitchin' Jaguar. Dennis loved basketball. I used to tease him, "Dennis, we're short guys—we don't like basketball." He'd say, "Danny, it's not a tall guys' game. Muggsy Bogues, Spud Webb—they are little, but they can hoop."

Most of the time, we'd meet at the Venice Café; Dennis would walk over to pick me up and we'd eat and walk the boardwalk with the kids if they were around. Dennis always walked fast so that people wouldn't stop him. I walk slowly and say, "What's up?" but that wasn't Dennis. On the boardwalk, if someone pressed Dennis for too much small talk, he'd get short with them. They didn't know if he was going to bite their tongue off or give an ass whupping. When he spoke to people, they'd think, *Is he furious? Is he joking? What was hilarious to me was I knew he was both.

Every day with Dennis was an acting lesson. He'd say, "Danny, if you drink a glass of water in a scene, *drink the water!* If you are walking across a room, *just walk across the room!*" He knocked performance out of performance—self-awareness in actors drove him crazy. "Just do your thing and don't worry about the cameras," he'd say. "If the director likes what you're doing, he'll shoot it again to make sure he's got it. And if you know you gave a good take and he asks if you want another take, say, 'No, you got it!'" He was a perfectionist, but he trusted that the director and the camerapeople knew their jobs.

Dennis liked having me and George around so much, he gave us parts in a movie called *Doublecrossed: The Barry Seal Story* that he was shooting in Puerto Rico. San Juan was beautiful. For me and George, it was like a paid vacation. We'd hang out at the beach and all these women would just flock to George. He was over seventy, but he still had his magnetism and silver-fox Portuguese looks. A lot of the women worked in the sex industry with the state of the economy being so bad in Puerto Rico in 1991. They begged George to take them back to San Francisco and put them to work.

I turned to George and said, "What do you think?"

He said, "Danny, are you crazy? I'm too old to be kicking some broad in the ass at one in the morning to go hit the street."

I nodded, then said, "What about ten p.m.?"

He laughed. Dennis Hopper had just returned from the day's shooting. He saw all these women around George and said, "What do you got, old man? What do you got? I mean, *what do you got*?"

Maeve and I finally split up for good. Zodiacally speaking, we were earth signs: dirt and water. Together we made mud. We fought so much. My son Gilbert says he learned to talk in full sentences before he was one because he was trying to referee our screaming matches. Maeve remembers Gilbert being four or five and yelling, "What is wrong with you people?" Sometimes, to be more diplomatic, he would say, "Dad, why don't you move downstairs? There's an open apartment."

When things were good, we'd go to the beach, play in the water, and get ice cream. When I think back on those days, that's what I remember. The kids started school and Maeve would make me get off my ass and be part of PTA nights and attend parent-teacher meetings. She was the one who was hell-bent on doing things the right way. Maeve was the cook, the shopper, the cleaner, the supermother. She was amazing at all those things. Because she was a vegetarian, we didn't go out to eat much, but we all liked eating at home better. Besides, I was out hustling work, or working weird hours, or hanging with my friends at meetings and going for coffee with newcomers afterward.

Maeve arranged with a photographer friend (I'll call him K to protect the innocent) to take a family portrait. Unknown to Maeve, K ran an illegal strip club out of his studio. Some of the biggest porn stars in the world used to dance there. I'd been there one night with George—now bear in mind this was a pimp who'd done six stints in San Quentin and had seen every type of human depravity—and that night at K's, George said, "Danny, can you feel that?"

I said, "What?"

"I feel the flames of hell licking at my feet."

When Maeve told me she'd arranged for K to photograph us, I called him and asked, "Did you tell Maeve we'd be doing a portrait at your studio?"

He said, "Danny, don't worry. That bad shit doesn't happen in the studio during the day!"

The portrait was going to happen. Maeve had bought Gilbert, Danny Boy, and me black pants, white shirts, and red ties. She got special dresses for herself and Danielle. We were dressed up nice, but we fought the whole time. In the photo, you can see what a shit show we were. The kids are crying and Maeve's so angry she's barely keeping it together. She's thinking, *I tied these ties! I bought these clothes!* She was always trying to give us experiences that "normal" families had, but I just couldn't do it. I could never just be normal.

One fight we had was around Christmas in 1989, when Gilbert was a baby. Compared to other arguments we'd had, it wasn't even that bad. George and I came home but planned to go right back out. Maeve said, "You were going to stay with the kids tonight." I guess she had something planned that I'd forgotten.

"But we'll be right back," I said.

Maeve threw the presents at me and we started jawing back and forth. Apparently, some neighbors heard the yelling and called the cops. California had just passed a mandatory arrest law that said if the cops were called for a domestic violence report, someone had to go to jail.

The cops pulled up when George and I were getting in his car. They said someone had called the police about yelling in apartment 22. We all walked back up to the apartment. The cops asked Maeve if she was alright.

"Yes," she said. "What's up?"

He repeated what he'd said—that someone had called about a disturbance in our apartment. We both said everything was fine, but he said, "Someone's got to go to jail. Who's it going to be?"

It sure as hell wasn't going to be Maeve; she'd done nothing wrong. So I said, "I'll go."

Maeve was distraught. "But we were just arguing!" she exclaimed.

An hour later, Eddie Bunker and George bailed me out and we went back home. Maeve was waiting up and made us something to eat.

It was a minor hassle at the time, but a bigger one long-term. Getting arrested goes on your jacket. That arrest was probably the one that caused me the greatest legal hassles when it came to working abroad. I'm not saying Maeve and I were right to argue, and I am in no way against police intervention when there is a need, but this was what it was, and what it was was an argument.

Maeve and I couldn't live together, but we couldn't be apart. We had been splitting up for ten years since we'd met in early 1986. I wasn't sweating it. I already had another old lady. Maeve was the one who called it. Jhonnie Harris said, "Danny, it doesn't matter who ends it, just that it ends." Later Maeve would tell me when she left she felt like she was setting me free. I made one last play for her, and she shut me down. I'd sent her to Hawaii with a couple of girlfriends, and somehow I got jealous because a dude drove them to the airport at the end of their trip. I had found yet another thing to be angry and jealous about, and Maeve was just done with it. I don't blame her.

By late April of 1997 we were done and I was indeed free, but it wasn't for long. I showed up less than a month later, shirtless, to pick up the children with another woman's name tattooed on my chest just to make her jealous.

I was fifty-three acting like I was seventeen. A few months after that, Maeve married someone else to get back at me, so I married someone to get back at her.

Chapter 28

HIGHS AND LOWS

1997

I met Debbie Shreve at a meeting. I don't go to bars and I don't go out with anyone who drinks. Debbie was different from any woman I'd gone with before. She didn't need me to save her, and I couldn't make her dependent on me financially. Debbie drove a Mercedes, made lots of money, and was extremely careful with it. In my relationships, I'd always been the breadwinner; this was a new dynamic that felt different. In a way I thought I was making a more adult choice.

Debbie was hell-bent on taking the street out of me. For years I'd carried a wad of cash in my pocket wrapped in a rubber band, making sure I had the biggest bills on the outside. When Debbie first saw that, she said, "Danny, poor people carry three thousand dollars in a rubber band. Poor people or dealers." I'd been both.

Things were good at first. We enjoyed each other's company. But a few years into our relationship, things started to turn. We had moved from Winnetka to a huge house near Chatsworth that was continuously getting remodeled and landscaped. It seemed a bit much, but I liked the kind of home Debbie was building for us. We filled it with antiques from Mexico, wrought-iron railing, and Mexican tile and carpets. Debbie owned a lot of rental properties when I met her, and together we bought more. Whenever I finished a job, I sent my work checks to our accountant and she put that money into acquiring new houses and apartments. Whatever she told me to do, I did.

A lot of the conflict we had was over my kids. Debbie and I couldn't have children. We tried, but we couldn't. I was in my mid-fifties. I had my children and didn't really want more anyway. Gilbert and Danielle came to stay with us every other weekend, but it soon became a problem. My kids were struggling. I don't know if they were cursed with the genes of addicts, or whether they made the wrong friends at the wrong time, or if the problem was that, unlike Danny Boy, Maeve and I had never managed to move them out of Venice. We hoped it wouldn't happen, but it did. They took to drugs at a very young age, just like I did.

Debbie wasn't their mom, and when she tried to rein them in, they didn't necessarily make things easy on her. She'd place them on a regimen of chores around the house and control their spending. I'd tell her to take it easy—I only had them for a limited amount of time. She'd say, "Danny, you are going to spoil them rotten if you don't come down on them and have them pull their weight."

"Pull their weight? Debbie, they're twelve and ten. They only see us every other weekend. They want to see me. We miss each other."

She did have a point, though. I had my own style of parenting, and Diana wasn't always a fan of it, either. When Danny Boy was around sixteen, he and a friend got busted in Lompoc for smoking weed. The cops got him and wanted him to tell them who the other kids were, but he refused.

Diana called and was yelling at me, saying, "Talk to him like a parent, not his best buddy."

I wasn't going to lay anything heavy on Danny Boy. Like I always say, sometimes *Let's go get pancakes* has more value than a lecture. But I couldn't take him out for pancakes, so I got on the phone and said, "I'm told I have to talk to you like a father right now, like a parent. So I don't ever want to catch you running with scissors and if all your friends jumped off a bridge, would you jump off it, too?"

He started laughing and Diana got back on the phone, furious. "What are you doing? Do you think this is a joke? What did you say?"

I said, "I told him I don't ever want to catch him running with scissors."

"You're a fucking idiot!" she exclaimed. But even she had to laugh.

I said, "Hey, when I was sixteen, I was busted for armed robbery. Who the fuck are we? You're Debby Boone all of a sudden? You just got out of the joint!"

Maybe I was too easy on all my kids, and the line between love and enabling became deeply obscured. Danny Boy was smoking weed, but for him, weed was enough. When Gilbert and Danielle started smoking weed and drinking, I prayed they wouldn't graduate to harder drugs. Maeve's and my response was to tell them they had to go to twelve-step meetings. They'd already been to so many recovery meetings as kids that Gilbert says that when he first smoked grass at age nine, he felt like he'd slipped, like he'd had nine years clean and now he'd blown it. I never thought of it this way, but later they told me they associated meetings with punishment.

Things started to slide. Their grades went to shit. I'm sure this is a story a lot of parents can relate to. You don't know if it's a phase and if it will pass or which way it will break, right or left. When I introduced my friend Timmy Sanchez to grass, he got sick and never used drugs again, while I was off to the races. For some kids, weed is a gateway drug. For others, it's just weed. But if their mother and father are addicts, there's a good chance they might be, too.

Unlike me, Gilbert and Danielle weren't fueled by rage. I got a thrill off scaring people; Gilbert and Danielle didn't. I'd raised them with a kind of love I'd never been given, and I'd hoped that would break the cycle, but here we were. Whatever the reasons, whether genetic, or a chaotic home life, or a combination of the two, they just took to it. Gilbert, who'd always been good at arguing, started using his skills to manipulate, triangulate, and gaslight in order to get high.

It may have looked like I wasn't dealing with the problem, but the way I saw it, I was fighting for time to figure out what play to make. Debbie's anger at me for enabling them was well placed, but it didn't sit well with me. I told an old friend of mine what was going on and he asked, "Do you two ever laugh anymore?"

I had to stretch my mind back to remember the last time we had. "Not really."

"Love has to be for fun and for free, Dan. Not an emotional hostage situation."

Maeve and I had fought, but we laughed just as much. There was passion in our life together. From the moment Maeve moved in—and she was the one who insisted Danny Boy be with us—we became a family. We made that tiny apartment in Venice a home. Before long it was five of us, and it never felt cramped. When we weren't yelling at each other, we had big laughs. I missed that.

But as I got older, I started to identify something messed up in me. I wanted my own space, but I didn't want to be alone. In the early days of our relationship, Debbie wanted to come everywhere with me for work, but since her own businesses suffered while she was away, she decided she had to stay home. That was cool by me, I liked the alone time, but Debbie started to guilt me about having to leave town and travel for work. Maybe *guilt* is too strong a word, but it became an issue. Like Maeve or any of my exes could tell you, I didn't like having to run my schedule past anybody. But my work travel was the least of our problems; the bigger issue was I fell sick with hepatitis C. The wreckage of my past, a past that included sharing needles and using toilet water to fix, had reared its ugly head.

It started after I wrapped *Reindeer Games* in Canada in 1999. Even though I dragged my ass to Austin to start *Spy Kids* in 2000, I still had a blast. On that film, I worked with two of the most talented kids I've ever known—Alexa Vega and Daryl Sabara. While we were filming there was a "bad word" jar by the sound cart. Every time an adult said a bad word, they had to put a dollar in the jar. I think the kids made as much money from the bad word jar as they did from their Screen Actors Guild salaries.

Carla Gugino and Antonio Banderas played their parents, Ingrid and Gregorio Cortez, spies who work for the Organization of Super Spies. Cheech Marin played their uncle, and I played Antonio's estranged brother, Isador "Machete" Cortez, who is an inventor of spy gadgets, like Q in the James Bond films.

Robert Rodriguez's films were like family reunions—I'd worked with Antonio and Cheech on *Desperado* and *From Dusk Till Dawn*. Antonio Banderas is just special. I joked if I looked like him, I'd just stay home all day and take pictures of myself. Cheech laughed at that one. He's younger than I am, but he grew up in the Valley and knew of me and my uncle Gilbert growing up. Cheech went to a private high school, Bishop Alemany, and I ribbed him about it.

"We used to take the Alemany kids' lunch money."

He laughed. "I know!"

I stretched my mind to remember if he was one of the kids we robbed.

After Alexa and Daryl, I found myself working with another brilliant young actor. I finished *Spy Kids* and went to work on *Bubble Boy*, a film starring Jake Gyllenhaal. I love how movie sets are a place where people anywhere from ages six to ninety become professional peers. In the film, I played a biker. But by the time I got to *Bubble Boy*, my illness had progressed. I was pale, I was weak. We went to the doctor, and he insisted I go on a cycle of interferon and Pegatron that made me as sick as a dog. If the hep C wasn't going to kill me, I thought the cure might. Debbie was there for me, and I will forever be grateful, but facing my own mortality made our disputes seem more like petty bullshit. My biggest fears were whether I could still work and if I could keep people in Hollywood from finding out about my illness. I was sure they'd express concern and send well-wishes, but there's something that happens in Hollywood when you get the label "damaged goods." And it was important to keep working, because who would take care of the children and Maeve? I didn't think Debbie could or would.

Every morning I'd inject myself with the drugs and go to work. I'd sweat, I'd puke. People noticed I'd lost weight. I didn't say, "Oh, yeah, it's the interferon and the Pegatron for my hep C." I remember being so out of it that I would first read the lines I was supposed to have memorized on the morning I was supposed to go out and perform them. I felt like I was letting people down. I was struggling. And when I got home and we got into shit about money, or kids, or whatever, it became too much.

Because of my role in *Spy Kids*, in September 2002 I was invited to the grand opening of the International Spy Museum in Washington, DC. Debbie's phone rang while we were taking the tour, so she stepped away to accept the call. When she rejoined us, she had tears in her eyes. "Danny," she said. "That was the doctor. He said you're completely clear of hepatitis C. You're cured."

After *Spy Kids* had wrapped and I was free of hep C, I started really enjoying life. Not that I don't always love my life and live it as fully and joyously as I can, but being that sick took a lot out of my soul. I feel like God kind of said, "You stayed grateful, you kept trying, now you can enjoy things a bit."

And with the release of *Spy Kids* I noticed a big shift in how people reacted to me on the streets. In the same way *Heat*, *Desperado*, and *Blood In, Blood Out* made me instantly recognizable with adults, *Spy Kids* did the same with kids.

Some years later I was driving in a van in South Africa and gangs of kids started chasing us. I was confused by what was happening and asked the driver what was going on. He said, "You are the uncle from *Spy Kids*; the children know this."

Wow, I thought, *I'm an international star to the children. What a cool responsibility to carry*. Overnight, with *Spy Kids*, I'd gone from being the bad guy, a Mexican stereotype, to someone kids could look up to. Over the years, I've probably heard, "Look, Mommy, it's the man from *Spy Kids*" in forty different languages.

The best part about playing Uncle Machete in *Spy Kids* was that the character was much closer to who I actually was than any of the violent gangster roles I had been playing. That gangster part of me had been dead since the late 60s.

While I was hitting a career high, Gilbert was sinking deeper into drugs. One time at the house Debbie and I shared on Hiawatha, I caught him coming out of the bathroom deeply high. I could tell it wasn't weed; I found out later it was cocaine. I grabbed him and shook him. I said, "I will break every bone in your body!"

It was exactly what my father had said to me when I was seven and he thought I had lied to him about my mom and Uncle David. And the weirdest thing of all was I had his smell. When my father got really angry, he'd get this smell—it wasn't body odor, it was a musk that was some kind of mixture of anger and fear. I was feeling both of those things in that moment.

I put him down and wandered outside and sat on the curb. It was awful to see Gilbert so messed up at so young an age, even though he was older than I was when I tried heroin. I was too hurt and too scared to cry. I went back inside and I said, "You know what, Gilbert? I will never grab you like that again, but you can't use drugs in this house." Even as I said them, the words felt empty. I couldn't control him. I knew the ride was starting.

At the same time as Gilbert's situation escalated, things with Debbie were coming to a head. She was concerned about someone I was starting to do business with, and we fought about it constantly. Turns out she was on point about that one, but I couldn't see it at the time.

And then Gilbert got busted. He had moved out of Maeve's, and when he wasn't with me on the odd weekend, he was living with a friend in Venice. Maeve tried to get him out of there, but he wouldn't listen. Then Gilbert caught a court case for a tagging charge, and I told him I would go to court with him. Maeve met us there. I told her we had everything under control, but she insisted on going in with us. In the courtroom, she told the judge that Gilbert was out of control and explained that she'd worked out a placement for him in a minimum-security lockdown rehab in Utah. The judge agreed. Of course Gilbert was furious. I was mad, too. But it was the right move. Gilbert finally got a chance at being clean for the first time in a few years.

Meanwhile, Debbie and I weren't getting along. When I came across a '38 Chevy my friend Ronnie Hernandez wanted to sell, I fell in love with it the second I sat inside it. It was fifteen thousand dollars, but Ronnie said they would give it to me for eleven. Debbie said we didn't have the money, that things were too tight. I was working so much I couldn't understand why we couldn't afford it. I'd made it through the interferon nightmare and I wanted to enjoy my life a bit. We had eight rental properties, for Christ's sake.

I dropped the issue, but a couple of weeks later Ronnie hit me up and said Debbie called him wanting to buy the Chevy on the down low. She said she wanted to give it to me as a present but insisted on keeping it in her name. It was a sneaky move, and an unnecessary one. Plus, if things were really that tight, how did she find the money to buy the car? It put me in a spot where if I said, "That was weird. Why'd you have to make it weird?" she could say, "I was just doing it for you." But I didn't feel like it was for me. It was about controlling the whole deal. Not just that car; she wanted everything in her name. We bought four houses together that were all in her name. My old truck was in her name. The only thing she had in my name was her name.

I hated feeling controlled, which is fucked up and ironic because I was a controlling asshole in all my past relationships. I joke that Debbie got me to get back for the way I'd gotten my exes. She just did it through finances. I'd hurt my first wife, Laura; the first Debbie, the beautiful cartoonist; and Joanne, that little firecracker I'd drop off at Sybil Brand Institute who helped raise Gilbert. I was jealous and I was a cheater. Now it was coming back on me. It was karma, the word I first heard after I pissed on that dude after kicking his ass in that bar. I deserved it, but karma's still a bitch.

My relationship with Debbie was the only one I was faithful in. I don't necessarily know why, maybe I just wanted to prove to others and myself that I could be. I was no angel, not even close, but I knew in my soul that way of living wasn't right. The deception was exhausting, not thrilling. There was no joy in hurting people who loved and trusted me with their hearts and souls. The old me, the one who didn't care if my first wife Laura's feelings were hurt, or Debbie's, or Joanne's, finally saw how destructive that kind of behavior is. And it wasn't just hurting them, it was hurting me, too. When you live a lie, your soul lets you know. For me, an alcoholic and addict, it starts whispering, *You need to take something to take the edge off this pain.* That's when I knew I had to get right. I didn't salvage our relationship, but I vowed to be a more honorable person whether I was in one or not.

One of the bright spots of that year was working on a film with Maggie Gyllenhaal called *Sherrybaby*. The film was written and directed by a woman named Laurie Collyer, and I don't mean to generalize, but I got the same kind of feeling working with Laurie that I had working with Allison Anders on *Mi Vida Loca*. Both of those women brought a beautiful understanding and perspective in their films about gritty subjects.

In *Sherrybaby*, Maggie plays a woman who's just gotten out of prison and is struggling to maintain sobriety. Having been used and abused by men in power (parole officers especially) and discarded by her family, she gets into a relationship with an older man she meets in Alcoholics Anonymous named Dean Walker, played by me. Nothing about *Sherrybaby* felt alien to me, from the real-to-life dialogue in the meetings to the difficulty of post-prison life I knew from my own experience. While *Heat* put me in with the Academy Award–winning big boys, *Sherrybaby* let me be me. I talked the way I talk in real life, I listened the way I listen. I was really, for the first time, inhabiting a role.

While working on *Sherrybaby* in New Jersey provided a good distraction from the problems I was experiencing in my marriage with Debbie, by late 2005 I'd had too much and I left, leaving behind pretty much everything I owned. First, I tried living with my son Gilbert in Venice. I lived in a small apartment with my dogs and teenagers who had to sneak around the corner to drink beer or get high because I was there. I was relieved as hell to be out of that house in Chatsworth, but it was clear living on my kid's couch wasn't going to work, so I rented a bigger apartment with space for Gilbert, his friend Jimmy, and me. Then it became clear that Gilbert really didn't want his old man living with him at all.

I didn't admit it to myself at the time, but Gilbert not wanting to live with me was a real gut punch. I was so used to all three of my kids needing their daddy, and while they could be in trouble or up to no good, they usually still wanted me in their corner. It was hard for me to accept that not only was Gilbert a young man, but he was a young man who actively did not want his pops around. Thankfully, Danielle didn't feel the same way, so I moved in with her in Marina del Rey.

Whether she ran away or got kicked out is up for debate, but when Danielle was fifteen, she left Maeve's. I went to pick her up and she had everything she owned in black trash bags. She tossed them in my Range Rover and said, "Dad, I need to take my dog."

I said, "There's no way we're taking a dog," but then Cash jumped up on the trash bags and looked at me. Danielle knew I could never say no to a dog.

When Danielle moved in with me, she was done with school. She had gone to Santa Monica High and then Venice High and back to Santa Monica. But when they told her she only had enough credits to be in tenth grade, not eleventh, where she thought she belonged, she decided she'd had enough.

She asked me to sign her out of school and allow her to drop out. I was okay with it, but Maeve and I had huge fights about it. All Maeve wanted was to see her kids graduate from high school. I screamed at Maeve, "What can I tell you? She doesn't want to fucking go!"

"She has to go!"

I said, "Maeve, I got my high school diploma for a can of Bugler tobacco in Soledad and I'm alright." (That was true. I got a diploma with a good GPA from a real high school for a can of tobacco.)

The three of us living together—Danielle, Cash, and me—was bizarre, but great. I hadn't lived with Danielle since she was a little girl, and now she was a young woman. But Danielle was like no woman I'd ever dealt with in my life. She wasn't afraid of me. She wasn't worried about hurting my feelings. I couldn't bully Danielle or control her by withholding emotion. And even though she was a teenager, Danielle was unabashedly a woman. Her friends would come by and start talking girl stuff about their periods and boys just to make me uncomfortable. I'd bang my ears and scream, "I can't hear you!" and they'd yell, "Period! Tampax!"

One night, Danielle was going out with her boyfriend wearing a black bra and a wifebeater and I said, "You can't go out like that." I was showing deep restraint by not saying what I really wanted to say.

But Danielle pushed. "What do you mean?"

"It's trampy," I said.

Danielle just said, "No it's not. It's cute! I was about to say something, but she shot me a look that said, *Shut it*, and *Don't you dare*, and *This is what women wear now, Dad, and you're going to have to get used to it.*

In an instant, Danielle made me rethink how I thought about and spoke to women. She dragged my double-standard male-chauvinist shit into the middle of the room and shined a spotlight on it. I realized that when I said things like that about women, I was saying them about her. I liked it when women were sexy, but not if it was my wife or my daughter. I might see a woman wearing something that made me say, "Oh, I like that," but if we ended up going together, I made sure as hell she didn't wear that same outfit again.

It was as unfair as it sounds, but at sixty-two years of age it was time for the double standards I held to die. It was Danielle who started cracking that open. She helped me see all the women in my life in a different light, with their own private intellectual and sexual lives. And that included my mom, who had tried to find comfort outside her marriage. I was beginning, in a way, to endow women with the humanity that they always deserved. The full spectrum. Everything I'd allowed myself to have.

Later, when Danielle's boyfriend saw her in the wifebeater-and-black-bra outfit, he said, "You have to go back and change."

Danielle said, "My own dad doesn't make me change."

He said, "Maybe he should," and grabbed Danielle's shoulder, so she whipped around and socked him in the eye.

A half hour later Danielle called me crying that she'd had a bad fight with this kid, so I ran over to his house. The second his parents saw me they knew he was in mortal danger. Immediately he came out on the porch with his hands up, saying, "It's not what you think, Mr. Trejo—*she* hit *me*!" Here he was, the tough kid in the neighborhood, and he was walking around with a big shiner Danielle gave him. I was proud of her for defending herself.

But him grabbing her roughly was unforgivable. She said, "Don't worry, Dad. He's gone."

While I was still living with her, Danielle was in a pharmacy in Venice one day and passed out from what turned out to be anemia and dehydration. The store called the paramedics, then me.

I found her passed out on the floor. But the first thing I noticed was this terrible tattoo on her hip. It was like a big blob of a flower. When she came to, I said, "What the hell's this?"

She said, "Dad, it's a tattoo. I don't like it. I regret it, but that's not what's important now. I have to go to the hospital!" Then she said, "You must really love me more than you love the boys."

I said, "Why's that?"

"If this had happened to one of the boys, you'd just say, 'C'mon, damn it, get up!'"

The pharmacist and the paramedics all cracked up.

The next thing I did was take her to get a tattoo by Freddy Negrete to cover the old one. As a guy who didn't like tattoos on women, I paid for my daughter to get a huge, beautiful peacock. (I know, I'm a hypocrite.)

Gilbert was back from rehab, but starting to slip into heavier drugs again. Heroin. He'd found it, and now I knew it would be a lifelong struggle to keep it at bay. The pressure was getting to me. One day, Danielle found me on my bed, clutching my head. I thought I was dying. She took me to the hospital, and a doctor told me I was having a panic attack. I'd made it through San

Quentin and Soledad without panic attacks; why did the stress of living with my daughter and her on-again, off-again boyfriend crush me? I knew that wasn't it, but to feel better I just moved out and got a room at the Bel Age Hotel in West Hollywood (now the London). After I paid Danielle's rent in advance, I had thirty grand left. I was sixty years old, with thirty G's and a used Range Rover to my name.

I know most of the people on earth will never know what it's like to have thirty grand and a car, but if you asked people on the street, they'd think I was a zillionaire. After working nonstop for twenty years in Hollywood, I didn't have shit to show for it. I didn't know how much longer I could work and earn. I thought I was entering the autumn of my career. I mean, who'd want an AARP bad guy in movies?

I was scared.

My response to fear was to say, *Fuck it.* The hotel was something like three hundred bucks a night. Even though the manager gave me a deal, it was still too expensive. In my own way, without using drugs and alcohol, I was in a free fall. I was sleeping around, chasing distractions. It was easy. I was in Hollywood, staying out all night, going to clubs, acting like I was twenty and just out of the joint. That shit is empty. I went to the bank to withdraw cash and the teller handed me a slip that said I had three thousand dollars left in my account. Standing there staring at the number was a harsh shot, but it wasn't like I didn't know it was coming. I was broke and could no longer afford to live the way I was living.

I decided to withdraw half my money in denominations of tens and twenties. I drove around in a spiral, feeling like my life was collapsing around me. I found myself downtown near Skid Row. I got out of my car and just started handing out cash. I don't know if I did it because I'd made a promise to God to help my fellow man, or to feed my ego, or a combination of the two. When I was leaving, I saw a Black woman with two children sitting by a little table. I remember thinking how clean and well taken care of the kids looked. The woman was selling these threaded bracelets she made that clasped together. I handed her a twenty and she freaked out. "No! I don't have change for that!"

I asked her how much the bracelets were and she said fifty cents. I told her to give me three.

"But I don't have change." She said it like I hadn't understood her the first time.

"I don't need change."

She cried, "My babies! Now I can buy food and shoes for them." I thought, *You can buy shoes for twenty bucks? I want to shop where she's shopping.* She was so grateful it made me understand why I'd gone to Skid Row, a place where human need couldn't be more evident.

When I got in my car, I realized I had less than a hundred bucks on me, but I knew I'd done the right thing. I didn't know what the future would hold, but I felt great. I knew my job was only to worry about what was happening that day. Taking things twenty-four hours at a time had served me well in the past, and I knew it was the answer to dealing with what was in front of me.

Part Four

FROM A SON

Chapter 29

MACHETE

2010

I took the 118 west to the Barrio meeting at the First United Methodist Church in San Fernando. The second I stepped in the room, I felt at home. There was a table up front with recovery literature, plastic chairs arranged in rows, and people loading up on coffee in Styrofoam cups from an industrial-sized urn in the back of the room. A guy clearly kicking dope was munching on a cookie.

"These are good."

The guy who's coming off drugs is always the most important person in the room. We're there to show them there's a safe place for them to get help because we were all in the same place once. Meetings were my church. They had been since I got out of the hole in August of 1968. The Barrio meeting was basically a bunch of hard people who'd been softened through recovery. They had turned their lives over to a power greater than themselves and decided to be better versions of themselves today than who they were yesterday. They went from people who might not piss on you if you were on fire to men and women who would help others through anything.

Out front, I saw Mario Castillo and Max Martinez. Max was a righteous *vato* from my neighborhood in Pacoima. I knew him through the program. Mario was the homeboy I first met on the pile in San Quentin when I was doing *Blood In, Blood Out*. Mario had been in and out of prison three times since I first met him, but I'd run into him at a recovery convention after he got out for the last time and was living at a rehab called People in Progress.

Mario asked me how it was going.

"I'm staying in a hotel in Hollywood trying to figure out what the fuck to do. I'm looking for a spot," I said.

Max said, "Two people just moved out of our house in Pacoima." I knew he and Mario were roommates. "We have a room open if you're interested."

"I'll think about it," I said. The second the word *it* left my mouth, I said, "I'll take it." I spent one more night in the hotel and moved my stuff into Max and Mario's the next day. I was back in Pacoima. That first night at their house was the best sleep I'd had in years.

The next day I had to go back to Venice to walk my dogs. Max said he'd come with me. We were walking down the sidewalk, waiting for the dogs to pee, when Max asked why I didn't just bring my dogs back to Pacoima, since we had a big yard. I don't know why I hadn't even thought of that as a possibility. I grabbed my dogs, along with my last few boxes of clothes, and headed back to my new home. For the first time in a couple of years, everything important to me was in the same place.

On top of that, my mom lived just five blocks away. The first time I stopped by to see her, I told her I was living around the corner and that Mario, Max, a friend named JoJo, and I were there for her. She was so happy, she cried. It hit me right then that she must have been so lonely for so long.

My journey to reconciliation with my mom came in stages. First, after my father died, I was there for her just enough to help her get through the funeral surrounded by my aunts and uncles, who couldn't stand her.

Then, after the time I went over to help her out, and she snapped at me about it being "her house now," I made my peace with God that my mom just wasn't going to be in my life. The way I felt was, she could have the house and be alone in it.

Years later, Jhonnie Harris, the man who had taken me under his wing all those years before in YTS, suggested I be the bigger person. Jhonnie told me, "Danny, your poor mom must have needed something so badly for her soul that she was willing to risk her life and your uncle's to do what she did. You should feel sorry for her and pray for her." He told me to man up and call her. In a way, my relationship with Danielle opened the door to my healing process with my mother. It helped me see her as a person with her own struggles and needs.

When I called my mom, she acted as if we hadn't gone years without speaking. It was nice, but I didn't trust it entirely. I didn't want to get too close. After Gilbert was born, I took him by the house with Maeve to meet my mom, but it was so cold, I never brought him back. She didn't know Danny Boy or Danielle at all.

Even now, back in Pacoima with Mario and Max, I kept my distance. I used Max, Mario, and JoJo as buffers.

She loved them. And I get it. When it's not a parent-kid thing it doesn't carry all the weight of past disappointments and expectations and everything else we pile on family members. With Max and Mario, Mom had her boys. All the ladies at CoCo's, her favorite restaurant, and at the grocery store would say, "Oh, Alice, it's your posse!" It was fun for her to be out and about with these stone-cold gangsters turned teddy bears.

More and more I went by the house and I started to notice it changing. It became a warm place. The plastic was off the furniture. I really forgave her. Not "I forgive her, but I'm still angry about her seeing David." I just flat out forgave her. She was doing what she felt she needed to do to survive whatever she was dealing with, the same way I have in my life.

The magic of forgiveness is so profound, and it starts with us forgiving ourselves. There were so many things in my life that I'd done because in the moment it felt like the only way to survive. I thought about the Lord's Prayer, which I've said every day since Soledad. When it came to my mom, it really hit home, especially the part where we ask God to forgive our trespasses, "as we forgive those who trespass against us." I realized I couldn't ask God to take that heat off me and love and absolve me if I didn't allow that for everyone else as well—especially my mom.

Going to the Barrio meeting and running into Mario and Max changed my life and opened doors just like meetings had done so many times in my life. On top of that, a couple of days after I moved in with them, I was offered a part in a movie called *Poolboy*. It paid just enough money to cover rent for the next few months and allow me to help Mario and Max take care of my mom, my kids, my dogs, and my life. The timing was perfect. Mario had just lost his gig at the Tarzana Treatment Center and Max was stringing together work in construction, but between the three of us we had everything covered.

At Max and Mario's I had everything I needed—we had a TV with cable, La-Z-Boy chairs, and a fridge full of food. Plus, we all knew the rules: take your shoes off in the house, wipe down everything after you use it, pick up after yourself, and respect the space. That's the convict code. And when I left town for work, Max and Mario couldn't give a shit. No one's feelings were hurt, my dogs and my mom were taken care of, and I didn't have to run my schedule past anybody.

My mom needed me, and I was able to give back to her. I'd stop by, or my friends would stop by, and she'd make us breakfast or dinner. She wasn't a prisoner anymore. Neither of us was.

Danielle and Gilbert were doing better. I had to thank God for that. I wanted to take advantage of the window of opportunity I was being offered and asked the kids if they'd like to do something together as a family. I was about to have the leading role in a studio movie for the first time in my life. I knew I would have some pull on the set and could get my kids work on the production. My agent, Gloria, called to say she had my plane ticket for Austin. She'd gotten tickets for Gilbert and Danielle, too. I was bringing them all to Texas to shoot *Machete*, a film in which I was to play the first Mexican American action hero. Mario and Max were going to drive Max's truck out there with my motorcycle to join us. A movie that had started as a conversation fifteen years earlier was finally happening.

I first met Robert Rodriguez when I auditioned for the film *Desperado*. When I walked into the office, the first thing Robert did was laugh. He said, "You remind me of the bad kids in my high school."

I said, "I *am* the bad kids from your high school." He looked me over, handed me a knife, and told me to get good with it. After I left, Gloria called and asked how it went, and I said, "He gave me a knife, so I think it went well."

I didn't know how much meeting Robert was going to change my life.

We shot *Desperado* in Acuña, Mexico, and even though Salma Hayek and Antonio Banderas were in the movie, it seemed like everybody in the town wanted to get an autograph and a picture with me. Robert was watching this go down and laughed. "They think you're the star."

"You mean I'm not?"

While we were doing *Desperado*, Robert told me the attention I was getting got the wheels turning in his head about creating a special character for me—a Chicano superhero. Robert said it was the combination of my look and the way people reacted to me that made him start thinking about the character Machete. He said, "Why shouldn't there be a Chicano Charles Bronson? Think about it, Danny, a Mexican James Bond."

Robert wasn't just a collaborator, he was family. When we were in Acuña filming *Desperado*, my relatives from Texas came across the border to watch us shoot. Both my dad and my stepmother's families were originally from Texas, so I had tons of Tejano aunts, uncles, and cousins. I remember we were busy shooting a scene when I saw my uncle Rudy Cantú talking to Robert by the video monitors. I thought, *Oh shit, don't bother the man when he has a job to do*. I walked over to see what was up and Rudy said, "Danny, meet your cousin Robert."

"*Primo!*" I said. "Now that we're related, you've got to make my part bigger."

The following year, in 1995, when we did *From Dusk Till Dawn*, Robert talked to me about *Machete* some more. I thought, *Hell yeah, he's been thinking about it*. I didn't know if he was completely serious. I didn't want to get my hopes up too much.

During the years after *From Dusk Till Dawn*, we were both busy and I wondered if the idea of *Machete* was going by the wayside. That didn't stop me from incessantly calling Robert about it and bugging him. I was in Vancouver, Canada, in '99, working on *Reindeer Games* with Charlize Theron and Ben Affleck, when Robert called and said he was making *Spy Kids* and wanted to introduce the Machete character as the kids' uncle. "Might as well get the character in there."

"Can we do that?"

"I wrote it. If anything, if we never get to make the Machete movie, he'll always be memorialized in film."

Machete came to life in *Spy Kids*, but it wasn't until *Grindhouse*, a few years later, that I really believed a Machete movie could become a reality. *Grindhouse* was an old-school, double-feature action flick codirected by

Robert and Quentin Tarantino. It was their love letter to over-the-top B movies of the 70s, a genre both directors dug to no end. Quentin and Robert were talking about trailers for fake movies they could stick in the film and Robert said, "I've got one, *Machete*. Pure Mexploitation!"

The plot of the eventual film was completely covered in the minute-and-a-half trailer Robert made for *Grindhouse*. In it, Machete is a former Mexican *federale* turned day laborer who gets paid one hundred and fifty grand to assassinate a senator. During the assassination attempt, he's double-crossed and seeks the help of his brother, a violent priest (played by Cheech Marin, maintaining the *Spy Kids* family), to take down the corrupt assholes who killed his wife and set him up.

I was sitting behind Robert during the *Grindhouse* premiere, and when the *Machete* trailer finished, the audience exploded with applause. Robert glanced back and gave me a nod. He knew he was onto something special.

To me, *Machete* wasn't about the first Mexican American action star or the first studio movie where the romantic lead was a sixty-five-year-old who looked like he'd seen a thousand miles of hard road. To me, being Machete meant I was going to be Batman. A stone-cold vigilante whose tactics might blur the lines between good and bad, but whose moral compass was on point. And also like Batman, I would be an icon in the world of pop culture. I even had my own version of the Batmobile, a Harley-Davidson motorcycle with a machine gun on the handlebars.

The first week we had wardrobe fittings, rehearsals, meetings with Robert. My kids got to be part of all of it. I noticed it had a deep impact on Gilbert. Gilbert was falling in love with filmmaking. As far as making films goes, I know simple shit like, "Learn your lines and don't bump into the furniture," but nothing about the lighting, the cameras, how the sound is recorded. I leave that stuff to the people who are good at it. Gilbert wanted to know all of it. He shadowed Robert and kept asking him why he did things the way he did. Robert would explain things I had no idea about—how he chose lenses, why he would reduce the lighting outside from this many thousands of kelvins to that many thousands of kelvins to mimic an overcast day. I didn't even know what a kelvin was (turns out it's a measurement of the heat of light). I had no idea what Robert was talking about, but Gilbert did.

I would pray to God, "Please, Lord. Take this passion this child has for making movies and put it strongly in his heart."

The first day of shooting on *Machete*, we had an early call. I stepped out of my trailer just as Robert De Niro was coming out of his. He smiled that world-famous smile and pointed at me. "Number one on the call sheet! One on the call sheet!" A call sheet is the daily schedule movie productions put out every night. The cast is listed in order of prominence in the project.

De Niro, one of the greatest film legends of all time, had been number one on the call sheet in *Taxi Driver, Raging Bull, The Deer Hunter*. He was number one on the "bad guys" call sheet for *Heat*, while Pacino was number one on the "good guys" call sheet. *Heat* was a movie with two number ones because how do you tell Al Pacino or Robert De Niro, "Ah, sir? You're number two."

I'd been far down the call sheet on so many of the hundreds of projects I've been part of. When you're "Convict Number 1" or "Mean Dude with Tattoos," you are so far down the cast list, you're almost on a separate page. And now I was at the top. I thought of the days on *General Hospital* when I crammed cans of Coke from the craft service table in my bag to bring home to my kids. Now I was on a set where all the trucks, crew, and equipment were there to help me carry an entire movie.

When Robert pointed at me and made a number one with his finger, he was saying I was the captain on this one and giving me his blessing.

I bowed. "Mr. De Niro, sir, can I get you a cup of coffee?"

He laughed. "Let's both get one."

Robert was excited about the job that lay before us, but it didn't mean we didn't reminisce about the past. We started talking about *Heat*, and I told him that Eddie Bunker had passed a few years back. Robert asked how and I said he was a diabetic; he went into surgery to repair circulation in his legs and never came out of it.

"He was in a lot of pain at the hospital; they had him on morphine, but they wouldn't give him methadone. He was kicking methadone at the end."

Robert winced. Everyone knows methadone's a bear to kick, even in small dosages. I told him a mutual friend snuck some into the hospital to mix with Eddie's Jell-O. He'd been on it ever since the end of his prison stints and at least he had a tiny bit at the end.

"An act of kindness," said Robert.

Gilbert approached us. He said, "What's up?" and I told him we were talking about his godfather.

Gilbert nodded his head. The loss had hit him hard. "I remember one time my father had to find me in Venice with some friends to drop me off some money and Eddie Bunker came with him," he said. "After they left, my friend turned to me and said, 'Who was that guy with your pops? He's the meanest-looking white man I've ever seen!'"

We laughed at that one. We all knew exactly what Gilbert meant. Eddie was a true hard man with the keenest intellect and a heart of gold. And notorious for hating film sets he wasn't working on. He wasn't one to twiddle his fingers. But regarding *Machete*, Eddie had said, "Danny, if they ever get around to making that one, I promise I'll be there."

Sadly, health and fate had intervened.

A few days into production, I was being driven in a van with Danielle back to the Omni Hotel. The driver was a young woman who didn't speak much. New to her job, she wanted to be a true professional. That day, she breached etiquette for a heavenly purpose. She said, "Danny, I never do this, but would you mind signing something for a friend of mine?"

I said, "Of course." She handed me a small bag with a paperback and a pen inside. It was Eddie's book *No Beast So Fierce*. As soon as Danielle saw it, she started screaming, "He's here with us, Dad! Eddie's here!"

All my kids loved Eddie so much. Maybe Danny Boy the best. He always remembered driving around with Eddie and me in my Cutlass Supreme when he was a little kid. He said, "Dad, every day with you and Eddie Bunker felt like we were doing a crime!"

I remembered what Eddie had said to me on the set of *Runaway Train*, when he told me that with my look I could make something of myself in this business. When the driver handed me his book, I knew it was Eddie's way of showing he hadn't missed *Machete*. Why would he? He promised he wouldn't. Our friendship, which had started with my buying robbery plans off him in '62, had come full circle.

Early into filming I was walking to set with Michelle Rodriguez and said, "Michelle, I just want to thank you so much for being in this movie." I just thought she was so bitchin' and so cool. Michelle has so much toughness and class, and I'd never met anyone so full of life energy (although Juliette Lewis comes close). I was a huge fan from when I first saw *Girlfight*. She stopped and grabbed my arm.

"Are you kidding? Danny, you're the number one Mexican in the world!" She laughed her crazy, big laugh. Man, I love that girl. I get to see her in my garage every morning. The artist Levi Ponce, who painted a mural of me in Pacoima, went on to paint a mural of the cast of *Machete* in my garage. Every time I have to drive somewhere, I'm reminded of my time making that film.

Machete was a joy. I'd never been in almost every shot of a film. Jessica Alba, Michelle, De Niro, Jeff Fahey, Don Johnson, Lindsay Lohan—every one of them was a pleasure to work with. Robert Rodriguez was so pleased he was finally getting to make the Mexploitation film he first envisioned during *Grindhouse*. While the days were long, they were filled with laughter. The gorier and bloodier the deaths, the more we laughed.

Machete wasn't just a franchise with a Chicano lead, it was a vehicle for so many amazing Latin actors—Cheech Marin, Jessica Alba, Michelle Rodriguez—brought together by a great Mexican American film auteur. Robert Rodriguez saw value in our world and brought it to a worldwide audience.

Machete opened my eyes, and it made me better understand where Edward James Olmos was coming from. Pedro Gonzalez Gonzalez, who appeared in a number of John Wayne movies, had opened the door for Latin actors, but it was Olmos who saw that we were taken seriously as actors and artists. The insecure part of me had looked at Olmos and thought, *You were never a zoot suiter. You were never in a prison gang.* But I didn't stop to consider what it had taken for him to get where he was, how he was representing Latinos and showing them as human and complex. Doing *Machete* made me appreciate what people like Olmos and De Niro had to do to get where they were, what an achievement that was, and what they had done for me.

Early into filming, Robert De Niro asked me to dinner. I told my children to be on their best behavior. "This is very important to me, so act cool, not like kids." We got to the restaurant and were talking about the film when De Niro said he thought Robert Rodriguez was an auteur. I didn't know what the word meant, but Gilbert did. They started talking about French, Italian, and Spanish directors, dudes I'd never heard of—Truffaut, Fellini, Buñuel. The whole dinner, Gilbert and Robert De Niro talked film. I didn't know Gilbert knew so much about art, history, literature, and cinema.

I made a note to myself: Always let your children read. The extent of my forays into literature had been limited to getting *Archie* comics in Eastlake and trying to erase the clothes off Veronica. I was so proud of my son, holding his own with Bobby. His excitement about making films got me excited. Gilbert had been clean for a few months. I was praying this time would stick. I thought, *Maybe he's found something he loves so much it will shove out his love for heroin.*

I think Robert De Niro felt the same way because he handed Gilbert a set of keys to the film archive at the University of Texas in Austin, where he had donated the catalogue of his life's work. He was sharing his love of cinema with Gilbert, something he felt my son was worthy of receiving.

Part of the reason I took the kids on the set of *Machete* was because Maeve needed a break. She had done the heavy lifting with the kids for so long and was back in Los Angeles with her hands full. Her second husband was gone and she had two young sons on her hands, Theo and Samuel, both with their own challenges. And we were both deeply concerned about what was happening with Gilbert and Danielle. We decided to divide and conquer. I needed to work, but I needed my children near me.

Sadly, when we got back from Texas, Gilbert and Danielle both fell back into using. They needed to find it in themselves not to use, and I couldn't be on them 24/7. Then, things got more complicated when my executive assistant, Mari, called and told me that my blood test had come back from a recent checkup and my doctor was concerned. He needed to run more tests. Having lost Dennis Hopper when I was away shooting *Machete*, I figured I'd better take my own health seriously.

I went with Mari to a hospital in the Valley and they did some more scans and blood tests. When the results came back, I was told I had to go to Cedars-Sinai, where three doctors were waiting for me and Mari. They sat me down in a room and put an X-ray–looking thing up on a screen that showed a ten-centimeter tumor on my liver. I'd been in good health for almost ten years, ever since I'd recovered from hep C in 2002, but some liver issues I'd thought I was past had come back hard.

"What's this mean?"

"It means if we don't start treating this right now, you're going to die." The first thing the doctor did was start listing off the side effects of the treatment.

I said, "Slow down. When?"

The doctors looked at each other like I was nuts. "When what?"

"How long until I die?"

"A year, fourteen months. It's hard to say."

I was ready to walk out of there. I didn't want to deal with any of that shit. I looked over at Mari and she was already on her phone, making appointments.

"What should I do?"

"We suggest a course of chemotherapy. But in your case, general chemo through an IV won't be as effective as injections we can deliver directly to the tumor."

"When can I start? I have work to do."

And did I have work. While I was on the set of *Machete*, I read in the trades they were doing *Predators*, a new take on the 80s action flick, and it was being produced by Robert Rodriguez. The casting notice said they wanted someone mean and intimidating "like Danny Trejo." I went straight to Robert and said, "What the fuck? *I'm* Danny Trejo. I'm the mean, intimidating guy you want!"

He said, "You're doing *Machete*."

I said, "So are you. We're going to be done."

The day after my last chemo treatment, I went to Hawaii to work on *Predators*.

There was going to be no slowing down for me. In addition to *Predators*, I was lined up to shoot the films *Death Race 2*, *Six Days in Paradise*, *Perfect Sunday*, *Justin Time*, *Food Stamps*, *Boston Girls*, *American Flyer*, *Recoil*, *Blacktino*, *A Very Harold & Kumar Christmas*, and the TV shows *Bones* and *The Cleveland Show*. I was in so many towns doing so many jobs, I didn't know where I was half the time. Robert Rodriguez loves telling people I called him one time and said I was doing a movie in Dallas. When he asked what it was, I said, "I don't know. It's a movie. How am I supposed to know what it's called?"

Machete opened in September. That Halloween, as we were handing out candy in my neighborhood in Mission Hills in LA, so many little Mexican kids were dressed up as *Machete*, Mario and I almost cried. People sent me photos of trick-or-treaters all over the country dressed in *Machete* costumes. They looked so cute with their fake Fu Manchu mustaches and plastic machetes. The greater meaning of this wasn't lost on me. We finally had a superhero of our own. A man who wasn't afraid, or cowed, and never gave up. And *Machete* did more than give these kids their own superhero to dress up as. It also gave their parents, many from first- or second- or third-generation immigrant families, a Chicano superhero to dress their kids as on Halloween.

There are forces we feel powerless to fight. Superheroes let us imagine that we can overcome those forces. During a movie, or on Halloween, we can fantasize: What if there really were Supermans or Batmans or Machetes? That fantasy gives us real hope and strength. And there is no greater gift.

Chapter 30

DOUBLE LIFE

2010

Right when I returned from Hawaii, I got an offer for a film called *Bad Ass*, directed by Craig Moss. Gloria said the production didn't have much money, but she liked the director and producers and felt it was something I should do. The biggest plus was the job was close to home. The snag was I was supposed to start the film in two weeks.

My doctor had told me, "We've been setting up your appointments with Mari and we should start as soon as possible."

"What if I don't?"

"It's too big to put you on a transplant list. We couldn't even do that until your tumor is at four centimeters."

"If I wait?"

"Well, then it can grow to a size where no treatment will have any chance of working. If you wait, you'll die."

Honestly, I thank God for Mari. She set up all my chemo appointments and I was going through chemotherapy the whole time I worked on *Bad Ass*. On the weekends, the doctors would put me under with anesthesia and shoot chemo directly into the tumor. So if you watch that movie now, just know I was sick as a fucking dog while we were shooting and doing my best to hide it.

Millions of other people have dealt with cancer. I reminded myself of that fact and kept my mind on the positives. I didn't obsess about treatments and prognoses. I didn't scour the internet for horror stories. I put my trust in the doctors, the plan of action they suggested I take, and, most importantly, God. That's not to say I didn't have moments of doubt and self-pity. After work one night, I went home shattered, wondering how I was going to make it through another day of work. I looked in my bathroom mirror and felt like screaming, *God, I do what You want! I say Your name every day. I help Your children every day! We had a deal!*

Then I walked out in the living room, and I swear to God, one of those commercials for St. Jude Children's Research Hospital was on TV. There was a beautiful little kid who couldn't have been more than six or seven, smiling. He said, "And if you donate, we'll send you this beautiful blanket." I felt like I'd been socked in the face. *You fucking punk, you've had this great life and there are little children who have this stuff and are going through chemo and they haven't even had a chance to live yet. You've had a great life. And they fight it, they don't feel sorry for themselves.*

Message received, loud and clear. From then on, I'd go to the children's hospital in LA and bring a carful of toys with me. The doctors at Cedars were amazed by my attitude. I told them God didn't pluck me from raging ocean waters to dump me on a beach to die of liver cancer. They couldn't believe my tumor was responding the way it was. When it got down to six centimeters they said, "We don't know how, but it seems like your tumor is dead." But they wanted to inject another round just to make sure it was, and I told them to go for it.

Just like when I had hep C, my biggest fear wasn't death, it was that people in the industry would find out and wouldn't offer me work anymore. I was also scared that I might not live to see who my kids might become, that I wouldn't meet my grandchildren, that I wouldn't be around to help them when they needed me.

To keep Danielle close, I got her a gig on *Bad Ass* as a wardrobe assistant. She would show up at five a.m. to start work. In the afternoon I'd ask her, "Are you tired? Do you want to take a nap in my trailer?"

"Dad, I can't do that."

"Why not?"

"I have to make my own way. You helped me enough. If I do stuff like that, I'll never get a job in this town again."

One of the last nights on *Bad Ass*, I sent Mario to get me some healthy food from a restaurant because I didn't want to eat the catering. One of the producers, Ash Shah, saw me eating the restaurant food and asked me if the catering on *Bad Ass* wasn't good enough for me. I said, "Ash, would you eat the food from a movie called *Bad Ass*?" We laughed. "I'm kidding," I said, "I just like to eat healthy, that's all." I couldn't tell him why I was being so careful about what I ate.

He said, "You should open a restaurant."

Joking, I said, "Yeah, Trejo's Tacos."

After the film wrapped, I went back to Cedars-Sinai for one of my last checkups and the doctor said, "We can't explain it, Danny, but your tumor has disappeared. We'll have to do annual checkups, but basically, you are cancer-free."

I knew how to explain it. It was all God. I had a new lease on life, but I never let the diagnosis stop me from moving forward. A diagnosis is just that. The result of a scan or a blood test or whatever is not reality; *reality* is reality. If you are sick and you avoid going to the doctor, that's not going to change what's happening inside your body. I wasn't afraid of bad news. But if Mari wasn't there setting the appointments up for me, I probably would have blown off dealing with them and I'd be dead. But I wasn't. I had shit to do. I'd just been offered a role in a TV series, *Sons of Anarchy*.

In the show I played Romero "Romeo" Parada, a high-ranking cartel boss who just so happened to be an undercover CIA operative tasked with bringing down the club's illegal gun sales.

I started doing *Sons* just after I came off treatment for the cancer. I was still feeling a little off and tired. The pace of the work on *Sons* was intense. Everyone was on point and everyone was prepared. I wanted to do a good job. I wanted Kurt Sutter to know that his faith in me wasn't misplaced, so I dug deep, and working on *Sons of Anarchy* was one of the coolest gigs I've ever had with some of the best people I've ever worked with. It was especially gratifying because I got to work with two close friends of mine: Emilio Rivera, who I'd first worked with on *Con Air*, and Donal Logue, an old friend I'd met in 1991 when he was working as a janitor at the West Hollywood Drug and Alcohol Center.

Sons was such a worldwide pop culture phenomenon; being on the show was like being in the Rolling Stones.

But the whole time I was on *Sons of Anarchy*, my kids were still struggling. I felt like I was fighting a war on three fronts: There was the me who had to show up to work every day and smile and take pictures; the me who went to chemo treatments at the hospital and in my private moments prayed for strength; and the me who needed to be there for my children, knowing I was powerless over their addiction but could do the only thing I knew to be right—give love. In 2011, Danielle went to treatment. She was in for nine months. Because I had so many connections within her facility, I started bending the rules as if my daughter wasn't just another client in need of help. For instance, there's a rule the clients don't get to have much cash on them—ten bucks, max. But every time I went to see Danielle, I'd slip her a hundred bucks. Money is the way I show people I love them. It's like, *Here, I love you, I care for you. Here's money!*

Looking back on it, my uncle Gilbert did the same thing with me when I was working at Carlisi's. He felt bad for me and dropped a grand on the counter like that was going to save me from my sorry life.

I was enabling both of my kids and undermining their recovery. One time Danielle skipped out of rehab with a friend and lied and told her counselor she was with me. She called and told me that she had lied. To make her story look credible, I drove as fast as I could to pick her up and bring her back. A week later her counselor called and said, "Danny, we had an unbelievable breakthrough. Danielle confessed she wasn't with you last week." I got mad and said, "Damn it, I told her never to plead guilty!"

Then Danielle got on the phone and said, "Dad, do you realize you are upset with me because I took accountability and responsibility—which is exactly what I should be doing and learning to do? You're undermining the process! You're an enabler!"

After that, I was banned from her rehab. In between gigs, I was still working for Western Pacific, petitioning politicians, speaking at big conferences with five thousand attendees and small rehab meetings with twelve teenagers. But in spite of all my years working in recovery, bringing countless people to rehabs (CRI-Help specifically), I was banned from Danielle's rehab. When it came to my own kids, everything I knew about recovery went out the window. And I know the fact I was so high-profile in recovery made it harder for my kids to get sober. People looked at them like it should be easy. Heroin addiction, alcoholism, none of it is easy. Addiction doesn't care if you think you are the king of recovery and you don't get extra ducats that keep your kids and loved ones free of that shit.

While I knew Danielle was safe, I had no idea where the hell Gilbert was. Neither did Maeve or Mario.

An ex–La Eme shot-caller, Rafael "Chispas" Sandoval, asked me to go to a high school in La Puente to talk to kids about staying off drugs and out of gangs and doing good in school. Chispas had been one of the leaders of the Mexican Mafia but had found religion and gone straight. That's the only way the Mexican Mafia lets you out: if you find religion and do good. And they don't just take your word for it. They check on you. They send people to church to make sure you're living the life and not just bullshitting them.

Chispas was righteous. Since getting out of prison, he'd fully dedicated his life to helping people. We settled in while kids started filing into the auditorium. I tried to think about what I was going to say, but I was distracted. How gangbanging was a guaranteed way to go from being down for your neighborhood on a Thursday afternoon, then finding yourself facing thirty to life on Friday. But I couldn't focus. I didn't even know why I was there. I felt like a fraud. Chispas noticed something was wrong and asked what was going on.

"Chispas," I said, "I don't know what the hell I'm doing. My own son Gilbert is on the streets somewhere, doing dope, and I'm here to tell other people's kids not to do the same. What kind of father am I?"

Chispas got quiet and said, "Danny, I know God wants you here today to tell these kids what it's like for a father to go through the pain of addiction with their own kids. They need to hear it from your perspective."

I was introduced, and the kids burst into applause. I was so nervous walking to the podium. I'd never felt nervous speaking to a group of people before. But I knew why. It was because I was hurting and about to get real. I told the kids, "Some of you here are probably already doing drugs and think it's cool. I just want to tell you what it does to the people in your life." I started tearing up. "I'm standing here in so much pain because my own son is on the streets, lost to drugs and addiction. I don't even know where he is right now. I don't know if he's alive or dead. I don't know what he has to do to get the drugs he thinks he needs. I can't describe to you what this pain feels like. I stay up all night—I can't eat, can't sleep. So know that what you do doesn't just affect you."

My words hit those kids hard. Wiping away my tears, I noticed the kids were crying, too. Chispas was crying. Those kids had never really seen the other side of addiction—the consequential pain it causes. When you're an addict you think the only person you're hurting is you. And that's not true.

I felt relief, if only for that moment. By helping others, I was healing myself. I knew it wouldn't necessarily bring Gilbert back, but it was helping me, because I was sick with grief.

All this was going down when my career was really taking off. After *Machete* and *Sons*, the offers poured in. Voice work for cartoons, movies, TV commercials. I was in demand, but my home life was falling apart. Gilbert would call from the streets and I'd be in Bulgaria, Romania, somewhere, and I'd call Mario to try and find him. He might be on Sunset Boulevard getting shaken down by some dude he owed money to, or he might be in a dirt lot, kicking, or he might be shaking down someone who owed him money. Whatever the case, Mario would find him and snatch him.

I went back to Austin to shoot the sequel to *Machete*—*Machete Kills*—but this time, Gilbert and Danielle weren't with me. Danielle was clean and sober and doing alright, but Gilbert was choosing a rough path. Michelle Rodriguez and Jessica Alba came back to reprise their roles, and we added Mel Gibson, Lady Gaga, Charlie Sheen, and Demián Bichir to the cast. Lady Gaga got involved because I was down at the Shamrock tattoo parlor one night while my friend Mark Mahoney was putting some ink on her. She saw me and got excited and said she loved *Machete*. I told her we were going to start the second one, and she said she wanted to be in it. I called Robert Rodriguez from the tattoo shop and he said to have Lady Gaga's people call him and he'd make it happen.

Gilbert was on the streets, beyond my help. There's a special place in heaven for parents of addicts. At some point you have to trust that they have their own God and that they are going to have to realize that and find the strength to do what's right. The whole time I was doing *Machete Kills*, I worried. Weeks turned into months. I was back in LA working on the sequel to *Bad Ass*, called *Bad Ass 2: Bad Asses*. I knew I couldn't change Gilbert's circumstances, so I focused on the job at hand. Luckily Danny Glover was with me on that one. He was a great guy and a good partner to do a movie with. When I first saw him before we started shooting, I yelled, "Danny Glover!" like I was this little fan chick, and it busted him up. I was just psyched to watch him work. But at night I'd look out on the streets and think, *My son is out there somewhere.*

My own kids' drug use made me feel like such a failure. I was a guy who was so well-known in recovery circles, so many people said things like, "You saved my life!" or, "You helped my cousin," but I couldn't help my own kids. I was pretty sure Danielle was slipping, too. All I could pray for was that they heard it for themselves somehow.

Years earlier, when I was living on Hiawatha with Debbie, just days after I shook Gilbert for being fucked up, I ran into a young guy named Johnny B at a meeting. Johnny was a cool kid who wanted me to sponsor him. He had a ring in his nose, three earrings in each ear, and his lip and nipples were pierced. I'm looking at this kid like *What the fuck?* I thought I was gonna make this fucker a Republican. Johnny had a big blue monster truck. I was going to go speak at a meeting in Santa Barbara, so Johnny and I drove his truck to my house. I got out of his monster truck and we went in the house, and Gilbert came out into the kitchen, wasted, with a druggie twenty-two-inch waist wearing size thirty boxers that were falling off him. He said, "Hey, what's up?" I introduced him to Johnny.

I took a shower to get ready for the meeting, and when I was done, Gilbert came up to me and said, "Hey, Dad, can I go to a meeting with Johnny?"

So I went to Santa Barbara by myself while Gilbert and Johnny went to a meeting in LA. My son didn't want to go to meetings with me, but he thought Johnny B was cool. I love how recovery works like that. Other people could do for my children what I could not. Just like I can help someone in a way that their own family can't reach them. I prayed Gilbert would run into someone in recovery who he related to like Johnny B.

While I was coming to grips with the fact that Gilbert and Danielle had their own battles they had to fight, my oldest child called. His mother, Diana, had died.

It was August 2012. Danny Boy said, "Dad, Mom died and I knew you'd want to know."

I asked how he was doing and he said alright, but I could tell it was super hard on him. I said, "Danny Boy, what do you need? Whatever you need, I got you."

He said, "There's going to be a memorial in two months out in Havasu." (Diana had moved to Lake Havasu, Arizona.) "It would be great if you could go with me."

I said, "Do you want to come stay with me till then?"

"No, I'm okay. Just come with me to Havasu."

"We're there."

Danny Boy and I flew to Las Vegas together. We got a rental car to drive to Lake Havasu. It was the first time we'd spent good alone time together in years. Of course Danny Boy had come down from Lompoc and stayed with me in Mission Hills from time to time, but this trip was different. The trip to Diana's memorial got us back on a plane, just like when we flew to San Francisco the time we hit turbulence and Danny Boy told a planeload of terrified passengers, "By the power of Grayskull!" and said, "They're not scared now, Dad!"

The drive to Havasu was emotional. Danny Boy was quiet. He loved his mother. That's one of my favorite things about him—how kind and loving his nature is. Sometimes I think that has a lot to do with Nanny. I know that's what Danny Boy attributes it to. The trip made me think of my time with Diana. I loved her, too. I didn't show it that well, but I loved her. I knew that God brought us together to make Danny Boy.

Danny Boy said, "Dad, thanks for caring about Mom." He knew there were exes of mine where we were neither civil nor anything to each other after we broke up—it was just better we were away from each other. But Diana and I could always laugh, even when we were arguing about parenting (like the time Danny Boy got busted for smoking weed). We worked together and she appreciated the years Danny Boy was with me and Maeve while she was in prison.

The wake was held at Diana's favorite restaurant in Lake Havasu. They reserved the patio for us. I liked the place—it was a real family restaurant with games for kids and stuff. The kind of place Gilbert, Danielle, and Danny Boy would have loved when they were young.

At the wake, people were sharing about Diana, so I got up and said that Diana Walton Hyde was a great woman and a great mom. I said we all have our demons, but I respected how she had dealt with hers and had blossomed so much in life and was in a great partnership, and that the greatest tribute to Diana was the kind of young man she raised Danny Boy to be.

Around five or six, people started drinking and Danny was ready to go. There were people at the restaurant who wanted pictures with me and autographs, so we decided we would split. When we were walking out the door, Danny Boy said, "Dad, I'm so glad you're here."

I was so glad I was there, too. But for me, not for him, because, selfishly, I needed that time with my oldest son. If memorial services hammer home anything, it's that the cycle of life can be so short and brutal, and we have to be there for each other.

Driving through the desert back to Vegas, Danny Boy said, "Dad, I have a few gray hairs. It's really bumming me out. Do you get gray hairs?"

I had to smile. My baby, my beautiful baby boy, the boy I would sometimes let swim in the pool at the apartment complex in Venice on hot summer nights after his bedtime, the boy who wanted "mac a cheese" from Nanny, the boy who I saw could be a boy in Lompoc so I had to let him go to be with his mother—that boy was asking me about gray hair.

I said, "Hell yeah, I get gray hair. On my driver's license under hair color it says 'Just For Men.'"

We laughed hard at that one.

"Thank God," he said. "It's not just me."

Chapter 31

WORRYING AND PRAYING

2013

Everything came to a head when I was in London working on *Muppets Most Wanted*. I was with Ray Liotta and Craig Balkham, a bodyguard we both worked with. Things with Danielle and Gilbert were tough. Maeve was struggling at home. My mother's health wasn't good. I was struggling, too. I felt the hurt closing in, but I wouldn't give in to it. I couldn't let it crush me. My faith saved me. I always went back to the mantra "If you're going to pray, why worry? And if you're going to worry, why pray?" I prayed and prayed. I prayed for Gilbert and Danielle, I prayed for my mother. I knew that if God saved me, presented a path for me to move forward, I could trust Him in this situation with my kids.

Maeve felt differently. She felt like she could turn her own life over to God, but with the kids, she was like, "It's up to me to fix it." But it was too much for the both of us. My friend Chris Davis told me whenever someone asks, "What's too much?" he says, "It's all too much; that's why we give it to God."

March 8, 2013, was Gilbert's twenty-fifth birthday. When I finished work, I went back to my hotel room to call him and wish him a happy birthday. I asked him what he was doing to celebrate and he said he was having breakfast at CoCo's with my mom.

That was incredible. Gilbert was still struggling with using, and my mom didn't know her grandkids well, so to hear that Gilbert took it upon himself to take her out for his birthday brought me a lot of joy. He put my mom on the phone and we talked for about twenty minutes. She asked me how London was and whether the people I was working with were nice. She was being a mom and I was being a son. I remember that phone conversation was Right Now in the way Quentin was, and by that, I mean in those twenty minutes we had no concern about the past or any worry about the future— we were purely present with each other. The cycle of forgiveness, me for her, her for me, had come full circle.

When we were getting off the call my mom said, "*Mijo*, I love you." I said I loved her back. And I did.

Four nights later, Craig Balkham knocked on my hotel room door and said, "Danny, I don't know how to tell you this. Your mother died."

My mom was taking the trash out, walking on the grass in the backyard, and she'd had a stroke. I was overcome with every fucking kind of emotion possible—sadness, anger, regret. I felt numb, broken. I knew her eventual death was inevitable, but it didn't lessen the body blow when the punch finally came. I wished JoJo, Max, or Mario could have been there with her in her last moments. Or that I could have been there. Her journey from Marfa to Arleta had been singular in many ways. I just wish she hadn't been alone at the end. But I was grateful she had me and all my boys around her in the years before she went. She loved those men. She called them her posse.

I went into the production office and told the producers to get me a plane ticket home. Craig was on the phone and said, "Hold on, talk to Mario and Mari." Mario, Mari, Gloria, everyone in my life, told me they were taking care of the arrangements—that Max, Mario, and Mario's son Mikey were there so there was no need for me to hop on a plane. Mari said there was nothing more to be done and if there was, they were doing it. Besides, I knew Production was worried. Acting can be a goofy job, but the size of the budgets and the scheduling are not. They were close to the finish line on the Muppets movie, and it would have cost them millions if I split. It was March 21, 2013; I'll never forget the day.

I went back to work. Everyone there knew my mother had just passed. People gave me a wide berth and walked on eggshells around me. They must have thought I was cold. I wasn't crying; I was quiet. I think that pissed my mother off, watching from heaven.

Muppets Most Wanted is a musical. That week we were filming a big number called "The Big House," where Tina Fey (playing a prison guard: genius) gives Kermit a tour of a gulag in Siberia with Ray Liotta and me as singing and dancing inmates. It starts outside, where Tina sings, "This is Russia's premier state-funded hotel / We're very proud of our eclectic clientele," and slaps me while we're doo-wopping behind her. We move inside to the chow hall, where she sings, "This is the dining room, the menu is minimal / What the cook does to the food is criminal / Pull a seat, grab yourself a stool, frog / May I recommend you try our famous gruel! / In the Big House / You'll never be alone . . . ," and I pick up Kermit and slam him on the table. Singing and dancing was nothing I'd ever done before. You have to commit fully to the hilarious goofiness of it, and I was dying inside.

Right before we started filming the part of the song in the dining hall, Steve Whitmire, the puppeteer who did Kermit, put the puppet close to my face and said, "I'm so sorry your mommy died, Danny." There's a rule Steve was abiding to that when you are working with the Muppets you have to always stay in character. Steve was sincere. Kermit was sincere. He scrunched up his little face and that puppet showed so much emotion it cut through all the layers of hurt I was holding on to. Even though the assistant director was just about to call "Roll" on a take, I bolted off the set and ran to the bathroom. As soon as the door closed, I burst into tears. I hadn't felt that much emotion since my uncle Gilbert died. Ray followed me in and waited with me until I got my shit together. We were two guys who had played the hardest motherfuckers in movies, and he was helping me get it together to go back out on the stage and sing and dance with a bright green puppet.

To this day I'm convinced it was my mother who told Kermit to say something.

We buried my mom next to my dad in the San Fernando Mission Cemetery in a beautiful ceremony. Gilbert was still using. Danielle wasn't much better, but she was still on and off the junk. After my mom passed, I was completely overwhelmed. And I was facing decisions that I couldn't handle—what to do with the house, what to do with her clothes, what to do with the dishes in the kitchen. Danielle was only twenty-three at the time, but I'll never forget this: she said, "Dad, I'll take care of the house. I'll sort through the things. I'll take charge."

Danielle says that when she told me that I sighed. Not a sigh of resignation—it was a huge exhalation of grief, relief, clarity, and regret.

Right there and then I gave Danielle my mother's house—the house where she'd offered me milk and cookies, the house where I'd buried the shotgun and hand grenade in the backyard, the house that had been so cold and complicated when I was growing up, that had since become a place of peace and reconciliation.

Maeve was broken over what was happening to our kids. The ups and downs were too much for her. She was almost incapable of working. She was struggling to raise her two younger sons. I was broken, too. I didn't know what was going to happen, but at least Danielle would have a place to live. After the funeral, Maeve said to me, "I don't know how you do it." She was talking about how I was dealing with everything, still showing up for work, still showing up for her and the kids. My faith was getting me through.

Gilbert was homeless. His shit was at my house, but he was on the streets. That's the way he wanted it. That's where his drug use took him. Drugs alienate and separate you from everything you love. Heroin is like a jealous girlfriend. Maeve couldn't have Gilbert's drug use around her other sons, and I understood. Gilbert was living around Silver Lake and Los Feliz; that was all I knew. The only thing I could really do was make sure he had a cell phone if he needed to reach out. For some reason, thanks be to God, he didn't sell the phone for drugs. Occasionally, we'd get word of him. Once my sister, my birth mother Dolores's daughter, Dyhan, called us to say she saw him. She was working for a needle exchange program on Skid Row and saw Gilbert slinking down the street. The same place with the tents and the cardboard houses where I'd passed out money to people was where my son had found himself. My heart was breaking. Whenever we'd track Gilbert down, we'd go grab him and throw him in detox. Then he'd get out and use again. It was a bad cycle that had been going on for almost ten years, but I was willing to do it for as long as it took.

During all this Gloria and I flew to Texas to see Robert Rodriguez. He called me to come to town because he was doing something super cool. Robert was hosting President Obama at his house. The Secret Service gave us the rundown on how to greet him, how much time we could spend with him, and so on. I was standing behind five other people when Obama stepped from the line, held out his hands like he was holding swords, and said, "I know this guy! Machete!" Gloria burst into tears. Later she said it was because she saw such an incredible change come over the president when he saw me. How excited he looked. How he broke with decorum. I was just incredibly happy I got to chat with the president. He was cool and easy. He felt like an old friend. I think the Secret Service guys were getting antsy that the president was falling behind schedule by talking with me too much, but he paid them no mind. As soon as I stepped away, I called Gilbert. He answered and I said, "Gilbert, I'm with the president!"

Gilbert seemed distracted. He said, "That's so cool, Dad." Then I heard someone say something. I didn't know what was going on, but I found out later Gilbert was standing in a vacant lot by Circus of Books where drug addicts would hang out. To get a homeless guy off his back, he'd just offered him a baby food jar with the residue of some crack cocaine he'd made.

I heard the guy say, "You just scrape it off from the inside?"

I heard Gilbert say, "Yeah, just scrape it off."

Then the line went dead.

I was so excited to hear his voice and then, when I heard those fucked-up people around him, I immediately got depressed. For so many years I'd prepared myself for the day when Gilbert couldn't answer a phone because he'd be dead. He'd have OD'd, or burned the wrong dude, or his abscesses might have turned septic. He'd answered this time, but he wasn't safe. Not now, not tonight, not tomorrow. Preparing myself for that possibility meant I accepted that his chances weren't good, but it didn't mean the fear of losing him was lessened. Not for a minute.

That was the roller coaster of my life. Sobriety had taken me to a place where the president of the United States knew who I was, and my son was making crack in baby food jars.

But then a miracle happened. Danielle got clean. It took a deep scare for her to do it. Danielle was living in my mother's old house with her cousin Christina and a girl named Molly. One night, Danielle shot up in the bathroom, went to bed, and OD'd. John Wesley Harding, a cute little terrier named after the Bob Dylan album, found her. He ran to Christina's bedroom and jumped on her bed until she got up to see what he was freaking out about. Christina woke up Molly, who dragged Danielle into a cold tub and gave her CPR. After that Danielle called Mari for money. Mari said, "Fuck you, you're going to rehab," and called 911. When she hung up with 911, she called me. These women saved Danielle's life. When I reached her in rehab, I heard something different in her voice that told me this was going to be the time. She was truly sick and tired of being sick and tired. I let myself hope, and my prayers were answered. She's been clean ever since. The strong, independent girl who taught me to see women in multiple dimensions was on track to build the life she was meant to have.

But it was one down and one to go. Gilbert was still using.

Maeve and I would talk about it. She would cry. She was convinced that there was no way God would be generous enough to allow both our babies to get better. She didn't trust that God gave with both hands. I knew He did, but Gilbert was in bad shape—he had abscesses, his mind was gone. He was so sick that even if he got clean we didn't know whether he'd ever be the same person again.

Maeve couldn't work; she couldn't function. I told her, "I got you," and I meant it. In a way, I was making good on the promise I made her the first night I met her. She was stronger than she knew. A few years earlier, before Gilbert was so bad, she told me about her struggle to find Independent Education Programs (IEPs) for her sons in the LA Unified School District. She said, "You have to be a lawyer to deal with this shit!" I said, "Why don't you go to law school? I'll pay your rent and put you through school."

And she did. She'd gone back to work as a nurse and was going to law school at night. When Maeve passed the bar we all went to the ceremony in Pasadena to celebrate, and this time we were all dressed up nice—Danielle, Gilbert, Danny Boy, Theo, Samuel, and me. We finally got to be the family we couldn't be back when we were living together in Venice.

When they called Maeve's name to come onstage and receive her certificate, she found me in the audience and mouthed, "Thank you." Right then, I felt like I had become the man my father really wanted me to be.

Gilbert was clean for the week his mom passed the bar, but he looked like a skeleton. Right after that, he quickly fell back into using and disappeared. At some point he called me and asked if I could help him out with some money for food. I met him at a gas station on the West Side and handed him a C-note. I was hoping we'd talk, but when he got what he needed, cash, Gilbert took off running. Afterward, Danielle asked how he was.

"Alive. I gave him some money."

"For what?" she asked, and I could tell from her tone that she didn't approve.

"I gave him one hundred dollars. The kid needs to eat," I told her.

"Dad, you shouldn't have done that. For a hundred dollars he can get a fix, a hotel room, and a hooker," she said.

"Really? You can get all that for a hundred bucks?" I asked.

"It's not funny," she said. "You're killing him."

She was right. He didn't want small talk, he didn't want me to save him, he didn't want anything but the money. I knew too much to expect anything different from an addict deep in their addiction. My heart was broken, but it had been for years. Part of me was just happy anytime I got to see him alive.

But luckily that $100 was Gilbert's last run. When I was in Atlanta working, he reached out to Mario to come get him. Mario found him in a dope house in Studio City where Gilbert was passed out on a couch. The house was full of dog shit, lawn furniture, used needles, and people fixing. Mario scooped him up, carried him out the door, and put him in his car. He took him back to our house just long enough for me to get him help.

I got home the next day and called a woman named Rene. I'd known her from the recovery world since she was thirteen; she now ran a detox called Rim of the World in a mountain town. I explained Gilbert was on my insurance and what he was going through. She said, "Don't worry about the insurance stuff, we'll deal with that later. Just bring him."

"Are you sure?"

"We'll make it work. He can share a bed if he has to."

"Thank you, Rene."

"You can thank me by speaking to our clients at one of our meetings."

Mario and I put him in my car and started to drive. He was asleep most of the way but woke up when we climbed above the cloud line. He looked around and said, "Well, there goes any plan of escaping."

I had to laugh. But, honestly, Mario and I were looking at each other like, *If he doesn't get it this time, he probably never will.*

Chapter 32

EL PADRINO

2014

Around then, something happened in my career—something that went beyond movie roles. I was hired to do a string of commercials for Old El Paso, a company that focused on Mexican cuisine. We were going to shoot them down in Mexico City.

On our second day there, I visited Plaza del Zócalo, which was built on the site of the ceremonial center of Tenochtitlan, the ancient capital of the Aztec Empire. I saw a statue of an eagle with a snake in its mouth. It was like seeing the American flag for the first time. It meant so much to me. The story goes that Huitzilopochtli, the god of war, told a group of wandering indigenous people (the Nahuas) that they should leave Aztlán and establish a capital for their new kingdom on the spot where they saw an eagle standing on a cactus eating a snake.

Almost fifty years before in Soledad, I'd made a mosaic of the Mexican flag for the Mexican Studies Center at the prison. It was the first time I felt like an artist. I remember putting so much care into the center of the flag that depicted the same thing that I was seeing in the statue. Making that flag really tied me to my Mexican heritage. Plus, the times were so heavy back then. In the 60s, the racial fights happening in the streets made their way into the California prison system. We Mexicans started to focus on our Aztec heritage—guys were getting Aztec tattoos; I finished my *charra*.

We believed we were descendants of a line of Aztec warriors that traveled through Pancho Villa and Emiliano Zapata.

In Mexico City I felt I was where I came from, where my ancestors were from. My bones felt like they were home. Craig Balkham and I went across the square to a cathedral where Mass was happening. We walked into this gigantic church and took up a spot in the far back. I swear to God, the priest stopped his homily, squinted, and said, *"Hola, Señor Trejo,"* without breaking stride. It was like he had expected me to show up.

Everyone in the church turned around. I nodded to them and told Craig, "Let's take off, I don't want to disrupt a church!"

I felt so embraced by people in Mexico. I was overwhelmed. I was humbled. I imagined my parents and grandparents looking down on me. I knew my dad would be so proud. We went to San Miguel de Allende and people were treating us like I was Zapata or something, crowding me and asking for pictures. Gilbert said, "Dad, you're like the Mexican Beatles or something."

I said, *"You* are." It was true. Barely clean, Gilbert looked like a totally different human. And he'd gotten clean because he wanted to live. He found it in his heart to make that change. I couldn't do it for him. Nobody could. Gilbert looked like a different human because he was, physically and spiritually. He'd surrendered to his addiction, accepted it, and stopped using because that was the only way to have power over it. He was so handsome, like he was an old Latin star. People were crowding him. Looking at his face, I was so proud.

The next day there was a picture of Gilbert and me on the front page of the Mexican newspaper. He so outshone me that I said, jokingly, "Don't ever stand next to me in a picture again."

But I was there to work. The Old El Paso commercials were the first time my career tied me to food and the family dinner table. The spots were funny takes on a big Mexican family getting together for meals. I played the crazy patriarch. It wasn't much of a stretch. We shot in the house of a famous old Mexican actor named Emiliano "El Indio" Fernández. Emiliano was good friends with Diego Rivera and one day he and Diego were getting fucked up and Diego's wife Frida Kahlo came by and started yapping at them about being assholes. Diego was so pissed, he painted a picture of Frida naked and when she came back and saw it, she stapled a dress to the painting to cover her naked body.

The painting is still hanging in the house. I may or may not have lifted the dress for a peek—I'm not saying—but I can tell you this: I've seen Frida Kahlo naked.

Shooting the shit over coffee, I asked one of the Old El Paso executives why they hired me and he said it was because they felt in Latin culture I was a *padrino*. I knew what *un padrino* represented—someone you went to when you needed help, assistance, advice; someone who was tough enough to handle business, and wise enough to give counsel. Most importantly, a *padrino* was someone who could be trusted.

I arrived at LAX from Mexico City late. By the time my driver, Bela, dropped me off at my house it was almost eleven thirty. I stumbled down the stairs into my bedroom and woke up on the floor in pain. I figured I'd just tripped on the stairs and lost my balance. I went to Mario's son Mikey's room and told him he'd have to take me to the doctor the next day because I'd hurt myself. I was worried because the following day I was leaving on a trip to New York and Rome.

We went to the doctor and X-rays showed I had a broken jaw. Despite my injury, I got on a plane to New York because I was scheduled to be a guest on *The Howard Stern Show*. Before I left, I asked the doctor what my options were. He said because the break was horizontal and not vertical, I could either get my jaw wired and wouldn't be able to talk, or I had to promise not to chew food. The choice was easy. I'd just drink smoothies.

On the flight to New York I had a bad headache, but I can deal with pain well. I was excited to meet Howard, since I'd been a fan for years.

Right off the bat Howard said, "When you grow up the way you did, it's incredible how you turned your life around. I don't know where you got the wisdom to do that. Do you believe in God?"

Immediately, he got right to the heart of my journey.

I said, "Absolutely."

"Do you believe it was divine—"

I cut him off. "Divine intervention, yes, that's what I call it."

We had a great conversation. I left Midtown Manhattan on a high and headed straight for the airport to catch a flight to Rome. On the car ride there my headache came back so bad, I thought I was going to throw up on the plane.

When I got to Rome I was exhausted, but I couldn't sleep. I went for a walk around the Colosseum, the square where Mussolini gave his speeches, the ruins of the Forum. I could hear history echoing through the streets. And I don't mean this in some kind of general, bullshit way. I had auditory hallucinations of Roman soldiers marching through the streets. I could even feel the ground shake. Outside the Colosseum, I heard the cheers of the crowd inside. My senses were heightened like I had smoked some killer weed, even though it had been so long since I'd smoked. It was such a trip. I could sense the ghosts of men who had died. Rome was so Right Now, it reminded me of San Quentin.

The movie I was working on was called *Hope Lost*. It was directed by an Italian guy named David Petrucci. He watched me do a scene and looked confused. After one take, he pulled me aside and asked, in a hilarious Italian accent, "Is the way you are talking an actor's choice?" I remember the way he said *actor* sounded like "act-oo-re," like it had three syllables.

I had been mumbling and talking out of the side of my mouth. I couldn't tell him it was because my jaw was broken, so I said, "Yeah, I think it sounds tougher."

He nodded and said, "Good, good choice-ah. *Grazie.*"

On the flight back to LA the headaches came back, so I pounded a bunch of Advil and tried to sleep. When I got to my house, I asked Mikey if we had any aspirin and he said he'd figured out that when I fell down the stairs, I bounced off my dresser and hit my fireplace because he'd cleaned up a bunch of pictures and stuff that had been knocked over in my room. I called Maeve and told her I was having bad headaches. In full-on nurse mode she asked if I was seeing double and a few other questions. Then she said, "Danny, you're exhibiting symptoms of having had a stroke. You need to go back to the hospital."

I didn't want to, but she insisted, so we went and the doctors told me the same thing they told me the first time—I had a broken jaw. Maeve started yelling at everybody, demanding they rescan me or reexamine the CT scan they'd taken before my trip. When they did, it revealed I'd suffered a massive subdural hemorrhage. Two of them. Two blood vessels had exploded on either side of my brain.

Before I could say anything, I was rushed off to the operating room for emergency brain surgery. I thought it was a joke. For some reason, when I was being wheeled down the hallway, I thought George Clooney, someone I didn't know well and only had worked with in *From Dusk Till Dawn*, had put a kind of *Punk'd* episode together. I was so convinced George Clooney was playing a prank on me, I called out in the hallway, "George, where are you? Clooney, why you pulling this shit?"

The nurses had to strap me to my gurney. I truly was out of my mind.

I came to twelve hours later to find a short Indian doctor in a too-tight, "Please Don't Rain on Me" suit. He was holding a clipboard. Danielle and Gilbert were in the room with me.

The doctor asked my name and I said, "Orville Stip," an alias I use when I check into hotels. He looked confused.

Gilbert said, "That's an alias he uses. Stop messing around, Dad, this is serious." That's when I noticed two huge tubes full of blood running down either side of my head. They were like those beer-bong hats assholes wore back in the 70s.

"What the hell are these?"

"That's blood draining from your brain," said the doctor. "Please answer my questions."

"Okay."

"Who's the president?"

"Muammar Gaddafi."

"This is not a joke."

"Don't mess around, Dad. This is serious," said Danielle.

I drew a blank. It was weird. "I hung out with him!"

"What's his name?"

"Ah . . . ah . . . the Black guy! He's my pal!"

The doctor looked suspicious. I thought, *Fuck, man, cut me some slack. I've got a brain bleed going on!* I honestly couldn't remember Barack Obama's name in that moment. Danielle said to the doctor, "If you knew my father, you'd know that was the right answer."

"Obama!"

The doctor said, "It's not funny to make fun of your neurosurgeon. I've never taken more blood out of anybody. Most people with your injury go to sleep and die. And you've been flying? It makes no sense."

The hospital kept me for a few weeks to monitor the bleed. Again I prayed. I'd most likely had the hemorrhage right before I fell down the steps to my bedroom. But I knew dying wasn't in God's plan for me.

I had so much time to think about my life in that hospital bed. I hadn't been nailed to one spot that long since my days in solitary. In some ways, my experiences being locked up made it easier for me to deal with being alone like that, but I really needed to get back to work. A big problem was my legs couldn't work—I couldn't walk. The surgery that saved me had knocked out my equilibrium and jacked my memory. After a few weeks in that hospital I was transferred from Northridge to St. Joseph Hospital in Burbank. I figured they specialized in helping rehab stroke victims because I was in a ward with a bunch of old people who'd clearly had strokes. What I couldn't accept was that I was one of them.

I was given a walker and assigned an older nurse who had to be with me when I tried to drag my body up and down the hall. She'd stand so close to me and say shit like, "You're doing so good today, Mr. Trejo!"

I'd get mad at her. I'd snap, "Give me some space!"

She said, "I have to be near you, or I will lose my job."

"Look, I ain't going to do this if you're standing next to me." I could tell she was scared, so I cut her some slack and let her follow a few feet behind. Even if it took me hours, I made sure I did round-trip laps of that hospital ward. We had a little gym on the floor, and I'd walk across it, dragging my legs, cursing at myself in a big mirror.

"Come on, you motherfucker! Weak motherfucker!" I was so angry. I'd relied on my body to cooperate with me my whole life. When I was boxing, I had such pretty footwork. I could run, I could move. My physicality was one of the things I always had going for me, but now I couldn't even make it ten yards with a walker. I saw an old guy who had had a stroke strapped to his walker, just standing there, not moving, watching me cuss at myself.

I told him, "We've got to do this." Weakly, the word "yeah" dribbled out of the side of his mouth. I could tell recovery was a bridge too far for him.

Privately, I said, *God, don't let that be my fate.* I knew I had to fight. I had to get well so I could earn.

I pushed out one more lap.

Chapter 33

TREJO'S TACOS

2015

By the time I left the hospital I was jamming across the gym with no problems. The doctors couldn't believe it. My nurse was so proud of me.

"You got to keep your job?" I asked.

"You didn't make it easy!"

Right when I got home, Gloria called and said Snickers wanted me to do a Super Bowl commercial that was a play on *The Brady Bunch* with my old pal Steve Buscemi. The Super Bowl is such a big deal. I knew everyone in America would be watching. In the commercial, I play a version of "mean" Marcia before she takes a bite of a Snickers bar and becomes her regular, sweet self. Gloria was worried I might not be well enough to do it.

"Hell yes, I can do it."

Now that I was walking again, nothing was going to stop me. While we were filming, one of the Snickers execs told me, "Danny, we didn't hire you because you are tough. We hired you because you're loved." I wanted to cry. God had just saved my ass from a double subdural hemorrhage, and here I was doing a Super Bowl commercial. It was around that time that Gilbert showed me a picture of a huge mural of me in a village in the Philippines. I just thought it was cool, but Gilbert said it represented something deeper. He said, "Dad, your image has seeped into the collective psyche."

*   *   *

Turns out, *Bad Ass* and *Bad Ass 2: Bad Asses* were so successful, Ash and his partners set up a third installment, *Bad Asses on the Bayou*. We shot it in Louisiana. I was in the production office getting my rental car keys when Ash handed me a binder.

"What's this?" I asked.

"It's a business plan for a restaurant. Trejo's Tacos," he said.

He'd been thinking about our conversation ever since the first *Bad Ass*.

I gave the plan to Gloria and Mari and they both said it looked like a pretty solid idea, so we moved forward. I never even read the business plan, but I was so confident in what Gloria and Mari thought, I said, "Let's do it." That's how Trejo's Tacos was born.

Ash brought in good chefs and management people and they listened to my input on the menu. I'm not an expert chef, but I know when good people are around me, and these guys were great. They asked what my mom, Alice, used to make at the house. Despite her problems, my mom was an amazing cook. She'd start making dinner for my dad just after lunch was finished. Her life was cooking, cleaning, cooking, then cleaning some more. I think food is where she exercised her creativity. Shopping for food, going to all the little Mexican markets, picking out the perfect chiles, meats, beans—that's when she could be free and get out of the house. When she talked about opening a restaurant, only half joking, Dad used to say, "What's wrong? You have a perfectly nice kitchen right there, with an O'Keefe & Merritt stove." Recently, Trejo's Tacos did a deal to offer our menu at every Live Nation concert event. For all my mother's pain and loneliness and whatever else drove her to find some moments of peace with my uncle David, I like to imagine that Trejo's Tacos is the fulfillment of one of her dreams. A place where the plastic is off the furniture, where people come and go and all are accepted and welcome. From heaven she can look down and I can tell her, *Mama, you got your restaurant, and now it's everywhere.*

The rest of 2015 was insanely busy. I was working all over the place. In the ten years starting with 2010, I did almost three hundred movies and TV shows, so the names and faces melt into each other. I mean, c'mon, I did a movie called *3-Headed Shark Attack*. I did everything that came my way. Sometimes a job in the morning and another the same night. Most actors are scared of what their next project is going to be, but that's never been a problem for me. I take the Michael Caine approach: it's all work, and all work is honorable. I'd done jobs on huge projects (a lot of them with Robert Rodriguez—the four *Spy Kids* movies, *Grindhouse*, *Machete*, and *Machete Kills*), and movies like *Heat* and *Con Air*, but a lot of my work in the 2010s was on straight-to-video movies, voices in cartoons, and television. A lot of people have written about this golden age of television, and as someone who has been around a long time, I can say it's true: the quality of the shows, the number of brilliant cartoons—there's so much good content for actors. I feel we are in a blessed era.

A lot of the jobs I've done are probably what people would consider to be B movies, horrorfests, schlock things. An interviewer once asked me if I liked working on bad movies. He wasn't trying to be rude, but I didn't love the question. I don't believe there's such thing as a bad movie. I see every movie and TV role as an opportunity for me to support Maeve, my kids, and the people who depend on me. If my involvement helps a movie get made, it creates jobs for crews that have families of their own to support. How can that be bad?

And a bad day on a movie will always be a million times better than your best day in prison.

With my health on track, I turned my attention to my cousin Gilbert's appeal. Gilbert had been in prison since 1979, when he was seventeen years old. He had served time in San Quentin with his father. Gilbert said he could tell from the sound of footsteps walking down his tier that a CO was bringing news of his father's death. He couldn't go to the funeral. When Gilbert was fucking up inside and using, he generally wouldn't write, and I definitely wouldn't write back. But when he reached out to me this time, I could tell this was a different Gilbert.

In one of his letters, Gilbert mentioned he was trying to get an appeal together. He had the name of an attorney in San Francisco, Tracy Lum, who worked on these types of things. I called Tracy and asked if she could help. After looking over his case history, she thought she could. That's when we started working on Gilbert's appeal. I started meeting state senators, US Congressman Tony Cárdenas, Senator Jim Beall, even Governor Jerry Brown. I wanted to change the law so that people who were given life sentences as juveniles could have easier access to the parole hearings they were entitled to. Most of these guys had been in prison for thirty, forty years. The laws sentencing juveniles as adults were supposed to encourage access to parole.

Gilbert had been in trouble since he was six years old. His dad was always locked up. He did well for that spell when Joanne and I had him on Osborne Street, but as soon as he went back with his mom, all bets were off. He had killed a rival gang member when he was seventeen, was tried as an adult, and sentenced to fifteen years to life in prison.

It hadn't been easy for Gilbert. He was the youngest prisoner in San Quentin when he got there, and because his father, his namesake, Big Gilbert, was so well-known in the prison system, there were expectations on him. Heavy ones. When he first got to San Quentin, a dude stabbed him while he was sitting at a table talking to shot-callers. The fact that the dude didn't kill Gilbert was his first mistake. He had missed his shot. His second (and third) was that he attempted the hit without receiving prior permission and did it in the presence of some of the biggest Mafia bosses in Quentin. Gilbert even got hepatitis because the shank he got hit with had been keistered. After he healed up there was pressure on him to kill the guy who tried to take him out. He wasn't even nineteen and that was the situation he found himself in. That's life in prison. Getting stabbed on the Yard in Quentin was his introduction to life in the big house. The Right Now.

So the path laid out for Gilbert was violent from the jump. He fought other prisoners, he fought guards. Years later, the system had a resentment against Gilbert for attacking a corrections officer. That crime had been committed when he was still a teenager, but it followed him for decades. Years later, Gilbert fought other inmates in staged gladiatorial contests in Corcoran Prison, where the guards released inmates from rival gangs on the Yard to fight each other just so they could place bets on them. It wasn't just the guards watching from the tower; administrative secretaries and prison officials were in on the spectacle, too. It's as sick as it sounds.

Gilbert was in hell, but if he won his fights, the guards would let him have Yard time at night so he could see the stars. That was his biggest desire. Gilbert's fascination with astrophysics set him free in his mind. When he was in solitary, Gilbert taught himself everything from algebra through advanced calculus. He taught himself to program a computer without having access to a computer. He learned advanced physics and became conversant in every-thing from Newtonian physics to string theory. Because the one thing you can't be denied in solitary is textbooks, and Gilbert read hundreds of them.

In Corcoran, Gilbert would fight to buy himself another day above-ground in the hopes someday his case would be heard. After all kinds of lobbying, meetings, and court dates, Gilbert's appeal finally went through. In 2015, Gilbert was found suitable for parole as a youthful offender under Penal Code 3051. Now there's a case that established legal precedent with Gilbert's name attached to it stipulating that inmates who were sentenced as juveniles and committed crimes inside before they were twenty-three are granted access to parole hearings. That I had something to do with helping pass a piece of legislation that resulted in meaningful prison reform fills me with pride and gratitude. Over thirty-five hundred men who had been sen-tenced to life as juveniles have now been released as a result of our work. It's poetic that the name Gilbert Trejo, which meant one thing in the California prison system for so long, now means that young offenders who committed crimes as juveniles have a chance to turn their lives around like Big Gilbert's son Gilbert did inside.

When Gilbert was in Ironwood, he was part of a group that talked to at-risk youths about what was waiting for them if they continued a life of crime and gangbanging. Knowing that the scared-straight method didn't work, Gilbert and the other lifers had access to the kids' files to find out not only what their crimes were but what their interests were. Gilbert saw one particular kid was a fan of science fiction like he was. When he met the kid, he said, "I'm a time traveler." The kid was confused. Gilbert said, "You like science fiction?"

The kid said, "Yeah."

Gilbert said, "I do, too, and I'm a time traveler. I'm from the future. I went to bed one night when I was sixteen, then I woke up in prison as a fifty-year-old man." That hit home.

Gilbert was fifty-five years old when he was released from Ironwood State Prison after thirty-eight years. Mario was driving sixty-five miles an hour down the 10, and I looked back at Gilbert and saw that he was quaking in the back seat, gripping the door handle. This man had been through the SHU gladiator fights in Corcoran, through wars in San Quentin and New Folsom, held his own on any Yard he was on, but he hadn't been in a car for so long that driving highway speeds scared him to death.

We took him to an IHOP to eat. When we walked in, he pulled out his prison ID card and asked the hostess, "Who do I show this to?" He wasn't joking. I'd been out of prison so long I'd forgotten about institutionalization. My last stretch was fewer than five years. I couldn't imagine what thirty-eight would be like.

He ate a breakfast and then asked us if he could order something else. Mario and I said, "Of course!" He ordered a lunch, and then he ordered a dinner. He had three meals for breakfast.

The first Trejo's Tacos finally opened on La Brea in Hollywood, right across the street from the church where my third wife, Joanne, and I got married. My partners were Jeff Georgino and Ash Shah. Jeff likes to say, "Danny's face will bring them in the door; the food will keep them coming back."

I've really put my heart and soul into Trejo's Cantinas, Tacos, and Coffee & Donuts joints. Mostly because I think my parents would have been so proud. They never considered acting a real job, no matter how successful I became. Not long before she died, I took my mom to see the mural of me that Levi Ponce painted in Pacoima in 2012. She kept looking at it, then at me, then at it again, like, *Why would the world do this?* I don't think most people realize the business aspect of Hollywood and how much of a grind it is for the crew and the production assistants. I'd always wanted my parents to see me as an entrepreneur. I felt like the restaurants gave me legitimacy as a businessman.

Besides, there is something gangster about owning a restaurant. You can invite people to come to your place; you can join people when they're eating with their families. It's like you've invited them into your home.

It was all happening so fast. We opened a Trejo's Coffee & Donuts shop on Santa Monica at an existing location that Ash and Jeff found. It was the old Donut Time, a shop made famous by being the main location in the movie *Tangerine*, the first film ever shot on an iPhone. To celebrate the opening of the Trejo's Donuts, we did a giveaway in the parking lot where I signed pictures and donut boxes. My son Gilbert came with me.

I was busy greeting people when I glanced up and noticed Gilbert talking to an old, Black homeless man with his arm in a cast. The man left and I called Gilbert over. I said, "Gilbert, that man looked familiar. Who was he?"

"He said he was in prison with you. He told the other guy with us, 'That man's a killer, a real OG, I did time with him.'"

"I knew I knew him! Why did he leave? We can hook him up with some food."

"I told him that, but he said you looked busy and didn't want to bother you."

"See if you can find him."

Gilbert ran off, but he came back alone. The guy had disappeared. I remembered him. I remembered him well. In Soledad he was an OG during the heavy days of George Jackson. Jackson had started the Black Guerrilla Family. Later, he was involved in a number of riots and was shot after a heavy standoff during which five prisoners and three guards were murdered in his cell. On that day, a warm day on Santa Monica Boulevard, all those years came back—good memories, bad memories. I didn't have many people left who I could kick it about that time in our lives. The homeless man with a broken arm had been a big-time dude in Soledad. He was political, got respect, and now he was living on the streets. I wondered how he'd broken his arm, what had happened all those years since the mid-60s when I'd last seen him; I wondered if he needed help. I wished he hadn't walked away. I wished we could have had a cup of coffee and cut it up. I wished I could have given him a hug.

Chapter 34

FROM A SON

2018

Two years ago, Gilbert came to me with an idea about a movie that centered around addiction. I read the script and was blown away. I couldn't believe my son had created something so powerful. Before we started filming the movie, called *From a Son*, Gilbert would show me pictures of him as a little boy—holding fake weights over his head in Venice Beach, me cradling him in my arms when he was just a tiny thing. In the movie, I play a guy trying to track down his son who is using. I knew that story well. The man was a hardworking handyman who was at the end of his rope looking for his boy. I asked Gilbert, "How'd you come up with this?" but I already knew the answer.

"We lived it, Dad."

We had. Both from the perspective of addicts who had put our parents through hell with worry, and from my perspective as a father who spent endless nights wondering where my kids were. Now, here we were, both clean, on a set, taking our respective journeys and making them into art. The passion that Gilbert showed when he followed Robert Rodriguez on the set of *Machete* had blossomed.

The experience of making *From a Son* gave me a view of my life through Gilbert's eyes, but, more surprisingly, it helped me see my life through my father's eyes. Dionisio Trejo was a tough man, a hard man, but probably more than that, he was a scared man. He was terrified that every time I walked out the door it might be the last time he ever saw me. He just could never find the words to share that.

In the film, Gilbert and Sasha Frolova, the actress who plays his girlfriend, are in the desert living in a squat, going from score to score. Gilbert shoots up and ODs, leaving this terrified little girl to figure out what to do. Seeing no other option, she buries him in the desert.

The whole time we were shooting the movie, Gilbert was on me hard to not fall back into old habits and just act tough and gruff, like one of the criminals I'd played in so many hundreds of films and episodes of TV. It had become a bad habit.

If I got tough, he'd hold out his wallet and say, "Here, you want my wallet?" He was breaking the gangster in me.

Early in the shoot, I was in dad mode, not in actor mode. After a few takes of a particular scene, Gilbert asked for another. I was tired and snapped, "You have enough!"

Gilbert pulled me aside and said, "Dad, I'm the director. If you don't respect my authority, no one in the crew will. And, no, we don't have it. You were falling into your old, bad acting habits." I realized Gilbert was no different from Michael Mann, Laurie Collyer, or Taylor Hackford. He was the director, I was the actor, and he deserved that respect. My job was to try and do what he asked me to the best of my ability.

Gilbert had shown me the pictures of him as a child to help me access emotions I'd buried deep inside. I pretended to be strong when Gilbert was on the streets with his addiction, but while I was working on *From a Son*, I was able to dip into that fear, safely, on a set, to help tell the bigger story of what parents go through when their kid is an addict.

From a Son was the first time I have really cried on a job. I was doing a scene where Sasha takes me out to the desert where she buried Gilbert's body. I ask her, "Did you kill my son?" and she says, "No. I really loved him." She breaks down. Through snot and tears she says, "He was my only friend."

That broke me. Something about her saying, "He was my only friend," hit me like a gut punch. So much of it was how much I love Gilbert. So much of my heart is him.

The scene was so real, it was uncomfortable. Tears poured out of me like a dam had broken. Before the scene started I had planned on crying like John Wayne, but I ended up bawling like Shirley Temple. I thought of all those times I'd looked at death, at a lifetime of imprisonment while waiting in Soledad to see if they were going to charge Ray, Henry, and me with a capital crime. I thought of the deaths of my birth mother, my father, my uncle Gilbert, my mother. I thought of the women I'd treated badly, the relationships I'd destroyed through ambivalence and selfishness, the fear for my children. All the times I never cried when I should have finally caught up with me. A certain set of rules helped me survive the first chunk of my life, the rules my uncle Gilbert taught me. Another set of rules kept me going all those years after I got out of the hole in Soledad. I stayed clean and sober by helping others get clean and sober. But there was a part of me I had never dealt with or accepted that I had to confront.

It all came to a head after work one night when Gilbert and I were driving home. We started arguing. What we were arguing about exactly I can't remember, but it got heated. Gilbert said all of who I was, my worldview, how I saw people, how I felt about women, how I had treated women in the past, how I needed to be the provider, a giver to people even to the point where it was pathological and hurtful to me, sprang from an environment of toxic masculinity that I was raised in.

"You can say you're different from the men you were raised by, but their influence stayed with you."

I was so angry, I called my friend Donal Logue, and I yelled, "Gilbert, what kind of environment did you just say I was raised in?"

"Toxic masculinity."

"Donal, what the hell is toxic masculinity? Because it's what Gilbert says I was raised in!"

Donal said there is a kind of misguided masculinity that poisons men and fucks up their relationships. He said it was beautiful I could still gain insight on my life and be set free from bonds and patterns.

It was true. I was seventy-four and I was finally understanding the engine driving so much of my behavior. It was a hard V-8 from the hood. As much as I hated the way my father and uncles were, their machismo, their *Chicanismo*, I was a *charro* just like them: unfaithful to my wives, violent toward other men, angry, guilty of playing the big shot. I knew I'd made great strides in other areas: I was clean and sober; I'd helped people in as many ways as I could think of; I was a loving dad who was not afraid to show my children affection; but somewhere down in my core I still carried a deep fear about being vulnerable and weak and being fucked over that immediately manifested itself in anger and control.

I was a bad man on the hardest prison yards but the most terrifying thing I ever had to face was my own emotions. I'd been taught to harden my soul against all those feelings, and I'd been afraid if I opened that door, it might never close. But now the door was open, and it was painful and scary and uplifting and right.

A week later, we wrapped up filming on *From a Son*. After the last take, Gilbert and I hugged. I thanked him for bringing so much of what I had buried deep inside to the surface. The act of creating together brought us closer than we had ever been. I was so proud. As a father, and even as an artist, it was almost like my life's journey had taken Gilbert and me to this place where we could examine the different hells we'd gone through, from both our perspectives as a father and son and as former addicts, to make a story that could help people going through something similar.

Besides his namesake, my son Gilbert has taught me more than anyone else I've ever known. I'd seen him go from an articulate five-year-old to a manipulative drug user to a brilliant film director. It wasn't a smooth path, but it made sense. Watching him work, and sharing my experience with my son, brought me deep joy.

After we finished filming the movie, I received a humanitarian award in Highland Park. We showed up to the theater in a procession of lowriders. The people I loved most in the world were with me—Mario, Gloria, Mikey, Mari, Gilbert, and Danny Boy. Unfortunately, Danielle was back in Ohio, but she was with us in spirit. I was with Chubby Hernandez, one of my oldest friends, who works on my cars. Chubby's dad, Keeno, was a mechanic in our neighborhood in Pacoima back in the 50s and 60s. Everyone took their cars to Keeno. Now I take my cars to his son.

One of the greatest things about that night was that my ex-wife Joanne was the one to present me with the award. She looked beautiful. She introduced me and told the audience that I had taught her how to care about people. I was overwhelmed. I had been through so much with this woman. Whatever else I was up to, our home was always open to homeless people, people coming off drugs, people who needed a meal and a meeting. I was proud of her. She's stayed clean since we were together in the 70s. After she introduced me, I said to the crowd, "How the hell did I let that one get away!" and everyone laughed. The hurts of the past were gone. We'd matured into adulthood, loving each other for what we meant to each other. Being reunited meant more than I can say. It was like the frayed ends of my life were coming back together and being made whole.

I've always loved music and it was always a dream of mine to get involved in the music industry. The first time I saw Baby Bash, an artist who'd come down from the Bay Area, he was all decked out in red. I thought, *This kid's got balls*. Here was this Northern Californian *vato*, deep in Sureño territory, wearing Norteño colors. It was almost as bold as when I first saw Mario working out on the pile in Quentin in shorts he made out of his LA County blues.

When we started the label, we wanted to help a young, talented singer named Tarah New as well as other artists in the Hispanic community. Tarah is a brilliant singer and an incredible human being who sings effortlessly in both Spanish and English. That's what we were going for with our sound—a combination of oldies soul and Mexican ballads.

Last year our record came out, *Danny Trejo Presents Chicano Soul Shop, Volume 1*. It featured Bash, Tarah New, Frankie J, Trish Toledo, Chiquis Rivera, and a young genius from San Bernardino named Joey Quiñones, who sounds like he makes music straight out of the 50s even though he's in his twenties. We cut it up in the studio, spent a ton of time together, and just basically pinched ourselves with how much fun we were having.

Within weeks, Bash had set up a performance with Art Laboe for Tarah in front of sixty thousand people. Standing backstage, I had to pinch myself again. It was all real.

Chapter 35

DANNY TREJO DAY

2020

January 31 was officially named Danny Trejo Day in Los Angeles. My love for this city runs so deep; the fact I get love back like this blows my mind. When a person gets off an airplane at Los Angeles International Airport, my voice is one that greets them over the loudspeakers, saying, "Welcome to LAX. I'm Danny Trejo. You might know me as Machete or have eaten at one of my Trejo's Tacos. Here's one more thing you should know—I love Los Angeles. It's the best city in the world. Enjoy your stay in the City of Angels!"

To me, Los Angeles is like Emerald City in *The Wizard of Oz*. It's a magical place where dreams still come true. Yes, it has Hollywood and the film industry, but every single part of the city reminds me of someone who got clean off drugs and got their lives together. Like every city, it's comprised of human souls. People slam LA for being shallow, but I call it Tibet. I call it that because I've seen thousands and thousands of people over the fifty-plus years I've been sober and out of the joint completely change their lives for the better as a result of leading simple, honest, spiritual, thoughtful lives. Whenever people say LA is superficial, I just have to laugh.

Last year an article came out about who has been the most-killed actor in cinematic history. I won by a landslide. I've died sixty-five times in films. It feels like more. I was eaten by a badger in *The Salton Sea* and by an anaconda in the Amazon. I was decapitated and had my head put on a turtle, which then blew up and killed the DA in *Breaking Bad*. I've been shot, stabbed, blown up, and hanged. You name it, it's been done to me. But it's okay, I've gotten more than even. In *Machete* alone, I probably killed a hundred people in the first ten minutes. I know some actors who refuse to have death scenes, especially older actors. Who knows why? Maybe they're superstitious; maybe they're afraid to push themselves to a place that can get intense. For me, it's fun.

The more I show up in films, the more people are curious about the story of my life. I hope people see through my story that it's possible to make a decision to live a better life, and to change. Once that decision is made, it's possible to stay true to it for the rest of your life. I had that window of opportunity in 1968. I asked God for help and He told me to stay clean and to help other people. That's the recipe. It's that simple. Drinking and drugs might temporarily bring some relief, but there is no problem in life that drugs and alcohol don't make worse—whether the issue is financial, emotional, or legal. If you are reading this and find yourself struggling, ask God to take the burden off your shoulders, reach out for help, and stop digging a deeper hole for yourself. There is a community of millions of men and women who have been in similar circumstances and will be there for you, stranger or not, because their own recovery depends on helping people like you.

To this day, I still work for Western Pacific Med Corp. After Dr. Dorr passed, he left the business to my partner Mark Hickman, who started there as a fourteen-year-old who skateboarded to work. Of all the things I've done, Gilbert's film, *From a Son*, and my association with Western Pacific are what I'm most proud of. Well, those and my role as a father.

I've given my phone number to thousands of people. A lot of them still call; it seems like some call every day. Sometimes I wonder what I'm doing, but by showing up for you, I'm showing up for myself. The restaurants have just become another way of being there for people. When we opened our restaurants, whenever I was in town I was down there, greeting people, meeting with them, eating with them.

As Sam Hardy told me, "You have got to do something for someone and not expect any kind of reward." The way he pronounced it was "reeeee-ward." When your motives are right, it seems like the world smiles upon you.

My film career is simply a vessel that helps me amplify a message to help a wider audience. Don't get me wrong, I love movies. Reenacting movies kept me sane in Folsom and Soledad. *The Hunchback of Notre Dame* and *The Wizard of Oz* still stop me in my tracks if I see them today. Movies teach us valuable life lessons. They teach us if we reach deep enough inside ourselves, we can overcome whatever problems we're dealing with, regardless of the odds.

But the most important thing to me about my life in the film world is that it helps me carry the message of God to as many people as possible. If people are interested in me because of the films, my hope is that they will dig a little deeper into who I am and what I'm about in a way that helps spread the message of recovery. If you think I walk as I talk, you might be more curious as to what I did to turn my life around.

Years before I got the role in *Runaway Train*, I was acting. I pretended not to be scared as a kid; I pretended I didn't see things I saw; pretended I didn't feel feelings I felt. You don't have to be from a bad neighborhood to have done that. For me, drugs provided a more direct and easier way to escape feelings I couldn't sit with.

Avoiding feelings and pretending not to feel them, that was what my life was about for so long. Prison was the same. Drugs, jacking off, anything to get out of my head for five or ten minutes, combined with never letting on how I truly felt. I acted mean till I believed it. Anybody that survives prison has to be a psychopath. When I got my first crack at acting on *Runaway Train*, I'd been in training for forty years. I was like a fish who'd found water. When Andrei Konchalovsky called "Action," time stood still. In the quiet and anticipation that followed, I was in control. It didn't matter if all the background prisoners were screaming; it didn't matter if Eric Roberts moved left when he should have moved right. I found I could control the action—just like in a robbery. In film, sometimes I play the hero; sometimes I play the villain. But the goal of films is to teach us you can prevail over your difficulties in life if you have courage. Through films and storytelling, as both viewers and artists, we get to work out our fears and examine the defects in our characters that hold us back.

Am I an unlikely movie star? Yes. It was unlikely that I would make anything of myself in any field. I wasn't a kid who'd fallen through the cracks,

I was a kid who'd fallen through the crack in the crack. My bottom was a piss-covered floor, an iron bed with no mattress, *Fuck God* scrawled on a wall, screams echoing through the cell block. Part of me feels like a fraud for having had success in Hollywood and another part of me thinks, *Who better?* The truth is few people can play a more realistic dude busting through a door with a gun in his hand besides me.

Today Gilbert's been clean for years. So has Danielle. She lives in Ohio and runs Dirty Water, a successful vintage clothing store. For many years I only felt safe when she had a boyfriend I knew would take care of her, but after her most recent breakup, when I said, "It's okay, I can help you like I used to," she said, "I don't need your help."

I pretended to sob. "You don't need me."

"Shut up, Dad," she said. "I'll always need you."

Danny Boy is in Lompoc and doing great. As often as he can, he drives down to LA to visit his old man. Maeve is still working as a nurse and an attorney and being a mother to her two sons and our two kids. Because Maeve works such long hours, her youngest son, Samuel, lives with Mario and me most of the time while her oldest, Theo, just moved into an apartment above my son Gilbert where Gilbert can keep an eye on him. My cousin Gilbert works as a union electrician and counsels at-risk youth, and I couldn't be prouder.

And Maeve. I used to point at a blank ribbon tattoo on my arm and say, "If you act right, your name could be there." By *act right* I just meant to do everything I said and have no opinion about it. Wow, I was so wrong.

But time is more powerful than tattoos and marriage licenses. If Maeve and I could have just stopped the war that came from insecurity, maybe we could have settled down and been a happy family. Life doesn't work that way, but it surprises you.

How it is now is that Maeve is one of my best friends. She and I are so close we talk every day and have laughs when we see each other. Her younger kids live with me a lot of the time when she's pulling long shifts in her job as a nurse in treatment centers. We're partners.

I love how Maeve and I are, regardless of how we got here. Thirty-some years later, Maeve is the love of my life.

If I've learned anything in life it's to tell the people you love that you love them every day. Especially your children. Kids just want to know that they are loved. Being an actor and a restaurateur is cool, but being a dad is the best.

I've got real-world problems. There are things about my life that aren't what people might think from the outside. I have living problems—I have obligations to the government, to my children, to my community. Life isn't worth living if you don't have some problems. But in truth, drugs and alcohol are really the only problems I have. If I touch either one of those, my life goes to hell and I can't take care of my obligations.

Donde hay vida, hay esperanza. Where there's life, there's hope, just like my grandmother used to say.

EPILOGUE

May 15, 2020

Friday is the day before my seventy-sixth birthday, and I get up a little later than usual. Two of the dogs are sleeping on the floor and five are snuggling in bed with me. Norm, my friend and stunt double, comes by to work me out and help me stretch. We don't do anything heavy, mostly just stuff to keep the blood moving.

When we finish, I see Donal in the backyard with my friend Sal. I met Sal in San Quentin in '65. He was a hell of a boxer. He still trains boxers, even at seventy-five. I saw him about three years ago at a meeting, after fifty-plus years of him being in and out of the pen, and asked him what he was up to. He said he was looking for a job, so I said, "Come work for me."

Mario is in the kitchen making breakfast, so I call out to the backyard, "All inmates report to chow!" Sal laughs. Mario makes enough for the seven of us: me; Mikey; Maeve's sons Samuel and Theo; Mario; Sal; and Donal. I have a quick bite and take a shower so I can be ready in time to go down to the Herb J. Wesson Community Center to hand out food to families in need.

Mario, Donal, and I take the 5 south, down a freeway strung with memories. To the left is La Tuna Canyon, where Gilbert and I used to go with .22 rifles and shoot shit up. To the right is my parents' home in Arleta, where

I was arrested after stabbing that sailor, where I buried the hand grenade, cash, and a shotgun in the backyard. We pass an off-ramp that says "Osborne Street," the street where Debbie and I lived and, later, Joanne and my cousin Gilbert lived as well.

The 5 merges onto the 170. My grandparents' house on Penrose is somewhere off to the left. That's where I smoked weed for the first time, where Gilbert taught me how to box, where I first shot dope, where I stole my uncle Rudy's car with Mike Serna to pull our first armed robbery.

The 5 and the 170 are like strands of a necklace draped around the neck of my wildest adventures—the robberies I pulled with Dennis, the house where I lost my virginity, the old North Hollywood Police Department substation where Rita tried to break me out of jail after Mullins busted me for selling drugs. Mullins. I had to laugh. I saw Mullins years after the bust when we both spoke at a youth conference in North Hollywood. He said, "Danny, I see you doing so good now. I'm proud of you."

A few weeks ago, Mario and I went to Cruise Night on Van Nuys Boulevard, an old Valley tradition that's recently been revived. We were trying to find a place to park. There were ten cops in this one spot, and one of them said, "Hey, Trejo."

I said, "Give me a parking spot!" I was joking, but immediately they moved a cruiser out of the way so I could have the spot. Mario's no youngster; he's done hard time. He couldn't believe it.

Turning enemies into allies.

I pray. I pray all the time, anytime, out loud, because why not?

Our Father, Who art in heaven, hallowed be Thy name. Thy kingdom come, Thy will be done, on earth as it is in heaven. Give us this day our daily bread, and forgive us our trespasses, as we forgive those who trespass against us. Lead us not into temptation, but deliver us from evil. For Thine is the kingdom and the power and the glory forever. Amen.

Farther down the freeway is my old drug-dealing spot, the Hole in the Wall, near where I lived with my first wife, Laura, and my uncle Gilbert's apartment, where I ran down the street screaming the first time I shot cocaine. Fifty-five years have passed, but I can still remember the feeling of my heart exploding out of my chest.

God, grant me the serenity to accept the things I cannot change, the courage to change the things I can, and the wisdom to know the difference.

I've traveled the world, but I'll never leave the San Fernando Valley. I hadn't realized the connection at first, but I bought a house on Lassen Street, forty-some-odd years after I lived in Lassen A in Soledad.

My prized possession is a beautiful blue '65 Buick Riviera. A blue '65 Riviera was what the federal agent was driving when he arrested me for selling bunk narcotics. That's the car I was transported in when they kicked my ass on the drive downtown to the Federal Building. And the '38 Chevy Ronnie wanted to sell me—when Debbie said we couldn't buy it, I wondered why I was so hurt, why it had felt so important. Looking back, I realize it was the same make, color, and model of my grandfather's car, the one Gilbert and I took to do my first drug deal, the car where I counted the songs on the radio.

No wonder I was so drawn to these things. I was revisiting my past through addresses and cars, closing circles, taking what had been bad in my life and making it good. We're headed downtown today, the same route Gilbert and I used to take to Chuey's on Temple Street to pick up the heroin we'd sell in Sun Valley Park. My grandmother would make us eggs before we left just like Mario did this morning.

Dear God, thank You for my life. Thank You for providing me with the ability to help Danny Boy, Gilbert, Big Gilbert, Danielle, Mario, Mikey, Maeve, Theo, Samuel, Chubby, Sal, Max, DJ, Mari, Gloria. Thank You for all my family, friends, and loved ones. Please look after them. Thank You for my dogs: Liam, Duke, Penny Lane, Sergeant Pepper, Raven, John Wesley Harding, Zeke, Dixie Wixie, and Whisper. Thank You for Ash and Jeff and everyone at Trejo's Tacos and thank You for the ability to take care of our employees and loved ones. Help my sponsees stay clean and safe. Thank You for Jack Bernstein at CRI-Help, Jimmy Peña, and all the people working in recovery. Thank You for helping Tarah New, Baby Bash, Twixxy, and Johnny and the boys, my artists, and thank You for Seniesa Estrada, the WBA and WBC boxing champion of the world, who Trejo's Tacos sponsors. Thank You, God, for everyone who helped me tell my life story in a book—Michelle Herrera Mulligan, Melanie Iglesias Perez, Shida Carr, Isabel DaSilva, and everyone at Simon & Schuster, Perri Kipperman, Albert Lee, Byrd Leavell, and Nancy Gates at the United Talent Agency, Lydia Wills, Hilary Liftin, Donal, and of course Gloria Hinojosa at AEFH Talent, under whose guidance my career and life have blossomed. God, thank You for Gloria, who's always had my back. Thank You most of all for looking out for everyone in the world struggling with alcohol and drugs today. Help them see there is another way . . .

We pass the Capitol Records Building on our right. Hollywood, Hollywood Boulevard. I remember punching the dude who ran up on the car when Diana was pregnant, the infection that almost cost me my arm. I see the block on Hollywood Boulevard where Frank, three Ulans, and I came up against a gang of eleven white boys who wanted to fight. I pulled a gun and the leader said, "What are you going to do? There's eleven of us."

"All I know is I'm going to kill six of you first. Then it will be five on five." I mention the story to Mario, and he laughs.

"White boys were always clowning us for our baggy clothes; they didn't know we did it just so we could hide guns. How the hell are they going to do that in tight jeans?"

Lord, I am not worthy that Thou should come under my roof. Speak but the word and my soul shall be healed.

We pull off the 101 on Western and head south. The neighborhood has changed, but it's still full of life. It's been years since I had the recovery house on Western and Third. The neighborhood seemed so much sleepier back then. They say memory is an unreliable navigator.

Pulling in behind the Herb J. Wesson Community Center, I notice the line of people waiting for food snaking around entire city blocks. People are compliant in social distancing and are wearing gloves and masks. Covid-19 has put a pall over LA, just as it has done to so many communities in the world. The economic impact is almost as devastating as the health issues. Councilman Wesson greets us with elbow bumps. Herb's been serving the community for decades. We chat for a minute before we get busy filling boxes with rice, beans, celery, cilantro, peppers, bread, apples, and candy for the kids. Our goal is to feed five hundred families. Looking at the line of cars outside the Manhattan Place entrance, I'm nervous we won't have enough. After we finish loading the last box they start coming—cars with grandmothers and grandbabies, husbands and wives, old people on foot with shopping carts. Everyone is patient, polite, and grateful. Every smiling face makes me feel good about myself. It's always been so simple: If you want to feel better about yourself, help someone else. A few women ask for diapers for their babies and I make a point of making sure I'll have some the next time.

A blue Dodge minivan is the last car to pull through. "Machete!" Little kids giggle in the back seat. I hand them snow cones and have Mario throw an extra box of groceries in the back.

We have just enough food for everyone.

Driving home, I feel tired in the best possible way. Mario puts the *Danny Trejo Presents Chicano Soul Shop, Volume 1* CD in the stereo. The tunes are fire. They remind me of the oldies from my youth. I call Bash and we cut it up about when we can get back into the studio to record *Volume 2*.

Retracing our steps home, we pass over where my grandmother's house used to be, over the graves of the Mudda Cat and Blackie. Have over seventy years passed since that day with Mary Carmen, Coke, Salita, and Toni in the alley?

When I walk into the house, the dogs go apeshit.

"Shut up! Okay, I love you, too! Who knows what C-O-O-K-I-E spells?"

They run in circles around the treats cabinet. After the dogs' snack, we settle on my La-Z-Boy couch. *The Searchers* with John Wayne is on TV. I turn up the volume and put out the leg rest. Liam settles on the floor by my feet and Duke jumps between my legs. I scratch Zeke. Penny Lane growls until I pet her and Sergeant Pepper paws my arm until I scratch his butt. My dogs all have very specific petting needs. I have to laugh. Dixie Wixie burrows in my shirt so she won't get crushed while John Wesley Harding snores by my side. When Danielle was a little girl, she used to love burrowing in my shirt. My kids are healthy, I'm healthy, my dogs are healthy. We're all happy. I think, *Tomorrow I'll be seventy-six and I still have so much living to do*, but in that moment, I'm content to let the world spin and enjoy being at home with my doggies.

I ask God one last question: I say, "God, how am I doing?"

God replies, *Great, Danny. You're almost out of hell. Keep it up.*

I smile to myself and thank Him for my life.

COLLABORATOR'S NOTE

The first time I remember meeting Danny was in the basement of a church in Prince George, British Columbia, on March 14, 1999. The group was composed mostly of indigenous First Nations men, and Danny fit right in. After doing a quick scan of the room, I did a double take when I saw him. I thought, *I know that guy.*

I immediately felt foolish. I didn't know him, I merely recognized him the way millions of people around the world did. By 1999, Danny's face was so familiar, his menacing presence so ubiquitous from the scores of movies he'd been in, like *Heat, Con Air,* and *Blood In, Blood Out,* I felt stupid I hadn't put two and two together. He was in Prince George for the same reason I was: to be in the John Frankenheimer film *Reindeer Games.*

It was my first night in Prince George and I was late to the party. An actor had fallen out of the project at the last minute and I was brought in as a replacement. The decision to take the job was agonizing. My first child, Finn, was only five days old, but I desperately needed the gig. My agency had dumped me and I had a family to support.

Prince George was the most remote town I'd ever been in. It was a mining and logging town dominated by a mill, a casino, and a prison. I ditched the pre-shoot cast and crew party to find a meeting and settle my mind. Looking for the church, I passed two men I thought were slow-dancing in the middle of a snowy street. Looking more closely, I realized they were blackout drunks engaged in the world's sloppiest slow-motion knife fight.

Toward the end of the meeting, Danny shared. He mentioned doing time in San Quentin and made a reference to 1968. I was confused by the math. I was born in 1966. He had a lot of mileage on his face, but was extremely fit. It was conceivable I was older.

After the meeting ended, I sought him out. Danny confirmed he was working on the flick and gave me some backstory as to what caused the casting change. Curious, I asked if he said he was born in 1968.

"What? No, holmes. I got sober in 1968 in solitary in Soledad. I was twenty-five years old."

I was stunned to find out that he was closer to sixty than thirty.

He said, "We met before, holmes."

"No way, I would've remembered that," I said.

"Didn't you used to be the janitor at the West Hollywood Drug and Alcohol Center?"

"Yeah."

"I met you there when you were cleaning a bathroom that looked like a crime scene. A toilet had exploded."

"What, did we talk?"

"Yeah. You were one of the angriest motherfuckers I've ever met."

I said, "If you were cleaning the bathroom at the Drug and Alcohol Center, I guarantee you'd be an angry motherfucker, too."

He laughed. "And now you're doing movies. You see what happens when people humble themselves and are willing to be a worker among workers, whatever the job?"

I nodded. It was true.

"How much time you got, partner?"

I told him I'd been sober a little under eight years, since I was twenty-five.

"You got a sponsor?"

I said I did, but he had recently gone out.

"I'm your sponsor now. I got your back. Stay close."

From that day forward, Danny called me one of his partners. I'd joined an elite group: his mentors Frank Russo, Jhonnie Harris, and Sam Hardy; his friends Little Tony Pastor, George Perry, Eddie Bunker, Max Martinez, and Mario and Mikey Castillo; his sons, Gilbert and Danny Boy; his daughter,

Danielle; Mari; Gloria; Chubby; Sal; Maeve; and others in his inner circle. Nearly everything he said was gold: wise, funny, pithy, at times clairvoyant. I gained more insight on life in those first few days walking around Prince George with Danny than I had in my previous thirty-two years.

One night, Danny knocked on my hotel door and said we were going for a drive. As the car wound down a snowy, wooded highway, I asked where we were going. He said, "Be patient. You'll see."

About a half an hour later, we came to a large house in the middle of a meadow. It turned out to be a home for troubled teens. Somehow, Danny had found out about it and called to say he was going to drop by, but told the guy who ran the place not to tell the kids.

When they saw him walk through the door, they were in shock. We spent two hours with those kids, and Danny talked with each and every one of them. His story of redemption left us all in tears—as many from laughter as heartbreak.

On the drive back to Prince George, I asked Danny how he found out about the place and he said, "Everywhere I go, I track down halfway houses and places like that. It's our job to reach out to these kids. Even dog pounds, holmes. Visit dog pounds. Just think, those dogs are doing time. And from someone who did time, the thing you most look forward to when you're locked up is a visitor."

The film itself was complicated for many reasons, the primary one being the weather wasn't cooperating. But, to be honest, there was a lot of stress on set. There was intense pressure to get everything Frankenheimer wanted on film on schedule. I remember meeting Ashton Kutcher. Although he'd finished the first season of *That '70s Show*, *Reindeer Games* was his first day on a film set. We did a take of him running out of a casino and he privately confided in me he'd forgotten to wear the sunglasses he'd worn in the prior take. He asked if he should say something.

"No."

It wasn't an environment where mistakes were tolerated. The main cast, which included Ben Affleck, Charlize Theron, and Gary Sinise, was great, but there were a couple of difficult personalities in the mix (none of the aforementioned, by the way).

I told Danny about the difficulties I was having on set and the guilt I felt leaving home so soon after the birth of my son.

"Fuck that asshole!" he said of one particularly problematic person. "He'll get his, just stay cool. You're here to provide for your son. You'll see him in two days. Your job is to do what God wants you to do: be a provider for your family and be happy, joyous, and free. If you aren't joyous, happy, and free, you aren't doing God's work for you." He finished his spiel by giving me a hug. "Don't worry, partner. I got your back."

The last day of shooting in Prince George, the cast and crew faced the monumental task of getting seventy-two setups in the can before losing light. The locations were so remote, if you stepped off the established paths, you'd sink in eight feet of snow. We'd already had more than a few crew members quit because of the intensity of the environment.

The final setup of the day was a shot where Gary, Danny, Clarence Williams III, and I rolled down the side of a hill in pursuit of Ben. The AD was screaming that we were losing light. The greens crew raked and brushed the steep hillside for almost an hour in a mad panic to clear it of boot prints and make the snow pristine. Balanced on the balls of my feet, I waited for the cameras to roll. After a series of delays, it was clear if we didn't roll in the next minute, we'd lose the shot. The tension was thick. In that moment, I lost my balance. The nanosecond my center of gravity shifted and I realized I was falling, I immediately thought of the wrath I'd incur of everyone who'd worked so hard to groom the hill, set the lights, focus the cameras. I knew Frankenheimer (who was brilliant and loving, but not shy about tearing you a new one if he felt you deserved it) would unleash a torrent of abuse my way, and in the eyes of my fellow, much more famous cast members, I'd be viewed as an idiot.

Pitching forward, arms flailing, I was internally gutted by the guilt of abandoning my child and failing at my job. Falling off that perch was my nadir, personally and professionally. Then, suddenly, miraculously, I found myself suspended in midair, my feet fully off the ground. Somehow, in the blink of an eye, Danny had grabbed the back of my coat and held me aloft as effortlessly as if I were a dishrag. I still don't know how he had the strength to one-arm me, a chunky two-hundred-pounder, suspended in air over a snowy cliff.

He gently pulled me back to my mark, to the exact spot my feet had been two seconds earlier, and whispered, "I told you I got your back."

The boom operator said, "Sound speed," and the AD yelled, "Roll cameras!" He's had my back ever since.

Donal Logue
Brooklyn, New York

Rest in peace to my parents, all my family members,
and everyone I've shared my life with who's no longer here,
and a special shout-out to my homies who are no longer with me:

George "Big George" Bustamente
Terry Roden
Johnny Martinez
Donald "Big D" Garcia
Robert "Robot" Salas
Rafael "Chispas" Sandoval
Joe Morgan
Joey Abasta
Chino Sainz
Ronnie Brown
Joey Bryning
George Perry
Eddie Bunker
Ralph Mata

ABOUT THE AUTHORS

Danny Trejo is one of Hollywood's most recognizable, prolific, and beloved character actors. Famed for his roles in series like AMC's *Breaking Bad*, FX's *Sons of Anarchy*, and director Robert Rodriguez's global, billion-dollar *Spy Kids* and *Machete* film franchises, Danny is also a successful restaurateur. He owns seven locations of Trejo's Tacos, Trejo's Cantina, and Trejo's Coffee & Donuts in the Los Angeles area, and is expanding his Trejo's Tacos franchise nationwide. Visit DannyTrejo.com to learn more.

Born in Canada to Irish parents, **Donal Logue** was raised on the Mexican border in Nogales, Arizona, and Calexico and El Centro, California. Donal studied history at Harvard University with the aim of going into foreign diplomacy, but theater intervened. He was happily sidetracked into the world of film, television, and literature, and went on to build a career in entertainment. A veteran of more than seventy Hollywood films and hundreds of television episodes, Donal won the Grand Jury Prize for outstanding acting at the 2000 Sundance Film Festival for *The Tao of Steve*. He stays busy between creative projects with his trucking company, Aisling Trucking, and hardwood company, Frison-Logue Hardwoods, in Southern Oregon. Visit DonalLogue.com to learn more.